MAPLE SYRUP

MAPLE SYRUP

A SHORT HISTORY OF CANADA'S
SWEETEST OBSESSION

Peter Kuitenbrouwer

DOUBLEDAY
CANADA

PUBLISHED IN 2025 BY DOUBLEDAY CANADA

Doubleday Canada, an imprint of Penguin Random House Canada Limited, 320 Front Street West, Suite 1400, Toronto, Ontario, M5V 3B6, Canada penguinrandomhouse.ca

Doubleday Canada and colophon are registered trademarks of Penguin Random House LLC.

The authorized representative in the EU for product safety and compliance is Penguin Random House Ireland, Morrison Chambers, 32 Nassau Street, Dublin, D02 YH68, Ireland, https://eu-contact.penguin.ie

LIBRARY AND ARCHIVES CANADA CATALOGUING IN PUBLICATION
Title: Maple syrup : a short history of Canada's sweetest obsession / Peter Kuitenbrouwer.
Names: Kuitenbrouwer, Peter, 1962- author.
Identifiers: Canadiana (print) 20250151677 | Canadiana (ebook) 2025015319X | ISBN 9780385698184 (hardcover) | ISBN 9780385698191 (EPUB)
Subjects: LCSH: Maple syrup—Canada. | LCSH: Maple syrup industry—Canada. | LCSH: Maple syrup industry—Québec (Province)
Classification: LCC TP395 .K85 2025 | DDC 641.3/364—dc23

Book design by Jennifer Griffiths
Cover and interior illustrations by Jonathan Dyck
Typeset by Erin Cooper

Printed in Canada

2 4 6 8 9 7 5 3 1

Penguin
Random House
DOUBLEDAY CANADA

For Mimi Maxwell, my sweetie

CONTENTS

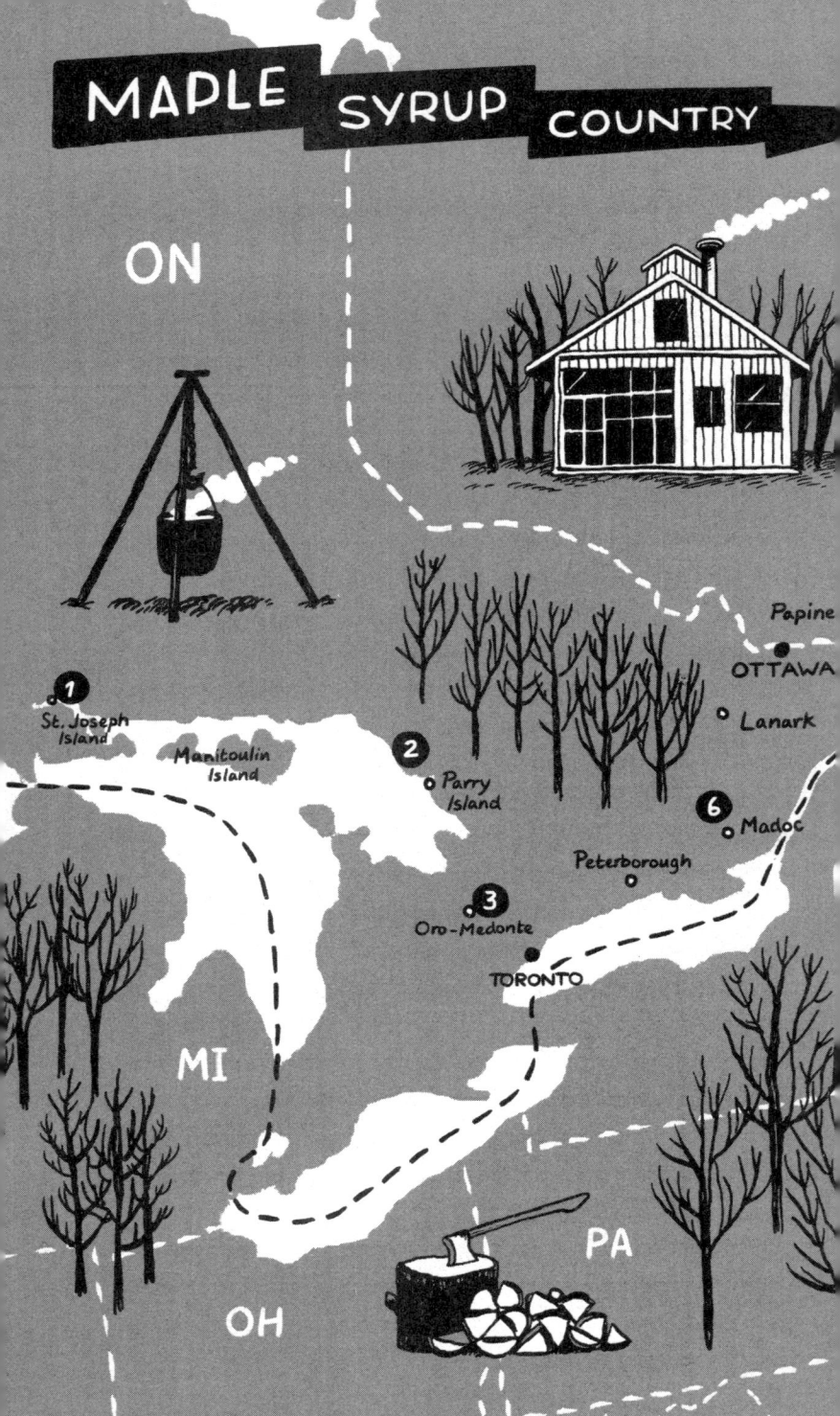

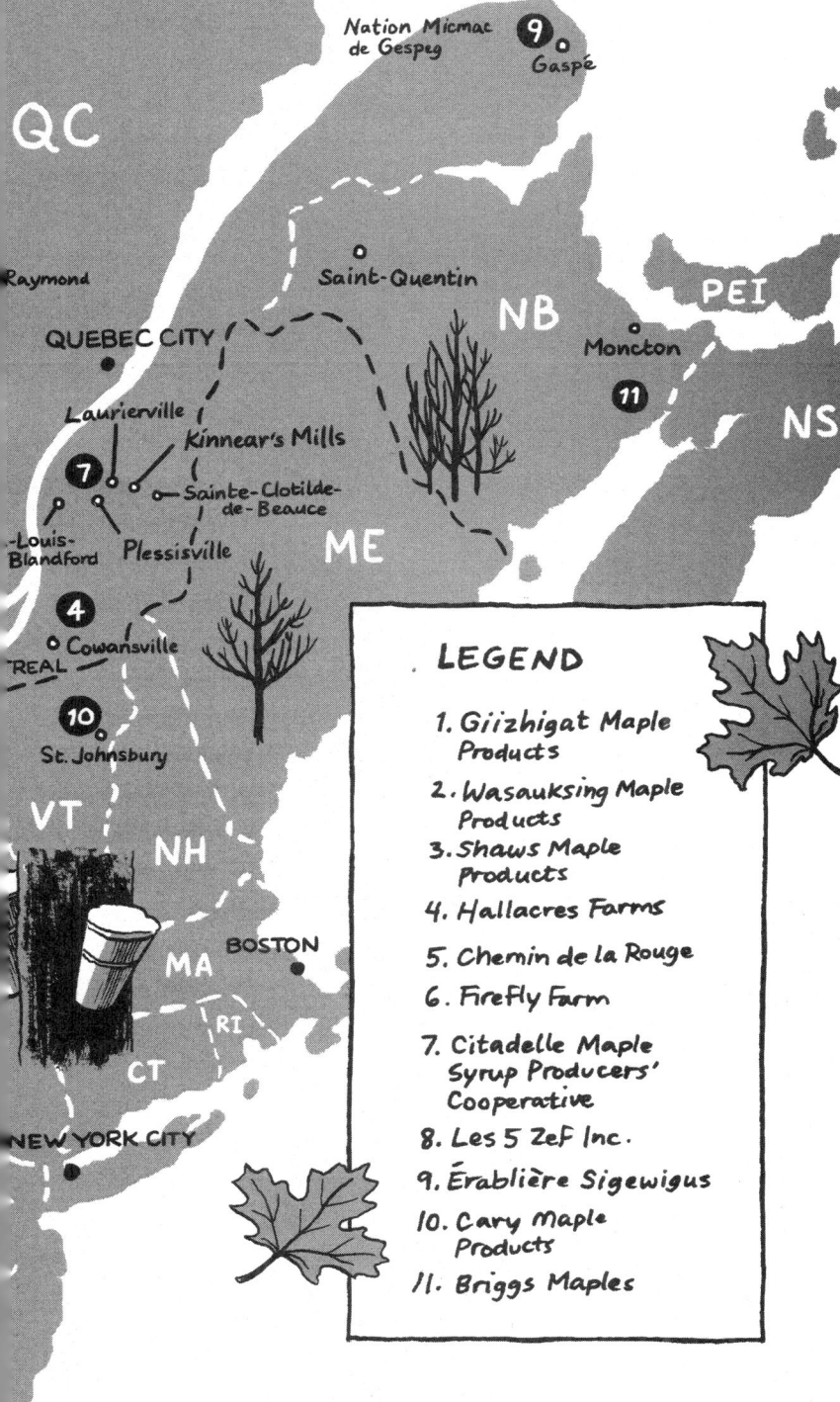

QC

Nation Micmac de Gespeg

9

Gaspé

PEI

Raymond

Saint-Quentin

NB

Moncton

11

NS

QUEBEC CITY

Laurierville

Kinnear's Mills

7

Sainte-Clotilde-de-Beauce

-Louis-Blandford

Plessisville

ME

4

Cowansville

REAL

10

St. Johnsbury

VT

NH

MA

BOSTON

RI

CT

NEW YORK CITY

LEGEND

1. Giizhigat Maple Products
2. Wasauksing Maple Products
3. Shaws Maple Products
4. Hallacres Farms
5. Chemin de la Rouge
6. Firefly Farm
7. Citadelle Maple Syrup Producers' Cooperative
8. Les 5 Zef Inc.
9. Érablière Sigewigus
10. Cary Maple Products
11. Briggs Maples

INTRODUCTION

A book about maple syrup has been taking shape in my head for a long time. The sticky stuff got into my bloodstream at an impressionable age. My elder sisters and I, children of immigrants who became itinerant hippies, weathered a tumultuous time as kids, rarely living anywhere for more than a year or two. Then my mother and stepfather bought a farm in a hardwood forest in west Quebec and decreed we would make maple syrup. In spring we struggled through snowbanks taller than us to gather maple sap. We boiled the sap into syrup. The endurance and patience the task required unified and gratified our family. Maple syrup lives in me as a proxy for happiness, stability and community.

After high school I left the farm and became a journalist. During the many years I worked at newspapers, I found myself increasingly drawn to write about the trees and forests of Canada, one of the world's great forest nations. After decades of interviewing the experts, I wanted to join them. In my fifties I graduated from the University of Toronto with a Master of Forest Conservation; I am now a registered professional forester. My deeper understanding of forests and how they thrive has driven me further to unpack the issues that underpin the success and the future of Canada's most unique forest product: maple syrup. My wife and I now have our own farm where our children and our neighbours help us make syrup for family and friends every spring. This ritual grounds me in a tempestuous world. But while I love the stuff, I had a lot to learn to tell the story of maple syrup.

History books have heroes. This book's first heroes are Canada's Indigenous Peoples, such as the Anishnaabe women of Manitoulin Island in the Georgian Bay who have known for millennia how to extract sap from the sugar maple tree and transform it into a sweetener, a skill they taught the colonists from Europe. Sugaring off, the English translation of the Indigenous word for this age-old ritual, has shaped the identity of Canada.

It was winter when I began research for this book. In these cold and dark months, one yearns for signs of spring. In Canada, syrup season is one of the earliest indicators warmer weather is on its way. During my commutes, I noticed that even in Toronto, where I live, maple syrup is ingrained in the collective psyche. In January a sandwich board outside a coffee shop announced "Welcome to the Sugar Shack," with photos of three drinks: a maple latte, maple chai latte, and maple cold foam espresso. In February an ad on the subway announced the Sugar Shack TO festival: "Tap into your inner Canadian!" beckoned the poster, with photos of smiling children in toques and a man in a plaid vest splitting wood. The poster added:

"March Break at Sugar Beach. Two sugar shacks, maple-infused food, lumberjack show. March 11–12. Sweet!" Interestingly, the festival was promoted by Redpath Sugar, a refinery on the shore of Lake Ontario that receives ships full of raw cane sugar from the Caribbean. Even though Canada imports most of its sweeteners from overseas, the company was celebrating our domestic supply, perhaps seeking to make itself seem more homegrown. Meanwhile, on the sides of buildings and on subway platforms, billboards declared "It's not Just for Breakfast," with an image of a hand tipping a bottle. Maple syrup poured out, initially heading for a stack of pancakes but then swerving midair to drizzle on a salad. "Maple from Canada" read the logo on the ad funded by Quebec's syrup producers. It's clear that our affection for maple syrup and what it represents runs deep.

For our iconic sweet treat, we must thank the mighty sugar maple tree. *Native Trees of Canada* cites twenty-six species of maple tree, including silver maple, red maple, Manitoba maple, Norway maple, and bigleaf maple. The book notes that the sap of the sugar maple, which grows only in the eastern parts of Canada and the United States, is the primary source of maple syrup and maple sugar. The distinctive leaf of this tree has become synonymous with Canada, frequently used on anything of Canadian provenance. Even Toronto's hockey team is called the Maple Leafs. And, of course, Canada's flag features a stylized five-lobed sugar maple leaf, which has become a ubiquitous all-season marketing tool for the maple syrup industry.

I travelled across maple syrup country to uncover a history that mixes Indigenous innovation, perseverance, know-how and religious zeal. In Quebec, north of Quebec City, I donned snowshoes along with a group of young men from Guatemala to repair maple sap tubing, a job that required climbing a mountain covered in wet spring snow. In Brome Lake, I careened through a muddy forest in a pickup truck with that rarest of breeds, a Quebec farmer who speaks—and cusses—in English, and nearly got stuck en route to a sap-pumping station. In Laurierville, I visited a warehouse owned by the Global Strategic Maple Syrup Reserve that sprawls the size of five football fields. Leaving Quebec, I visited Wasauksing First Nation a few hours' drive north of Toronto where residents use contemporary methods to continue a tradition started long before colonists came to Canada: boiling sap in spring to make maple syrup.

In search of maple syrup's origin story, I visited Ottawa to read through research material housed in Library and Archives Canada, which is located next to the Supreme Court. Security is tight in our national archive. Upon arrival, a commissionaire dispenses a locker key and a clear plastic bag to registered visitors. Personal belongings are to be stored in the locker; anything needed in the library goes in the bag. Past security, a marble staircase leads up to the collection. Surfaces have been polished to a hard shine, and the place has a timeless air. Windows in the research rooms look north over the Ottawa River to Quebec. I had ordered material ahead of time. I donned a pair of the archives' white cotton gloves and untied the white ribbons to access the material I had requested: 19th-century illustrations of syrup-making from newspapers; a hand-written petition from one First Nation in what is now Ontario, who pleaded for permission to continue their tradition of tapping sugar maple trees; yellowing government syrup-making pamphlets;

black-and-white photos of syrup-making techniques of days gone by. Handling these relics gave me a thrill, reminding me of the intrinsic importance of maple syrup from the very beginnings of this nation's story.

Sugaring off first appears in the historical record in 1600, when a Jesuit missionary reported on Indigenous women who in spring collected maple sap in bark vessels, but this ritual predates the arrival of colonists in what is now Canada by millennia. In recent years some archaeologists and historians have argued that colonists from Europe taught Indigenous Peoples to make syrup, since the First Peoples lacked the iron pots needed to boil sap. The facts disprove those arguments. The First Peoples venerated the sugar maple tree, whose sweet sap they used to season meat and as a remedy for heart, stomach and breathing problems, among many other uses. The colonists copied the Indigenous techniques to make sugar and syrup from maple tree sap. Then, colonists removed the First Peoples from the sugar bush and cleared the maple forests for farms or restricted them for settlers' use. Indigenous Peoples I've met have spoken to me of both their trauma and their resilience as they reconnect with the sugar bush.

For farmers in eastern Canada, as for Indigenous Peoples, syrup-making has long been the first outdoor job in spring. Thousands of families—mine included—head into the forest when the snow begins to melt at winter's end. The ground is too soft for logging and the nights too frosty for any crops. But it's the right time to collect sap. Sap-collecting is, however, back-breaking work: One must haul and boil forty buckets of sap to make one bucket of syrup. Canada's sweetener is a symbol of rugged self-sufficiency.

For the First Peoples maple sugar was both foodstuff and medicine. In colonial times it became a staple. When I was a kid maple syrup was our only sweetener, since we practised subsistence agriculture and had no money to buy cane sugar. Today maple syrup lives at the intersection of refinement, authenticity and decadence. Martin Picard, the Quebec chef, published the *Au Pied de Cochon Sugar Shack Book*, about his seasonal restaurant in Mirabel, Quebec, a lavish, reverential tome complete with a photo of a woman in her birthday suit reclining in a bathtub of maple syrup. Picard celebrates sugaring-off season, alluding to Quebec's long history with the Catholic church when he writes, "After 40 days of fasting, it's a revenge against Lent."

A luxury product around the world, maple syrup, even in Canada, is something of a treat. A friend said that when his three children were little and the family sat down for pancakes on a weekend morning, they guarded the maple syrup for adult use only. The kids got corn syrup—until they were old enough to demand the good stuff, that is. Our family lucked out: At the French public school our children attended in Toronto, a parent had an uncle in Quebec and would take orders for pure maple syrup, bringing it in by the case.

Canada and the United States produced equivalent quantities of maple syrup until World War II. After the war Canadian production increased, while in the States syrup production flatlined. Today the vast majority of the world's maple syrup comes from Canada, specifically Quebec. This concentration of sweet maple wealth in a system controlled by a powerful federation has led to theft, rebellion and debate about quality versus quantity. Furthermore, foresters like me worry what effects climate change will have on maple syrup, dependent as the industry is on the freeze–thaw cycle of spring. We must reduce our greenhouse gas emissions to save the national lifeblood that is maple syrup.

The future of the sticky stuff is anything but clear.

ACER SACCHARUM

O ne of Canada's largest forest regions is the vast Great Lakes–St. Lawrence Forest, which grows from Manitoba to the Gaspé Peninsula. It is second only to the immense boreal forest region, which stretches from the Yukon to Newfoundland. While the boreal forest is largely dominated by evergreen trees, the Great Lakes–St. Lawrence Forest includes hickory, beech, birch, oak and, importantly for this book, maple. Of the 124 species of maple trees growing in the northern hemisphere around the world—from the Himalayas through Europe, China and Japan—10 varieties of maple are native to Canada. A bigleaf maple growing on Canada's west coast, for example, can live to be 250 years old. A Manitoba maple is so resilient to the indignities of urban life that it has become a weed tree in central Canada. Unique among leaf trees, all maple trees—red maple, silver maple, Norway maple, mountain maple and sugar maple, among other varieties—produce a sweet sap. The sweetest maple sap, and the preferred species to make maple syrup, comes from the sugar maple tree, known in Latin as *Acer saccharum* and sometimes called hard maple or rock maple. It is one of the tallest hardwoods in Canada and grows best in moist, rich, well-drained soil. This tree, which can live for more than two centuries, is a symbol of Canada. Sugar maple forests, often called sugar bushes, cover parts of Nova Scotia, New Brunswick, Quebec and Ontario, and spread through the northeastern and north-central United States, as far west as Minnesota and as far south as Missouri and Tennessee. The riotous colours that maple leaves turn in autumn draw tourists across North America's northeast, giving rise to the term "leaf peeping" and generating huge profits for the hospitality sector and tour operators.

Beneath the maple's beauty lies its bounty. Through a complex series of interdependent factors—the tree's physiology and the climate conditions of North America's northeast—the maple tree generates a sap that can be transformed, with great effort, into a delicious syrup.

Trees need water to survive. They use their roots to suck water from the ground like a big drinking straw. As in all trees, both water and sap run under the bark of the sugar maple. The water travels through a network of tubes, called xylem, which connect the roots to the branches and leaves in the crown. Xylem is a band of tissue in the tree's sapwood, beneath the bark.

All trees and plants use a process called photosynthesis to grow. Once the water that the tree has sucked from the soil reaches the crown, the tree's leaves go to work. In summer the sugar bush is a shady place. Standing amid the maple trees you can hardly glimpse the sky, thanks to the splendour of billions of green leaves that make up the forest's canopy. Each maple tree fights with its neighbours to push branches skyward, rising to the height of church steeples in the hopes its leaves might capture a little scrap of sunlight. This light is vital to the tree's survival.

The scene is quiet, save for the chirping of birds and the chatter of squirrels, but amid this serenity the trees, from their wide-spreading roots to the tops of their crowns, are working harder than the most industrious of factories, in shifts that last from sunrise to sunset. Leaves are nature's chemical manufacturing plants. The leaf opens small pores on its surface, and carbon dioxide from the air diffuses into the leaf. Using the energy of the sun, chlorophyll in the leaves breaks the carbon dioxide into its two parts: carbon and oxygen. The oxygen dissipates into the air. The leaves' chlorophyll molecules use the carbon to manufacture sugar: the food the tree needs to grow. Dissolved in sap, this sweetened liquid then moves down to other parts of the tree to build cell walls. What it doesn't immediately use the tree converts to starch and stashes in its trunk and roots for later use. Some water in the leaf evaporates, which creates negative or vacuum pressure in the tubes in the tree's bark. This pulls up more water from the soil. And in this way the hard-toiling leaves produce the sweet sap in the tree.

In autumn the maple tree, like all deciduous trees, lays down its tools. As they cease their season of labour, the leaves turn brilliant colours and then retire, fluttering down to carpet the forest floor. When winter arrives, the maple tree enters a kind of hibernation, using its sweet sap as an antifreeze to protect itself from plummeting temperatures.

Then spring arrives. In the morning when the weather warms compressed gas in the tree expands. The rising

Oh Canada, dear Canada
none can compare with thee;
'Neath sunny skies the Earth replies
and laughs with harvest glee;
Thy winters cheer with air so clear
but best of all to me,
The summer and the sunshine
and the spreading maple tree.

HENRY HERBERT GODFREY,
The Land of the Maple, 1897

temperature draws the sap up to spur growth in the tree's buds, until the leaves begin to produce food. The pressure in the tree is greater than the pressure outside. Excess sap descends the tree, due to gravity. Make a hole in the trunk and some liquid, or sap, will come out. Boil this sap for a very long time, since maple sap is just 2 percent sugar, and you get maple syrup.

FLOW OF MAPLE SAP IN SPRING

This temperature swing, from cold nights to warm days, is at the crux of what makes maple sap flow in spring, from February up to May, depending on the latitude of the forest.

"The thaw days, you want some sunshine with that," as Tom Shaw, a syrup-maker I met from Ontario, told me. "The reason you want sunshine: it's the temperature shocks that create the pressure in the tree. A +7 cloudy day isn't going to get you as much sap because there isn't the shock. A +7 sunny day, it goes from a freezing night to all of a sudden that sun hitting those dark branches and shining on them, the temperature changes immediately, and it's 'cause the branches themselves will be so much warmer than they were. It is the little small branches on the top that really do the sucking and the pulling and the this and that of it all."

The long, cold winter of North America's northeast—distinct from the weather patterns of Europe, for example—creates the conditions necessary in spring to make maple syrup: good flows of sap with a reasonable sugar content. Without this freeze–thaw cycle, the sap will not flow. Europeans have tried to make maple syrup at home and failed. During the Napoleonic Wars in the early 1800s, the British blockade prevented cane sugar made in the Caribbean from reaching the European continent. Germany, Austria and Sweden experimented with planting maple trees for sugar, but the short springs on the continent proved incompatible with the endeavour. The Europeans tapped their maple trees, but the sap did not run. After Napoleon's defeat at Waterloo in 1815, Britain lifted the blockade and Europe, once again awash in Caribbean sugar, abandoned its attempts to make sugar from maple trees. One also cannot make maple syrup in warmer parts of the United States. Thomas Jefferson, the second US president, brought young maples from Vermont to his plantation in Virginia. But the location was too far south to provide the needed combination of freezing nights and warm days. The trees lived but Jefferson got no syrup.

SUGAR MAPLE RANGE

That syrup-producing sugar maples are exclusive to just one part of the world adds to their mystique. Many plants eaten worldwide originated in the Americas: cacao, corn, peanuts, avocados, squash, tomatoes and potatoes. After colonization these foods became ubiquitous, and now farmers grow them everywhere. Other plants are adaptable too: Sugar cane comes from Southeast Asia; now farmers grow it across the tropics. Grapes originated in the Middle East; today winemakers around the world grow grapes. Dairy cattle come from Europe; now cows live everywhere. But sugar maple trees only produce maple syrup in the northeast of North America, and nowhere else on Earth.

To make maple syrup one must, of course, tap maple trees, preferably sugar maple trees. Unfortunately, it can be hard to distinguish maples from other tree varieties during maple syrup season, which occurs before the trees have leaves. One giveaway is the symmetrical branch arrangement: on a maple tree, wherever a branch or twig or bud grows, a twin grows on the opposite side (branches alternate on most other leaf tree species). It's a good idea to mark sugar maples with flagging tape during the leaf season. One year I tapped an oak tree by accident; it gave no sap.

Enterprising experimenters in the forest have made yummy syrups from birch, butternut, hickory, sycamore and walnut trees, but only maple trees—and palm trees, in the tropics— contain enough sugar for its extraction to be profitable. Unfortunately for the syrup industry, there are other ways to profit from maples, all of which involve cutting down the trees and sending them to the sawmill. Woodworkers prize sugar maple to turn into furniture, flooring, veneer, plywood, cutting boards and even the pin block that holds the tuning pins of a piano.

In one key way, maple syrup differs from other crops. Almost all agriculture as we practise it today would be unrecognizable to our ancestors. Laser-guided tractors; sensors on cattle; planting drones; herbicides and pesticides that scrub from the landscape everything but the desired crop; genetically modified strains of corn, wheat and other plants; as well as irrigation, drainage, and the increasing use of climate-controlled greenhouses—we have learned to industrialize and regiment almost every detail of food production. By contrast, the sugar bush grows much as it has through history: Syrup producers do not plant, irrigate or fertilize their woods. Sure, they thin the forests to give light to the best of their maple trees. But the vistas of a sugar bush—an irregular expanse filled with rocks, hills, creeks, ponds and underbrush, with trees of every age from sapling to grand old ancestor, with leaves and logs strewn to rot on the forest floor, and with woodpeckers hammering trunks in search of insects—remain largely unchanged. And perhaps it is this untrammelled, romanticized image of the pristine forest, growing as evermore, that lends a cachet, a kind of imprimatur of purity and sanctity to maple syrup, a product not of mechanization but of Mother Nature.

Tom Shaw described the connection he feels with his ancestors during the season: "What's cool about this business is I'm still tapping and making syrup from the same trees. See that tree, the third one back in there? That's a 250-year-old tree, or 200-year-old tree, so close to the sugar camp. That tree has been tapped by five generations of my family and has made syrup every single year since 1904."

Given both its good looks and its generosity, in timber and sweet sap, it is no wonder that we prize the very tree that has sustained and delighted us for centuries: the beloved sugar maple.

LA ROUGE

The anticipation that I start to feel as maple syrup season approaches is something that my friend and Toronto neighbour Oona will never understand. When the days lengthen and the snow starts to melt, I'm like a thoroughbred in a paddock before the gun goes off to start a race. I champ at the bit and paw my hooves, eager to get into the forest and tromp around in the thick, wet spring snow tapping trees. One March my wife and I invited Oona and her husband, Ward, for sugaring off at our farm east of Toronto, near a village called Madoc, Ontario. This invitation proved a mistake—a slightly comical mistake.

Oona, though born and raised in Quebec, wants nothing to do with maple syrup season. She may even count it among her reasons for leaving the province. As we walked from our family cottage to the maple forest along a snowy trail, Oona, clearly triggered, recounted nightmarish memories of the obligatory annual pilgrimage made by Quebec schoolchildren in spring, when teachers load them onto yellow school buses and then disgorge them at the sugar bush to schlep around.

"It was always freezing cold," Oona recalled. "They would make us walk through the forest in the snow and our feet would get wet. The wind blew, sometimes snow or rain fell. We would shiver past all the trees with the buckets hung on them, and then get to the sugar shack. There they would serve you plates of food—beans and pork and eggs and pancakes— everything slathered with maple syrup. And pea soup. I hate pea soup! Absolutely disgusting. Inedible. And the worst part was the taffy. They would pour the syrup on the snow, and you were supposed to scoop it up with little wooden paddles or popsicle sticks. But it was all sticky. I always had long hair and I would get the maple taffy stuck in the strands. Everything about it was awful!"

It was ever thus. In his book *Le temps des sucres,* Jean-Claude Dupont counsels those en route to a sugaring-off party to wear warm, old clothing since, he writes, "A maple taffy party never ends without a session where people get smeared with syrup and soot." And Hazel Boswell in her book *Legends of Quebec* warns of boys chasing girls with the goal of gumming up their hair with gobs of what Québécois call *la tire.*

Oona's husband, Ward, derived a more philosophical observation when he saw how we make maple syrup on our farm. He and I for years have taken our sons on a summer canoe trip to Algonquin Provincial Park, north of Toronto. It often rains. We wake up in soggy tents and, slathered in mosquito repellent, stand around a smoky campfire as we try to warm up and dry off. On that day in our sugar bush, Ward stood quietly. He watched the flames lap the sides of a

"We think we are rediscovering the secrets that some of our forebears . . . knew so well: the secrets of simplicity, adequacy, decency, neighborliness, self-respect, and a never-ending attachment to the marvels of the life of nature and of society that we contact on every side and of which we are integral parts."

HELEN & SCOTT NEARING,
The Maple Sugar Book, 1950

rectangular pan I had placed across some iron bars over a cement base. There boiled the sap, on its way to becoming maple syrup, while snow fell around us. "I see how this works," Ward observed. "It's a lot like camping in Algonquin. We stand around in inclement weather, drink beer and try to keep the fire going."

That said, neither of our friends has ever returned to our farm during sugaring off.

Why am I so devoted to syrup season? On the surface my affection for it defies logic. I have my own hard-lived childhood memories: During sugaring off, my sisters and I suffered more than Oona ever did. We got wet. We got cold. And yet, for me, making maple syrup became a compulsion. I have spent decades trying to unpack my seemingly irrational affection for it. The answer, I think, lies in part with the warm embrace I felt as a little boy stepping into the timeless, stoic hardwood forests of eastern Canada and the sense of togetherness I garnered from sugaring as a family. Oona was a spectator, an outsider; I was a participant. I adopted the Québécois' cultural bond to the sugaring rituals of spring.

The poet William Chapman in 1904 published a collection titled *Les aspirations*. One of his cloying, sticky-sweet poems, "L'érable," celebrates the importance of the maple tree to Quebec (the poem rhymes in French).

> *Its leaves, in mid-September*
> *As the boreal winds start to blow*
> *Cover themselves in gold, purple and amber*
> *And glow like a royal robe.*

In April the peasant pierces
Its flank, softened by the thaw
From this wound the tree sheds
All month long, tears of honey.

These tears are a richness
They make us take many steps
But the farm is distressed
If the maple does not cry.

Because it is fertile, we love it,
And our ancestors, in their pride
Took its leaf as the emblem
Of their citizenship.

This devotion to the maple tree, and affection for its bounty, are sentiments that I, the son of immigrants from the Netherlands, grew to share. Having been uprooted many times in my childhood, I searched for stability, and I found it in the sugar bush. The forests welcomed me. I *belonged* there. The resilience of the rugged maple tree, with its deep, wide-spreading root system, was a comfort. And the forest was generous, a generosity we repaid through our gentle methods and our care. The maples on the Quebec farm where I grew up sprouted from the earth long before my birth and are set to outlive me by a century or more: Soaring taller than houses, taller than barns, these regal giants exhibit the kind of steadfastness or permanence that I craved. They weren't going anywhere; they stayed put.

There was something else, too. The Dutch call it *gezelligheid*—a combination of comfort, togetherness and well-being. The

Québécois find it in raucous gaiety of family gatherings in spring, in the sugar shack. And when my family moved to the dirt road, the Chemin de la Rouge, we connected with this feeling—not quickly, nor smoothly, but in our own bumpy way.

I had yearned for this embrace without even knowing that I sought it. My childhood was nomadic. My Dutch parents met on a ship from the Netherlands to Canada. They settled in Vancouver and had three children. The pair separated when I was two; my mom took her three kids to live near a sister, in California. One year we moved six times. In La Jolla, a beach town near San Diego, my mother met her second husband. We travelled across Canada by VW van several times and lived in Banff as well as a number of places in the Montreal region. My mom studied ballet in Montreal. One of the teachers at her dance school had a huge farm for sale in western Quebec, just north of the village of Papineauville. Pooling some small inheritances, my mom and stepfather bought 250 hectares of Quebec's forest, with a few fields and a few old wooden houses in the hills north of the Ottawa River. The river divides Ontario from Quebec, with Quebec lying on the river's north bank.

In the spring of 1971, my mother, stepfather, two elder sisters and I left the house we had rented in a suburb of Montreal. We packed what worldly possessions we owned, plus two cats and a stray dog who had adopted us, and moved to the countryside. I was eight years old. We arrived on May 2. There was still snow on the ground. The truck that brought our meagre belongings got stuck in the snow on the front lawn. Winters were colder then.

To explain our move to rural Quebec, my mother told me that many in her generation longed to shrug off the strictures of their parents, and find freedom and independence. People wanted to be left alone. Our flight to the forest made our family part of the back-to-the-land movement of the 1960s and '70s. In her song about the 1969 Woodstock music festival, Joni Mitchell sings about the yearning to escape the smog and life as a cog in a wheel, and get back to the garden. Such was our goal.

The spot our family chose—thickly forested, resolutely French and, at the time, staunchly Roman Catholic—is called La Petite Nation. The sluggish, brownish Rivière de la Petite Nation bordered our farm on its way to drain into the Ottawa River.

We moved into a drafty, sagging wooden house at the foot of a hill that saw our basement fill with water each spring. The rural community had a timeless quality. The neighbours— dairy farmers named the St. Denis—had a daughter followed by eight sons. Every morning before school the children crossed the dirt road to their barn. There lived twenty Holstein cattle in a stable. Above them was a loft filled with bales of hay. Each boy milked two cows by hand, morning and night, distributed the hay and shovelled the manure. This was the standard for family farms at the time: everyone had chores.

All those kids meant lots of companions for this young boy. Here at last was the *gezelligheid* for which I had thirsted. I'd somehow squeeze in alongside the throng of loud and gangly youth as they sat on handmade wooden benches around their red Formica kitchen table and passed around the pies Mme. St. Denis would bake—*tarte au sucre, tarte aux pommes, tarte aux raisins, tarte aux framboises* . . .

Our stepfather made his living as a potter. He and my mom decided, with all the land we had, that we would grow all of our own food. We also acquired goats, chickens, a milk cow and, eventually, a horse.

That first autumn we gasped in wonder as the leaves on the maples that covered the hills exploded in a riot of reds, purples, oranges and yellows. We went for the first of many annual Thanksgiving walks and gathered leaves to decorate the table for our autumn feast. It was a beautiful time of year on the farm.

Then winter arrived. The wind tore the remaining leaves from the trees with contempt and then brought snow that hammered the farm with a raw savagery unfamiliar to us. Our house sat just 10 kilometres, or about 6 miles, from the village where we attended French school, yet one afternoon a storm slammed into the region with such ferocity that we had to spend the night in the school gym. Snow days, when the snowplow could not come and school was cancelled, came as a blessing. We read the *Little House* books by Laura Ingalls Wilder and realized that we didn't have it so bad.

Winter endured.

In March, the calendar said it was spring. It still looked like winter. We scraped snowdrifts off the windows to let sun into our house. Undaunted, my mother and stepfather decided to embrace "subsistence agriculture." The other euphemism my parents used for our lifestyle was "voluntary simplicity." We did not have much, not even a TV, but we had a heck of a lot of sugar maple trees. We would make maple syrup. Woefully underequipped, as my mom later admitted, we headed to the forest.

Perhaps part of the appeal was that the maple trees were already there. No preparation needed. The goats we had to corral—few pens will contain a goat—and feed and milk; the chickens we had to protect from the foxes; the garden we had to plow, and disc, and sow, and hoe, and weed and harvest. But the maple trees thrived on their own, not needing any watering or weeding or compost or manure, or even protection from bugs or weeds. Just vibing, as my son would say, in the forest. Drill a hole in spring and the sap drips out. And that's what everyone else on our road was doing, too.

For guidance, my mother and stepfather turned to *The Maple Sugar Book* by Helen and Scott Nearing. About a century ago, Scott Nearing, a prolific author and scholar, had been chased out of academe in Pennsylvania and New York for his socialist views. He and his partner Helen, a violinist, in 1932 purchased a Vermont farm in what is known as the Green Mountains, which stretch south from the Canadian border. The Nearings' book, an exhaustively researched epistle referenced in just about every book I consulted to write this one, taught my parents how to make maple syrup, and also offered a kind of mantra or set of guiding principles that vindicated the path our family had chosen. In the last chapter of the book, titled "A Life as Well as a Living," the Nearings wrote of rediscovering the secrets of their forebears in the Green Mountains, adding that "the occupation of sugaring has been a thorough-going education and broadened our contacts with life in its many aspects."

On our dirt road in west Quebec we set about broadening our own contacts with life. While it still looked like winter outside, we could smell, even feel, that spring was in the air. Although it had been well below zero overnight, we could tell when the sun came up that it was going to be a "warm" day— that is, the temperature would rise above freezing. A feeling of anticipation, of excitement, accompanied this knowing— we would be freed from captivity (the shelter of the house).

My sister Noelle recalls: "You go 'Oh, it's sugaring-off time again,' and you feel a little rush."

The families on our road—the Poulins, the Labelles, the Lecots—all made maple syrup. The St. Denis family didn't make maple syrup so their sons went to help their aunt and uncle, the Lecots. My family, with our amateur fumbling around in the sugar bush, must have amused our neighbours; even so, they showed huge generosity in teaching us the complex and time-honoured rituals of *le temps des sucres*—literally, "the time of the sugars." In English it's typically referred to as "sugaring-off season," a phrase whose roots harken back to the Indigenous tradition of maple sugar–making. Before there were cans and glass bottles, most people boiled maple sap to the point it granulated into sugar, which is shelf-stable and easier to store.

On La Rouge, our sugar bush grew mainly on a hill on the south end of the farm, up the dirt road from the existing house. My mother and stepfather decided to build a new house at this end of the farm. To practise construction they built a sugar shack on the hill just a few steps up from the new house site. (A sugar shack is a building that houses an evaporator, which is used to boil down sap into syrup.)

My parents were able to equip our sugar shack at minimal expense as a consequence of one of the bigger Canadian governmental boondoggles of the 20th century: the 1969 expropriation of a vast area of Quebec farmland (almost the size of the city of Montreal) to build Mirabel Airport, an international passenger airport that later failed in spectacular fashion and has since been demolished. Many of Mirabel's maple syrup producers were dispossessed. My stepfather went to the auction and for $25 bought a huge evaporator

MAPLE SAP EVAPORATOR

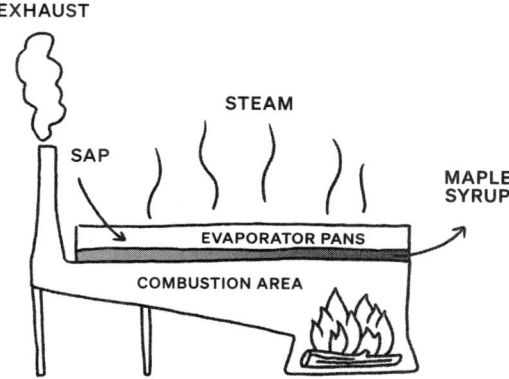

along with hundreds of buckets and taps: everything. He came home with an enormous amount of equipment.

In researching this book I've come to realize that most of my family's sugaring equipment and techniques belonged in the 19th century. My stepfather used a brace and bit, for example—a drill you crank by hand—to make holes in the maple trees. Then he used a hammer to tap into the hole a metal spile, which had a ring around it with a hook. We hung a welded tin bucket on each hook and affixed a lid on top to keep out rain, snow, insects and other impurities. Our buckets were already hopelessly outdated: In 1935, the US government sought to ban syrup imports from Canada because of the lead content, which leeched solder that held the buckets together. In response, the Quebec and federal governments offered a subsidy to producers willing to turn in their old vessels, paying two-thirds of the cost for new aluminum buckets. Although eighteen million sap buckets were switched out in that period, we ended up with the old, lead-soldered ones (perhaps explaining my dim wit . . .).

We had more pressing matters at hand: trying to eke a little sugar from a lot of trees. Like anyone else who takes up syrup-making, we were dismayed at the paltry results of our herculean efforts. After collecting back-breaking volumes of sap, cutting and stacking big piles of firewood, and then burning said wood to boil the sap for days, we ended up with just a few little bottles of syrup. Still, we persisted. A couple of years later my stepfather acquired a tractor, a small but indomitable grey gas-powered Ferguson from the 1950s. On the back of the tractor he attached a barrel to hold maple sap. Despite its age, the tractor was technologically light years ahead of the rest of the gear that we used for the job.

My parents didn't hesitate to put us kids to work, either. While we sat in school, the sap would slowly drip, drip, drip into the buckets and gradually fill them up. At the end of the day, the school bus would drop us off at the sugar bush rather than at home. While other kids watched *The Brady Bunch* and *The Six Million Dollar Man* on TV, we'd change our footwear and head into the forest. In a bid to keep our pants dry, we'd tuck our jeans into rubber boots, the kind with a red strip across the top and a red sole (made in Canada and typically sold at Canadian Tire, these boots are wrong for the job). We began the sap collection job at the sugar shack. Our stepfather would steer the tractor into the deep snow, and we would follow the deep tracks carved by its fat rear tires, each of us carrying two 20-litre, or five-gallon (US), white plastic pails. The chains on the tractor tires jingled in the quiet frosty afternoon air. On our arrival in the woods, we'd plunge into snowdrifts, forging a path to the maple trees. Every laboured footfall would see us waist-deep in snow. Arriving at a tree, we would pour the sap from the tin buckets into the plastic pails. Our stepfather would idle the tractor and we'd run to catch up and pour the sap into the tank.

Snow, in spring, gains a crystalline quality. This gravelly snow would pour over the lip of our boots and find its way down to our wool socks. As we'd struggle back to the tractor to pour the sap into the steel tank on its back, the brimming pails of cold sap would slap against our legs and slosh into our boots, mixing with the snow and soaking our jeans and socks. Never since have my feet felt that cold.

Sometimes we'd get lucky with the weather, and a rain-storm followed by a hard frost would top the deep snow with a thick crust of bumpy ice that would make it possible to walk as though we were on pavement. But it wouldn't last. Inevitably, I'd think I was on solid ground and then, without warning, my boot would punch through the crust and I'd sink up to my waist in snow, pouring sap onto my jeans as I plunged.

I cannot say I fell in love with the sugar bush during those moments. Mostly I remember the labour and the cold. But there was also magic. Every day the sun got brighter and the snow melted. Although late-winter blizzards did wallop us with bleak regularity, the trend was to warmer weather. I remember those spring afternoons when we would jump off the school bus and run toward the sugar shack through the slowly receding snow, a carpet of dead leaves and grass beneath our feet. Birds in song. Water running in little creeks and ditches beside the road.

We'd clamber up steep hillsides. Sugar bushes often thrive on hills, located in areas settlers never bothered to clear since their slope makes them unsuitable for agriculture. At the top of one of our hills my stepfather had set a vintage dairy can. He had drilled a hole at the bottom of the can and attached a black plastic hose, which ran down the hill to the collecting basin behind the sugar shack. We'd pour crystal-clear, ice-cold sap through fine cheesecloth tied across the mouth of the milk can, and the sap would rush down the hill. The can would make a satisfying deep sucking noise as the last of the sap departed on its journey. My sister Noelle remembers us calling back and forth so nobody had to walk to a tree where the buckets had already been emptied—the job required teamwork. We bonded in the maple forests.

Gradually, we'd fill the tank. Our job was mostly done. Sometimes we could hitch a ride on the rear fenders of the tractor as it trundled back to the sugar shack. At the shack we'd tip the spout on the tank that sat on the back of the tractor and pour the sap into the reservoir. Then my stepfather would light a fire in the evaporator using the wood he had worked all winter to cut and stack in the adjacent shed.

Our recompense came after dark. We'd hang our sopping wool socks to dry by the warmth of the fire crackling in the evaporator. Steam, smelling very slightly of maple sap, would envelop us. On occasion, before bed, we'd get a sip of fresh, hot, golden, sweet maple syrup.

Just as spring, usually much later than we'd prefer, finally overtakes winter, my family, against very long odds and with many setbacks, succeeded at maple syrup. And maple syrup—*sirop d'érable*—found its way into my bloodstream. Ever since, sugaring off has had, for me, a spiritual quality. It's one of the things that helps to define me.

For my friend Oona, going to the sugar bush as a child was boring, cold and uncomfortable. It sucked. She didn't see the point. For me, the sugar bush made me feel as though my life finally had a point. In the years before we settled on the farm, my siblings and I felt like we were a bit of a burden to our parents, getting in the way as they sought to enjoy the Summer of Love in Haight-Ashbury, San Francisco, or whatever late-sixties, early-seventies follies had beckoned. But once we moved to the farm, we kids became an indispensable part of the equation. For the first time, I felt needed.

I asked my mother why we pursued making maple syrup when we had so little experience and resources. She answered: "Why did we make maple syrup? That's the time it was. It was the *temps des sucres*." After a pause, she added, "After living here for more than fifty years, there is very little that I connect with about the feeling of what it is to be a Québécois. I will be a foreigner 'til the day I die. But maple syrup was one point where we saw eye to eye with our neighbours. For you and for me it was a shared cultural experience with the people around us, and it was a shared family experience."

The first year we made just a few bottles of syrup. Later my parents had two other daughters, who as they grew up began to help out in the sugar bush. By the time I moved out at age sixteen, our family made all the syrup and sugar we needed, and even had some for sale. We usually stored it in old whisky bottles or brown gallon jugs that had held Algerian red wine. After weathering five grade schools in six years before moving to the farm, the toil of collecting cold sap in deep snow and transforming it into sweet syrup became my redemption story. The bliss I felt then has always stayed with me.

My whining about wet socks seems infantile when I think of the farmers along our dirt road who taught us to make syrup: Lecot, Labelle, Poulin. They were the original back-to-the-landers, as my stepfather reminds me. Totally pure old Quebec: raising families of up to ten children with no electricity. They made maple syrup because they had no other sugar. When we vote for leaders with plans to fight global warming, that's the Canada we seek to protect. A rugged landscape where we overcome obstacles to thrive, where icy winters give way to the miracle of spring and bring us the first harvest: maple syrup.

THE FIRST SUGAR-MAKERS

P arry Sound lies north of Toronto on the eastern shore of the Georgian Bay of Lake Huron. The town is home to the Bobby Orr Hall of Fame. The great hockey defenceman for the Boston Bruins learned to skate on the Seguin River where it flows into Parry Sound. *Sports Illustrated*, in a story on Orr in 1966, wrote that every winter day Orr and the other kids from town played hockey on the harbour, where the ice can freeze a metre thick. The children played against each other or the Indigenous boys from Parry Island, who skated onto the ice brandishing saplings for hockey sticks.

The boys from Parry Island, just offshore of the town of Parry Sound, hailed from Wasauksing First Nation; Wasauksing means "Place that Shines in the Sacred Light." In the 19th century, settlers moved these Anishinaabe people, whose members belong to the Ojibwe, Odawa and Potawatomi Nations, to the island. Perhaps Wasauksing's most famous son is Sergeant Major Francis Pegahmagabow, who fought for Canada in World War I, becoming the deadliest sniper on either side of the war.

Today, though, I am here to research something else, a subject as central to Canada's history as war or hockey: the Indigenous manufacture of maple syrup.

Many books on maple syrup begin with the assertion that the First Peoples of North America pioneered the extraction of sap from maple trees in spring, to be boiled down into sugar. In *The Maple Sugar Book*, Helen and Scott Nearing are definitive: Indigenous Peoples taught colonists to make maple sugar. But where are the Indigenous maple syrup makers of today? They are hard to find, for a simple reason: colonizers claimed the forest as their own, cut down much of it, pushed Indigenous Peoples onto reserves, and then sent their children to residential schools to strip them of their culture, causing unimaginable suffering, death and intergenerational trauma.

The road to reconciliation and a better future for Indigenous People in Canada is long. Recently, First Peoples have been finding their way back into the syrup business, one tree at a time. Many are adopting technology to extract sweet water from those maple trees to which they have access. Rebuilding their ancestral connection to the sugar bush is a long journey—but the result tastes very sweet. And that is what brings me to Wasauksing: an opportunity to meet Indigenous maple syrup makers.

Winter in Parry Sound is a serious business. I once had to stick my mittened hand in a snowbank to excavate a parking meter just so I could drop a quarter in the slot, so I am glad my visit is falling at the turn of the season. On this

April morning, ice covers the sound. With the warm sun the ice has begun to melt. The only access to the island is the Wasauksing Swing Bridge, a steel relic built in 1895, wide enough for one car. Oncoming traffic must wait at a stoplight for its turn. A sign announces that the bridge belongs to the Government of Canada, with operation by Wasauksing First Nation.

The largest of 30,000 islands in the world's largest freshwater archipelago, Parry Island is bigger than Manhattan but sparsely populated: The Anishnaabe community—a term that refers to a number of First Nations concentrated around the Great Lakes—counts a few hundred souls. Settler cottagers hold leases on the island's northwest shore. The scarcity of people leaves a lot of room for trees. As instructed, I turn left at a substantial graveyard, where historic headstones stand sentinel. My car bounces down a wet and rutted gravel road covered in snow and mud, and lined with birch and poplar forests. A sign points left to the Wasauksing Marina and Wasauksing Maple Products.

The sugar shack sits in a hillside clearing surrounded by maple trees; it's a barn-sized structure covered in corrugated tin. A half-dozen steel chimneys of various diameters and heights jut from its roof. Guy wires run from the largest smokestack to points in the forest to ensure the tall and vital chimney remains upright. A cupola—a smaller raised roof intended to let vapour from boiling sap out of the shack—crowns the roof. A ladder leans against the roof. I learn later that staff had climbed up to install wire-mesh fencing over the opening of the cupola to deter the raccoons who had discovered the yummy syrup inside. Plastic tubes, blue and black, run from the forest into the building. Bars cover the windows. Next to the sugar shack, in a big open-sided wood-shed, tower stacks of corded dry firewood.

On that crisp clear morning no smoke curls from the chimney, nor does steam billow from the cupola.

The structure's twin plywood doors, like barn doors, stand open. In the doorway stands a tall man with broad shoulders. He introduces himself: Marshall Badger. He wears tall black rubber boots and thick black gloves that taper halfway down his forearms, with reflective silver stripes. Badger, who has a weathered, square and craggy face, is busy at the front of the evaporator—a noble beast, bigger than a pickup truck, made of a cast-iron firebox on which rest stainless-steel sap pans and crowned with a range hood that glitters in the morning light.

Badger opens the evaporator's iron doors. Beside him wait chunks of maple firewood, each as big as a toaster. Badger places one on a chopping block. With a small sharp axe he splits off kindling. Then, over crumpled newspaper inside the firebox, he builds a teepee using those thin sticks and lights a match. As a merry little fire catches, Marshall relates a brief version of his biography: "I was adopted into a non-native family," he says. "But my parents always kept me close to my culture." After studies in sports psychology at Seneca College, where he majored in tennis, and at what was then Ryerson University in Toronto, he found work as far south as Oklahoma, helping troubled youth. And now he is back where his ancestors came from, building a fire, as his people have every spring for much longer than anyone can remember, to boil sap into maple syrup.

Up until the 1960s almost every family on Parry Island made maple syrup. They tapped trees with metal spiles, hung cans to catch the sap, and boiled the sap outside in cast-iron pots on oven racks over open fires. The Anishnaabe have for centuries gathered for spiritual celebrations of the sugar season. Under colonial influence the locals replaced their ancient traditions with the Parry Island Maple Fest, where they competed in pie-baking and voted for the cutest baby, the best chili, the tastiest scones, and the best Mr. and Mrs. Sapsucker. "One guy used to win all the time," recounted Dave Rice, a community worker and hockey coach at Wasauksing. "He dressed like a voyageur, in a checkered wool shirt, with teeth darkened so it looked like he had missing teeth, carrying old snowshoes and a pail."

Today Wasauksing calls its sugaring-off party a Sweetwater Ceremony. The celebration of Ninaatigwaaboo, or maple sap, takes place at Enji-nooj-mo-haad, or "A Place of Healing" in the community.

In the 1960s Wasauksing built this sugar shack. The enterprise has had its ups and downs. Generations of Indigenous Peoples have had to leave their communities to find work: a quarter of the Wasauksing population left the island between 2011 and 2016. The syrup operation is part of the effort to create opportunity at home. There is plenty of hope and goodwill, but challenges are many and funding is tight.

As I stand talking to Badger, while the first flames lick the bottom of the evaporator pan, a sturdy man with a moustache and goatee walks over to introduce himself. The sugar bush operations manager is dressed in a stained brown padded vest over a black fleece, work pants and thermal rubber boots. He offers me a big hand to shake and tells me his name is Chris Chomyshyn, pronounced "Commission."

Wasauksing's syrup season has gotten off to a slow start. Just as the sap began to run at the end of March, mechanical failure shut down the pump that creates vacuum pressure to suck sap from the maple trees. The sap still flows by gravity— slowly. Chomyshyn has ordered a new plate and roller bearing, and is waiting on delivery. This mechanical failure had a silver lining: Contemporary sugar shacks are noisy places, a bit like the furnace room of a high-rise. With the pump down, all that's left is the sound of the fire crackling in the evaporator, rendering the sugar shack a lovely place to conduct my interviews.

Chomyshyn's own story epitomizes the tortuous route of many First Peoples: pushed away from their traditional territories and, in some cases, making their way back. Chomyshyn's grandmother Adrienne King, born on Parry Island, lost her Indigenous status when she married a Ukrainian man. Chomyshyn grew up in British Columbia. He became a tree-planter. Later his father, a property manager, moved to Wasauksing to work in the community's real estate division and learned that the community sugaring operation needed love. He told his son. In 2012 Canada updated the Indian Act, and Chomyshyn was able to get Indian status. This offensive term is the precise legal language for Indigenous people eligible for registration; the word is wrapped up in a long history of official government policy that aimed to disenfranchise and assimilate the First Peoples.

Chomyshyn had spent his whole career in the forest, so the sugar bush job sounded good to him. He traded the evergreen forests of British Columbia for the hardwood forests of Ontario. He is determined to move any obstacle, including the heavy weight of history, to make a success of this sugaring enterprise. "I feel like I am taking my skills that I have learned somewhere else and bringing them back to contribute to the community," says Chomyshyn. "Forestry skills, leadership skills. I lifeguarded for years on Vancouver Island so I am familiar with pumps. The opportunity came up, and I couldn't turn away the chance to make maple syrup. I'm lucky. I worked as a tree-planter for twenty-three years. I'm not afraid of hard work. I manage forest crews. It wasn't too much to switch from an eighteen-man crew of tree planters to a six-man crew for maple syrup because it's mostly forest work." How did he learn to make maple syrup? He pulls out his tattered copy of the thick, authoritative *North American Maple Syrup Producers Manual*, published by the University of Vermont. "I read this," he says. "When I started I just researched the hell out of it." Chomyshyn inherited the evaporator; he added the vacuum pump and reverse osmosis, a technology that removes some water from the sap to reduce the length of time needed to boil sap into syrup.

The year I visited, the Wasauksing Maple Product team put about 2,700 taps into sugar maple trees over a two-month period. That sounds like a lot of taps to me, thousands more than we'd tapped when I was a kid, but, as we'll see later, that is a comparatively small sugar bush by contemporary standards. The Wasausking staff drilled holes and put a spout or spile in each hole. Attached to each spile, a pale blue plastic tube feeds sap to larger trunk lines that then bring the sap either directly into the shack or into a separate pumping house down the road.

The struggles faced by the Wasausking workers to make maple syrup in spring would feel familiar to their ancestors. The tools may have changed, but one constant remains: It takes a lot of effort to reduce 40 pails of sap into one pail of syrup. The job is so demanding that, over the centuries,

Indigenous Peoples across sugar maple country have passed down similar versions of a parable to explain the toil needed to make a sweetener from the maple tree.

The hero of this fable is Nanabozho, in the accounts I read from the Ottawa and Chippewa Nations. The Abenaki Nation, in what is now Vermont, call him Gluskonba. For other Nations he is Manabush. Long ago, this hero went from village to village to keep an eye on people for the Creator. One day he arrived at a village that looked abandoned, with overgrown fields. Cooking fires had gone cold. He heard moaning. He followed the sound to a stand of maple trees, under which people lay on their backs. They had broken tree branches, and thick, sweet maple syrup dripped into their mouths. The syrup had made them so fat and lazy that they could hardly move. Disgusted by this sloth, Nanabozho/Gluskonba/Manabush fashioned a large bucket from birch bark, scooped into it a lake's worth of water, and poured the water into the maple trees. Finding the sap no longer thick nor sweet, the people got up and asked where their treat had gone. The hero told them they would now only get syrup through much hard work: make birch bark buckets to collect the sap; gather wood for fires to boil the sap into syrup. And henceforth, sweet sap would only run from sugar maples for a brief period in spring.

It was this laborious effort by the First Peoples to make sugar from trees that the first Europeans observed on arrival in what is now Canada. Settlers often belittled the First Nations techniques. A booklet, *The Maple: Pride of Quebec*, produced in 1920 by the Maple Syrup Producers of Quebec, notes that the "primitive methods" that the First Peoples used to make maple products "were quickly improved by the Whites."

Addressing a maple producers' conference in Rigaud, Quebec, in 1916, Joseph Lefebvre, of Quebec's Ministry of Agriculture, came up with this patronizing line: "Long before civilization came to the Americas, people made maple syrup and maple sugar in Canada." The First Peoples, Lefebvre explained, cut the maples with a tomahawk, put a stick in the slit, and the sap dripped into a bucket made of birch bark. They then boiled the sap in earthen cauldrons. "They made this way small quantities of dark and thick syrup."

Incredibly, some writers have questioned whether Indigenous Peoples were the first to make syrup. A history chapter in the *North American Maple Syrup Producers Manual*, a book in the Wasauksing Maple Products kitchen—on which the staff relies for technical detail, not for its take on history—states that archaeologists and historians have no solid proof that the First Peoples made maple syrup or sugar before Europeans arrived. The Producteurs et productrices acéricoles du Quebéc, the syrup producers' group that controls most of the world's maple syrup, writes on its website that the Europeans and the Native Americans discovered maple syrup together thanks to the iron cauldron brought by settlers from France.

The speciousness of this logic lies in the suggestion that the First Peoples could not boil anything before colonists brought metal vessels. As a corollary to this line of reasoning, some authors, such as Tim Herd in the book *Maple Sugar* and Maxime Caouette his book *Histoire acéricole*, who say Indigenous Peoples were the first to make sugar from maple sap, describe a technique that beggars belief: The authors report that the First Peoples would pour maple sap into wooden troughs, birch bark vessels or hollow logs, and then add red-hot rocks from a fire to slowly evaporate the water and leave behind a dark sweet sugar.

Anybody who's stood shivering in the woods in the snow in early spring by a pan of maple sap, stoking the fire for hours, if not days, to distill the liquid into maple syrup, knows that the hot rock method would never succeed. It's actually a silly suggestion.

Brian Chenevert, Tribal Historian for the Nulhegan Band of the Coosuk-Abenaki Nation in Vermont, calls the hot-rocks-in-wood-trough description "insulting." In an essay on sugaring published by his community's history department in 2021, he writes that ascribing this technique to his ancestors suggests that they were primitive and lacked the technology to boil food before settlers brought brass and iron pots. In fact, Chenevert states, the Abenaki boiled the maple sap into sugar in clay pots hung over the fire, as they had cooked soups, stews and tea for thousands of years. To put rocks covered in ash into maple sap, he points out, would ruin the stuff.

There is evidence of clay pots in the written record. In his voyage of discovery of 1632, F. Gabriel Sagard-Théodat, a Franciscan friar and missionary to Quebec, describes how the First Peoples with whom he visited cooked corn into *sagamité*, a stew: "When they want to cook it, they put it in the bouillon, where they had already cooked some meat or fish which is cut up, with a quantity of pumpkin, or in clear broth, and cook it until the sagamité gets thick enough, and stirring it constantly with a spatula, which they call an *estoqua*, and then they spoon it into bowls, with a bit of oil or grease on top. This sagamité is delicious, and it fills you up." He adds, "Our Hurons, and other sedentary nations, had, and still have, the use and the knowledge of how to make clay pots, which they use to cook in, and which are good and strong, and don't break when put on the fire, even if they are empty."

Other early adventurers in the New World also tell of eating meals cooked in clay pots over the fire: The method sounds effective, even if some didn't much care for the results. "Nothing more disgusting," wrote Father Sébastien Rasles when describing his visit to an Abenaki village in Quebec in 1689. "After having filled their boiler with meat, they let it boil at most three-quarters of an hour, after which they take it from the fire." Clearly boiling foodstuff was routine for these Nations.

One afternoon I caught up over Zoom with Dominic Beaudry from Wiikwemkoong, an unceded Anishinaabe settlement on Manitoulin Island in Georgian Bay. Beaudry is associate vice-president of academic and Indigenous programs at Laurentian University in Sudbury. He told me that historically his people practised agriculture; colonial rewriting of history tends to turn the Anishnaabe into primitive savages. In that narrative, he said, "The brave Europeans are going to arrive to civilize us. But there were already complex agricultural communities that existed in the Lake Huron region."

Denying that the First Peoples made sugar from maple before colonization is part of this erroneous settler narrative, he said. His people boiled sap to sugar in clay pots—a fine technique. "Even some of the world's best chefs today use ceramic and pottery pots," he said. "It's not a primitive process. This is high culture, comparable to Italians processing grapes. It was part of an economic enterprise. These are people who planned well for their communities." He granted that his people gladly switched to cast-iron pots after contact with Europeans: "Metal pots were trade items during the fur trade era. We adapted to change."

"Indigenous people throughout the Northeast have been sugaring for thousands of years. Each year, we waited for the perfect time to start tapping maple trees."

BRIAN CHENEVERT,
Maple Sugaring Among the Abenaki and Wabanaki Peoples, 2021

For the First Peoples, maple sugar and maple syrup were much more than condiments: Maple sap, maple sugar and maple syrup sustained them. Maple syrup was used as a remedy for breathing problems. Maple sap, syrup or sugar was used to treat heart and stomach problems. Sap straight from the tree has diuretic properties: it helps reduce fluid buildup in the body. Indigenous Peoples sweetened herbal teas with maple sugar, and sometimes healers secreted medicine in sugar cakes (a strategy later popularized by Mary Poppins). The Haudenosaunee, also known as the Six Nations Iroquois Confederacy, added black raspberries or thimble berries to maple sap, making a non-alcoholic beverage they drank for rituals in the Longhouse, which was their centre of communal life. Haudenosaunee women dried and pounded bark from red maple and sugar maple trees to make a powder that they baked into bread. The Meskwaki, who are of Algonquin origin, used syrup to season meat. Across the region where maple trees grow, First Peoples carved maple's hard and tight-grained wood into bowls, cooking stirrers, paddles, and bows and arrows, as well as using the wood as fuel. Continuing today, First Nations cherish maple syrup for its healing and nourishing powers.

The sugar bush was a woman's domain. Women made the wood spiles, ladles and birch vessels used to collect the maple sap. Women moved to the sugar bush in spring, where they tapped the trees, boiled the sap and taught their daughters to do the same. Men would set up the poles over the fire, to suspend the pots of sap to boil, and cut firewood to feed the fires.

The ancestors of Wasauksing's sugar bush staff depended on maple sugar as a staple in their diet. They used maple sugar to season meat, fish, fruit and vegetable dishes. The

Europeans who arrived quickly gained a taste for the sweetener, and bought it in quantities that dwarf the amounts Wasauksing makes. The Ojibwe of the 17th to 19th centuries sold maple sugar in blocks packaged in birch bark, known as *makaks*, that could weigh up to about 12 kilograms, or 26 pounds, each. Their first non-Indigenous customers were French *coureurs de bois*, the first fur traders. Later, over a two-century period up to around 1873, the Ojibwe supplied sugar to the three main fur trading companies in eastern North America. The maple sugar that European traders could obtain from the industrious and skilled Indigenous sugar-makers, in exchange for cloth or alcohol, among other goods, was cheaper and more abundant than cane sugar, which was coming from much farther away. The European fur trading companies redistributed the sugar to their trading posts.

But not all traders paid the First Peoples for the sweetener. In his journal of 1802–1804, *My First Years in the Fur Trade*, George Nelson, a teen who travelled as a clerk with the Montreal-based XY Company, described how his party ran low on food while on a trip near Grand Portage, Minnesota. They knew of the Ojibwe custom of leaving sugar for the dead and took from a gravesite a bark box containing about 18 kilograms, or 40 pounds, of sugar.

In my school our Canadian history books told stories of the First Nations, Métis and Inuit Peoples trading furs with the Europeans for pots, knives, axes, guns, blankets, cloth and thread, but they did not mention maple sugar. Still, records show that the growing colonies bought all the maple sugar that the Indigenous Peoples could spare. The First Peoples had the know-how and the manpower and the trees. "We are not talking about the little trees we have today," noted

Beaudry. "These were huge maple trees." The settlers provided iron pots to hang over the fire, a useful improvement over the clay pots the Indigenous Peoples were using, one that boosted their output of maple sugar.

Sugaring is woven into Indigenous culture. The annual move to the sugar bush signifies the beginning of spring. The Anishnaabe name for March is *iskigamizige giizis*, or the Month of the Sap-Boiling Moon. Alexander Henry, an American fur trader and adventurer in the 1760s, in his book *Travels and Adventures in the Years 1760-1776*, describes moving with a group of Chippewa to a sugar bush along Lake Huron's St. Martins Bay, south of Sault Ste. Marie. In one day the group built a 6- x 4-metre, or 20- x 14-foot, house. Then the Chippewa gathered birch bark to make vessels "to catch the wine or sap," Henry writes. He adds that the locals tapped the trees and put in "spouts or ducts," and caught the sap in the birch containers. The sugar-makers transported the sap in 100-gallon reservoirs made of moose skin and poured it into a dozen boilers under which fires burned. Within weeks, he reports, the group returned to Fort Michilimackinac—a stronghold of the period at the strait between Lake Huron and Lake Michigan—with "six hundredweight of sugar and 36 gallons of syrup."

Authors of colonial maple syrup histories may disagree on the origins of maple syrup, but they agree on one point: the virtuous and morally superior nature of maple syrup during the colonial era, in contrast to the taint that clung to sugar made from cane, grown mainly by the slaves that European powers brought to the islands of the Caribbean. This theme, contrasting righteous maple syrup with immoral white sugar, comes up in many histories of maple syrup.

Benjamin Rush, a celebrated physician who signed the US Declaration of Independence, wrote in a letter to Thomas Jefferson, the third president of the United States: "I cannot help contemplating a Sugar Maple Tree with a species of affection, and even veneration; for I have persuaded myself to behold in it the happy means of rendering the commerce and slavery of our African brethren in the sugar islands, as unnecessary as it has always been inhuman and unjust." During the US Civil War, maple sugar gained popularity in the Union States, which had abolished slavery.

But our maple syrup is not so pure. The relationship between the settlers, who had viewed Indigenous Peoples as trusted partners to supply vital foodstuffs, such as maple sugar, changed around the 19th century. Improvements in technology lowered the price of cane sugar, decreasing the settlers' need for maple sugar. Settlers dispossessed the First Peoples of their lands, including the maple forests across eastern Canada and the US northeast, cleared the land for agriculture, and cut the maple trees for timber—or set about making maple syrup themselves. The forced displacement of Indigenous Peoples from their lands is a pivotal point in Canada's history that clouds, discolours and even embitters the taste of our national sweetener.

One place in Ontario encapsulates the settlers' attitude shift from viewing Indigenous Peoples as economic and military partners to consigning them as an awkward anachronism: Manitoulin Island. Manitoulin, in the Georgian Bay north of Wasauksing, is the world's largest freshwater island, more than five times the size of the Island of Montreal. The ancient Anishinaabe creation story says that when G'chi Manitou, the Great Spirit, created Turtle Island (a First Nations word for

North America), he set aside a place to rest, taking the bluest waters, the fluffiest clouds, the most fertile fields and the lushest forests to make Manitoulin, or Great Spirit Island. The island remains a sacred place for the Anishinaabe Peoples.

Before colonization, thick forests of leaf trees covered the island. Every spring, Indigenous communities on Manitoulin gathered sap from the sugar bushes to make *ziinzibaakwad,* or maple sugar. This tradition endured for millennia. Then the settlers arrived. After initially buying maple sugar from the First Peoples, the settlers pushed them out of the Manitoulin sugar bushes to make way for farms.

At first, the British had promised to leave Manitoulin alone. Sir Francis Bond Head, a hot-headed soldier whom the British appointed as lieutenant-governor of Upper Canada in 1835—and recalled two years later after his tempestuous and vindictive tenure—negotiated a treaty with local First Peoples around Lake Huron in what is now Ontario. Bond Head persuaded the Saugeen First Nation to surrender 600,000 hectares, or 1.5 million acres, and move to Manitoulin Island, which Bond Head protected for the exclusive use of Indigenous Peoples, including the Huron and Moravian Nations as well.

But the deal to set aside Manitoulin for Indigenous Peoples proved short-lived. In 1862, the British Crown changed its mind. The Crown adroitly excluded from talks on the fate of Manitoulin the people of Wiikwemkoong, its main settlement; thus negotiators obtained most of the island for settlers by agreement of less than half its population. The deal consigned the First Peoples to six reserves on Manitoulin. The Indian Act of 1876 forced Indigenous Peoples to live on these reserves—small, unproductive land tracts—and required them to seek permission to leave the reserve. This displacement severed the Anishinaabe connection to their ancestral home: the sugar bush.

The Government of Canada's Indian Affairs Central Registry holds a file with the title "Manitoulin Island Agency—Correspondence Regarding Land Sales in Howland Township that Was Being Used as a Sugarbush by the Indians." The letters in the file capture the anguish of the Indigenous Peoples on Manitoulin when barred from something they had always done: make maple sugar in spring.

Canada became a country in 1867. The maple chapter in the Manitoulin story begins just after the nation's birth. The Canadian government under the Indian Act had appointed an administrator called an Indian Agent to live on each reservation and enforce the Act, with ultimate decision-making held by the superintendent-general of Indian Affairs, in Ottawa. In 1875, the Indian Agent for Manitoulin reported the distress of the Sheguiandah First Nation as settlers cut down or burned the sugar bushes to make way for agriculture. The agent, in a letter to the Department of the Interior in Ottawa, handwritten in ink with a quill pen, described a "Council of Indians" held at Michijueedinong:

> Chief Taibosegar . . . enquired whether an Indian would be allowed to buy a piece of land for the purpose of sugar-making, one of the Indians present being desirous of purchasing a piece of land outside of their reserve where he had been accustomed to make sugar.
>
> The Indians have been accustomed to make sugar anywhere on the Island where they pleased, that as the land becomes settled, disputes occasionally occur, and

whereas it sometimes happens while clearing the land their camps containing their kettles and sap troughs are burned, much ill feeling is caused; to prevent the growth of this feeling between the settlers and Indians, which might lead to trouble, I respectfully submit that by allowing the Indians the use of certain shared lands for sugar-making, and withholding such from sale, that the liability of trouble growing out of this matter would be avoided. This branch of industry is of great importance to the Indians—the quantity made by an average family being five hundred pounds annually, which represents the value of about fifty dollars, adding greatly to their domestic comfort, and I promised to bring to your notice their requirements, assuring them that in this and other matters their interests would be cared for.

A month later a bureaucrat in Ottawa wrote back to inquire "what quantity of land you consider would be sufficient to allow the Manitoulin Island Indians the use of for the purpose of making sugar?"

The agent suggested reserving several lots in a township then called Sandfield—a total of 351 hectares, or 868 acres—noting that the land had been sold to two settlers named John Shipper and Noah Shipper, but added that they "are quite willing to give up the lots and take land elsewhere."

Notwithstanding the agent's words, it is clear that the vast majority of settlers insisted on unfettered access to all the land on Manitoulin (minus the reserves). That April, dozens of settlers on Manitoulin signed a petition, appending: "Your petitioners feel satisfied that Indians will never make use of this land. They then humbly ask that you will cause it to be put into the market for sale."

But the Canadian government did not sell the forest—not yet. Robert Thorburn, the Indian Agent, took up the band's cause, writing that the Sheguiandah "are not accustomed themselves to the changed conditions of life. The maple products are used very much as a food and any surplus that they can make finds a ready market at 10 cents per lb for sugar and $1 per gallon for syrup. The sugar season comes just at a time when there is no work and considering that the area occupied by 14 sugar camps has been burnt over and the camps destroyed . . . I would ask that the department consider the matter and if possible grant their wishes."

In April 1875, the Government of Canada "set aside" about 140 hectares, or 350 acres, on Manitoulin—less than half the land the agent requested—for the local Indigenous Peoples to make maple syrup and maple sugar, but never returned title to this forest to them.

During this period, many Indigenous communities sought to retain access to their historic maple forests to make sugar. An Indian Agent's report from 1874 in what is now Wisconsin recorded that, even as government policy forced them onto reserves, the Anishnaabe ventured into the forests that surrounded seven reservations and produced over 200,000 pounds of maple sugar.

Dominic Beaudry of Wiikwemkoong Unceded Territory on Manitoulin Island told me: "Our people were called the Sugar Kings before the settlers over logged the region." Once colonization began in earnest in the mid-19th century, the government moved to weaken the economic structure of the Indigenous Peoples. He added: "The settlers burned down our forest because we wouldn't sign the treaty." Beaudry compares the destruction of the sugar bush in his part of Ontario to the settlers' eradication of buffalo from the Great Plains across North America's West—a genocidal removal of a linchpin of Indigenous survival.

On Manitoulin Island, the ultimate disposition of the forest that the Crown "set aside" for use by the Indigenous Peoples helps to illustrate colonizers' relentless efforts to control all the land and stifle the Indigenous Peoples' sugaring industry. Letters in the Ottawa file describe how, over the ensuing decades, settlers continued to illegally log that forest. In the early 20th century, the Government of Ontario cut a road through the land and gave the hardwood timber to settlers for firewood—without permission from Indian Affairs. Meanwhile Indigenous sugar-making on the land waned. A 1907 letter from the Indian Office at Manitowaning notes: "The main reason that those who used to go there to make sugar quit doing so was on account of the treatment they got from the settlers who apparently took delight in destroying the property of the Indians." In the 1930s the Manitoulin Island Rural Telephone Company received permission from the federal government to install a line across the lots.

Over the years Canada's federal government repeatedly asked the West Bay Band, known today as M'Chigeeng First Nation, for permission to sell the reserved forest. The West Bay Band Council passed a resolution in 1937 saying they would accept a minimum of $3,000 for the property. Ignoring the Council, in 1943 the federal Department of Indian Affairs sold it to several settlers for a total of $1,200. The outraged West Bay Band Council wrote to the Indian Agent: "I would like to know who sold this and why the Indians were not notified." The Indian Agent passed the question to his boss, the Superintendent for Reserves and Trusts of Indian Affairs, who responded that the First Peoples had surrendered the land in 1861; that it had been reserved for their use as a sugar bush but that since "the Indians made no use of this reserve land for sugar bush purposes . . . its sale in the Indian interest was strongly indicated . . ." A further letter notes: "The $1,200 which was added to the capital account of the owners of the land is in the judgment of this office of more value to them than the possession of this surrendered land which they are not using for the purposes for which it was temporarily reserved." It's unclear who got the $1,200; "the owners of this land" appears, by the government's logic, to be the Government of Canada.

Indigenous Peoples were forced from sugar bushes across eastern Canada. In Quebec, after the Government of Canada moved a Mohawk community to a reservation called Caughnawaga (now known as Kahnawake) on the south shore of the St. Lawrence River in Quebec, across from Montreal, the Mohawk people, who relied on their sugar bush to make syrup and sugar, appealed in 1874 to the government for help to protect their forest from young men on the reserve who had begun cutting the trees in the sugaries to sell to settlers.

In 1876 Canada had passed the Indian Act, the goal of which was to disenfranchise and assimilate Indigenous Peoples into settler culture. In 1881 the Act was amended to forbid anyone from cutting sugar maples on the Caughnawaga reserve, a move that lays bare a certain absurdity. For millennia the Mohawk people had a sufficient supply of maple trees to both heat their hearths and produce maple syrup; Canadian government policy put the Mohawk in the bizarre position of having to ask the government for help to look after their own forests, reduced as they were from vast stretches of wilderness to a postage stamp hemmed in on all sides by the rapidly growing suburban area surrounding the city of Montreal.

There is a crushing irony in this saga. Canadians trumpet maple syrup production as an emblematic Canadian pursuit. At the same time, Canadian government policy aimed to wipe out the culture of Indigenous Peoples—in short, to make them less Indigenous and more like the settlers. But government policy took away the First Peoples' ability to perform that most "Canadian" of rituals: making syrup. Outnumbered and outgunned—the Indian Act prohibited the sale of ammunition to First Nations—Indigenous Peoples from Montreal to Manitoulin to Parry Island protested this restriction on their spring access to the sugar bush. Sometimes the government heard them. In 1888 the Government of Canada, reacting to complaints that community members near Parry Sound were logging the Indigenous sugar bush, issued an order-in-council, signed by the prime minister, Sir John A. Macdonald, that, "the cutting, carrying away, or removing of any hard or sugar maple tree or sapling from Parry Island or by the licensees of the timber on that Island, or by any other party or parties . . . are hereby prohibited under pain of the penalties in the said section mentioned."

Today, save for land leased to hundreds of cottagers on its north and west shore, Wasauksing First Nation occupies most of Parry Island and its sugar maple forests. While the lumber industry cut most of the forests around Parry Sound, the island's forests remain reasonably intact.

I AM KEEN to see the rest of the Wasauksing Maple Products operation. I join staffer Justen Tabobundung in his truck for a trip down a dirt road to another part of the sugar bush. We park and walk down a laneway too muddy for even his pickup. We stop at a pump house, placed here to gather the sap on this side of the road. Shrouding its tanks of maple sap is an innovation that Chomyshyn has adapted from his years as a tree-planter: a curtain made from a Silvicool tarp. Tree planters use Silvicool tarps to cover caches of tree seedlings, to keep the sun off until planters can get the trees into the ground. In this sugar bush, to protect the cool maple sap from the warming rays of the afternoon sun, as the sap accumulates in the collection tank prior to boiling, Chomyshyn has hung a Silvicool tarp across the front of the pump house.

In the pump house we find snowshoes, which we lace up. Tabobundung, a bearded man with plenty of enthusiasm, then straps on new canvas tree-planting bags, another Chomyshyn adaptation taken from his days in British Columbia. Chomyshyn ordered six sets of these shoulder bags. In the back bag, rather than tree seedlings, Tabobundung puts a coil of blue maple sap tubing; the side bags hold his tubing-repair pliers, tape, connectors and spiles. He also carries a small aluminum stepladder.

On our trudge through wet snow to a forested area beside a swamp, Tabobundung tells a bit of his story. His mother comes from the Vancouver suburb of White Rock. At age eighteen she visited Parry Island with the Beavers to build a library. On the island, she met Justen's father. Then she went back to White Rock and he was born. Tabobundung grew up in the West, working in oil and gas exploration in Alberta and Texas, until his father, still living in Wasauksing, got sick. "I came back three times. Then he passed, and I was liking it—being around my sisters." He caught the sugar bug: Along with his work here, he has put seventeen taps in his own trees—on the weekend he boiled for fifteen hours and, he told me with pride, made 1.75 litres of syrup.

Tabobundung climbs the stepladder to tap a spile into a tree. The snow has receded a metre since the Wasauksing team tapped these trees. Even on the ladder he cannot reach one spot above the pipe line to drill a hole. "Okay, buddy," he tells the tree. "You get to heal. You get to take the year off." He adds: "I try to be nice to the trees because I believe in karma. If you're not nice to them they might drop a big branch on ya."

As he walks, he listens. Sometimes, over the wind whistling through the branches of the maple and yellow birch trees, we hear a faint hiss—a leak in the vacuum pressure in the tubing. Tabobundung's job is to seal the leaks. He starts with the biggest leaks. "It's like triage," he says. The tubes are vulnerable to falling tree branches as well as to wildlife; earlier this season, a bear had stormed through and made a mess of the lines.

Tabobundung stops. He hears a hiss. He pulls electrical tape from a planting bag and wraps it on a tube to seal a hole. Every patch counts. Wasauksing made about 2,500 litres, or 2,640 quarts, of maple syrup in 2023, most of which they sold in Parry Sound, a popular summer tourist destination, or gifted to their community.

Other Indigenous Nations are also returning to the maple syrup business in a big way, including Ziibaakdakaan Maple on Cape Croker northwest of Toronto, and Giizhigat

Maple Products on St. Joseph Island near Sault Ste. Marie, Ontario. Another burgeoning Indigenous maple syrup operation belongs to the Nation Micmac de Gespeg on the tip of Quebec's Gaspé Peninsula. In 2020, after obtaining a quota to make syrup from Quebec's syrup producer federation, the Nation sank about $1 million into a project to build a sugar shack, with solar panels on its roof, in the public forests of the region, which the Nation calls Gespe'gewa'gi, or unceded territory. The Nation first had to thin the forest, build roads, and find the maple trees to tap.

Frédéric Basque, a forest technician and member of the Micmac Nation of Gespeg, works closely with CDL, a Quebec syrup equipment supplier, and took courses to learn the syrup trade. The sugar shack operation grew quickly, to 6,000 taps by 2024. That year they produced thirty-eight 34-gallon barrels of maple syrup. Basque worked seventy hours a week at the sugar shack during sugaring off, and described the myriad off-season jobs, among them cleaning the tubing and making stovewood to fire the evaporator. "*On parle d'un Moses de travail,*" he says, employing the semi-profane "Moses," which translates loosely to "It's a ton of work."

Terry Shaw, former Chief of the Nation Micmac de Gespeg and forest technician, calls the project sustainable development that respects nature and the territory. "We come together, become closer to one another," says Shaw. "We get back to our roots and back to the land."

This Indigenous community calls its sugaring operation Sigewigus, which translates to Sugar Moon. Sigewigus staff transform the syrup into maple butter, maple sugar, maple pie, maple popcorn, maple and pumpkin seed butter, maple and sunflower seed butter, plus a frozen delicacy called a maple butter and maple taffy cone. They sell these sweet wares online and at events such as the local ribfest and summer music festival. They also hold sugaring-off parties with traditional treats and Indigenous food. They are experimenting with other products, too, such as a forest pizza with locally foraged mushrooms and maple syrup, said Jonathan Desjarlais, the interim sugar bush co-ordinator. "We're making products that are a bit more wild," he said. "We have fun. We are making different things."

It is heartening to see these communities build back their legacy in the sugar bush. The bleak history of Canada's treatment of Indigenous Peoples stares us in the face. News media inundate us with stories of Indigenous people in custody, of suicide rates, of Indigenous communities forced for decades to boil contaminated water, and of bodies of murdered Indigenous women dumped in landfills. Centuries of official government policy have left deep scars in battered and wounded communities.

During my research for this book I attended a daylong workshop called "Indigenous Cultural Mindfulness Training" with a retired Ontario Provincial Police officer, who is Ojibwe. George Couchie told the audience of about forty people: "We need to get through this. But we need people to come with us to move through this." We *come with* the First Peoples when we seek out Indigenous maple products. Sugaring off allows Indigenous communities to heal and feel pride and make something that everybody likes to eat.

In comparison to the Nation Micmac de Gespeg operation, Wasauksing's sugar shack is quite analog. Other than cellphones, there is no information technology in sight: It is a few steps behind its non-Indigenous competitors. No big deal. The place has a sunny, relaxed, natural vibe, of people reclaiming their traditions and creating new ones. Chomyshyn does not see this as an arms race to make the most syrup with the least effort. He sees the whole project more philosophically; its goals are more wholistic than mercantile: "This allowed me to be a part of a community that I am pretty proud of, and apply my skills in a way that is beneficial to Wasauksing." As he speaks, his employees drift off. It's 4 p.m.—quitting time. The staff head home. Chomyshyn is in the shack, feeding wood to the fire that crackles under the syrup in the evaporator. He smiles. He plans to stay later, to keep boiling sap.

Chomyshyn is optimistic. "We are applying for federal funding to improve our building," he says. "We would like to add a new kitchen. This has so much potential, but it takes capital. It brings a lot of pride to the island because as Anishinaabe people we have been making maple syrup since the beginning of time, as far as we are concerned. It wouldn't be a bad idea to make some more money and put it back into the community."

COW-PILFERERS AND CARELESS SUGAR SENTINELS

In March in the sugar bush, a crisp, frosty night followed by a warm day is perfect weather for maple sap to run; on such a day a syrup-maker can find themselves with a great deal of sap to boil. The best-tasting maple syrup comes from sap boiled right after collection; bacteria in sap begins to multiply quickly in a holding tank. Waiting too long before boiling sap can result in darker syrup and taint its flavour. But boiling takes a long time. Maple sap contains on average about 2 percent sugar. The rest is water. Boil off half the liquid, and your sugar content goes to 4 percent. Keep boiling: Maple syrup is 66 percent sugar. A big sap run often requires a syrup-maker to boil all night.

Before electricity, reverse osmosis or efficient evaporators, the job of boiling maple sap into syrup while alone in the deep, dark woods, thick with snow, cold and with the stars sparkling through the tall leafless trees above, could—and still can—be a spooky occupation. I have been spooked myself in these conditions. It's hardly surprising that sugarers have passed down a thick catalogue of ghost stories from colonial times that take place in the sugar bush.

One such Quebec folktale tells of Carisse Bélanger from Saint-Antonin, east of Quebec City: One night Carisse found himself alone in his sugar shack, surrounded by snow in the deep woods. At 2 a.m. when he was about to fall asleep, he heard a ghost faintly calling out: "Where shall I put it?" Then the voice got louder. Carisse got mad. He slugged back a drink of hard liquor to give him some of what in English we call "Dutch courage." Then he grabbed his axe and walked toward the noise. When he heard yet again the plaintive cry "Where shall I put it?" he yelled back, "Put it where you found it, damn you!"

A man walked up to Clarisse and held out his hand. He recognized Charles, a man from his village who had died twenty years earlier. Charles said, "Thank you, Monsieur Bélanger, you just opened the gates of heaven for me. When I died, St. Peter kept me out and condemned me to walk in the sugar bush at night, with a property boundary marker in my hand, waiting for a syrup-maker to hear my cries. When I was alive, to enlarge my sugar bush, I moved the marker between my forest and the forest of my neighbour. I died before I could put it back. St. Peter told me, 'Only when a sugar-maker tells you to put the marker back where you found it, will you come into heaven.' Thank you, you have helped me to pardon my sin."

Ontario has its own spooky stories from the early days of sugaring: An old man from Scotland who had settled in Lanark County, east of Ottawa, in the early 1820s set up a kettle and boiled sap for several days but never got any sugar;

he suspected a neighbour's sorcery. He told the Reverend William Bell, the first minister in Perth, "I'm sure my sugar could na gang awa [could not have gone away] without somebody that had a connection with witches." No witches were ever found who would admit to stealing the old man's syrup.

The frosty phantom fable and the saga of the sugar sorcerer underline a few truths about the early days of settler sugaring: It was a solitary and endless job; the early syrup-makers could be devout in their religious faith; and sugarers guarded their section of the forest closely, the source of their spring bounty.

This kind of spooky sugaring-off season, with all-night boiling sessions in the cold snowy dark woods, was a common rite of spring for Canada's settlers in the early 19th century. One who would have found such a scene familiar was Catharine Parr Traill. Traill, born Strickland in England, married Lieutenant Thomas Traill, a Scottish veteran of the Napoleonic Wars. Traill, her brother and her sister all emigrated to Canada from Scotland, along with close to one million others who moved from Great Britain to what was then British North America in the first half of the 19th century in search of a better life. This mass migration came as the British Crown moved Indigenous Peoples off much of their ancestral territory and gave the land to settlers. Forest covered most of this land. In colonial days, just about all those who moved to the rural northeast of North America—from Nova Scotia to Ontario and across the northeastern United States—tapped their sugar bush in spring. Among Ontario settlers the Strickland family, all gifted storytellers, managed quite successfully to monetize their adventures of trying to hack homesteads and some sort of a living out of the seemingly impenetrable forests that covered the colony. Their books about early rural life inevitably include intricate descriptions of making sweetener from the maple tree.

In July 1832, long before Canada became a country, Catharine and Thomas Traill set sail from Greenock, a port west of Glasgow in Scotland, bound for Canada, a journey described in Catharine's book *The Backwoods of Canada*, which was written as a series of letters home to her mother and illustrated with woodcuts. The Traills' choice of sailing vessel suggests a snobbery that befitted Thomas Traill's rank. They boarded the *Laurel*, what Catharine describes as a "fast-sailing brig." The fare was steep—15 pounds each—but Traill says they had no choice, since the only vessel in the river en route to Canada was a passenger ship crammed "chiefly of the lower class of Highlanders."

Fast-sailing as this brig may have been for its day, the two-masted vessel took more than a month to reach Montreal. Cholera raging in Quebec City prevented the couple from visiting that port during their voyage. Still, Traill writes with colourful and optimistic language about the trip and the promise of the territory. The *Laurel* travelled behind a steam vessel through the St. Lawrence River: "Our brig with her white sails followed like a butterfly in her wake." Night falls. She rhapsodizes: "Then came forth the stars in the soft blue ether, more brilliant than ever I saw them at home, and this, I suppose, I may attribute to the superior purity of the atmosphere." The pair travelled by steamboat and stage-coach and wagon lined with buffalo robes to approach the place where the British Crown had deeded them land, near the present-day city of Peterborough, Ontario. The last part of the journey was rough: A scow deposited them at night in a forest 5 kilometres, or 3 miles, short of their destination;

"The female of the middling or better class, in her turn, pines for the society of the circle of friends she has quitted, probably for ever. . . . She has little time now for those pursuits that were ever her business as well as amusement. . . . She must become skilled in the arts of sugar-boiling, candle and soap-making, the making and baking of huge loaves, cooked in the bake-kettle."

CATHARINE PARR TRAILL,
The Backwoods of Canada, 1832

they climbed over fallen trees and Catharine fell in a swamp before they finally arrived at an inn where they found all the beds taken. Locating their land in the forests beyond proved even more challenging.

Traill was a hardy soul, based on her descriptions of the privations of settler life. Over the course of her first few months in Canada she had to sleep in smoky, dark log buildings alongside the other families in the area, often sharing space with the pigs. The mosquitoes were a constant bother, and there was a complete lack of any provisions, even flour. Slowly, with the aid of sixteen neighbours and "the help of plenty of Canadian nectar (whisky), the honey that our bees are solaced with," the Traills were able to raise their house and make a home for themselves.

The neighbours were not Traill's only friends. Given the cruel treatment of the First Peoples by colonial officials, it is refreshing to read Traill's descriptions of her relationships with Indigenous people, whose beauty and skill she admired. She writes of her delight at night as she watches the canoes, lit by torches, glide in silence over calm lakes; the women paddle the canoe with skill while men with spears skewer fish. The settlers prized the warm moccasins that the First Peoples made from deerskins; Traill secured one pair, decorated with porcupine quills and ribbon, in exchange for four yards of printed cotton.

Along with baking, sewing, and cooking, Traill makes maple sugar. Like all settlers, Traill initially copied Indigenous techniques. To traverse the thick snow in the forest and get to the maple trees, the sugar-makers wore snowshoes, an Indigenous invention that remains vital in the sugar bush today. The earliest spiles were chips, perhaps the length of an adult hand, carved from pieces of cedar or sumac wood and curved a bit. The settlers, imitating what they saw, used a hatchet to cut two gashes in the maple in the shape of a V and tapped the narrower end of the wood chip into the bottom of the gash. The Indigenous Peoples collected sap in buckets, which the Ojibwe called *mokuks*, fashioned from birch bark sewn with strips of bark from elm, tamarack or larch trees and set on the ground below the tree. The settlers hollowed out logs to make troughs they would place on the ground to catch the maple sap. It was an imperfect technique. The old-timers recount that sometimes the snow under the trough melted and it would tip over, spilling the sap, or it overflowed and then the sap would freeze the trough to the snow, or the sap froze and split the wooden trough.

The settlers over time began to innovate. Instead of making a gash with an axe, they began to drill a hole in each maple tree with a hand-cranked half-inch auger.

One key tool for the early colonial sugar-makers, also quickly adopted by Indigenous Peoples, was an iron cauldron. In 1751, the British Parliament passed an Act to encourage colonists in the Americas to make potash. Industries in England had a high demand for potash to process wool and cotton and make glass; the colonists had lots of wood to burn to make it. Settlers made potash from the ashes of trees that they burned to clear their land: first they leached the wood ashes with water to create lye. They then boiled the lye in a cast-iron pot—known as a potash kettle—to create a residue. This residue was then heated to a molten mass and then cooled into a kind of pink and grey powder. By the 1850s, settlers were shipping thousands of barrels of potash to England every year. During syrup season, the iron or copper potash kettles did double duty when settlers tapped what maple trees they had not yet burned and used the kettles to boil the sap for sugar.

Twenty years after penning her book on her first years in Canada, Traill elaborated on the rituals of the sugar bush in *The Canadian Settler's Guide*, offering advice for "the wives and daughters" of emigrants to Canada about "the particular duties which they are designed to undertake."

Colonial women in Canada should know that life will involve challenges, and they will have to do without many of the creature comforts to which they had become accustomed, and work jobs that they have never tried before, Traill writes. The women don't know what they are getting into, and thus tend to fail at it. "Disheartened by repeated failures," Traill warns, "domestic happiness disappears. The woman toils on heart-sick and pining for the home she left behind her. The husband reproaches his broken-hearted partner, and both blame the Colony for the failure of the individual."

Well, "wives and daughters," never fear, Traill is here to help. And one of the duties for which her book offers pages of instructions is the making of maple syrup and maple sugar. For an immigrant from Europe unaccustomed to hollowing out logs as receptacles or spending days—and even long nights—trying to keep a fire going, in the snow, in March, in the dark forest, one can imagine some tests to the ideal of domestic happiness.

"In the backwoods the women do the chief of the sugar-making; it is rough work, and fitter for men; but Canadians think little of that," Traill notes. She instructs her readers to dig out troughs from pine, ash or basswood logs (though, as we will see later, Traill's brother rejected this last tree species) and place each trough under a maple tree in which one has made an incision with an axe, inserting a splinter of cedar so that the sap drips into the trough. Then one fixes two "stout forked posts into the ground" over which to lay a pole (no explanation of how one drives these posts into the forest floor, which surely is frozen solid and covered in snow in March). Then, hang a kettle from the pole. Fill the kettle with maple sap. Hang a piece of pork or bacon over the pot to keep the sap from boiling over. Build a fire under the kettle. The book warns: "The one who attends to the boiling should never leave his business; others can gather the sap and collect wood for the fires. When there is a good run, the boiling down is often carried on far into the night" (cue the ghost stories).

These days syrup-makers use a thermometer to know when the boiling sap has become syrup; one takes off the syrup at 104°C, or 219°F. In settler times syrup-makers used the spoon test: unfinished syrup drips off the spoon; finished syrup "aprons" or sheets from the spoon. In another technique, the sugarer licks his thumbnail and wipes it on his pants. Then, he puts a drop of syrup on his nail, which he then turns over as though to let the syrup fall off. If the syrup runs, it is not yet ready.

Traill also describes how she converted the sap into maple sugar. Among the First Peoples and settlers alike the sweet product of the sugar maple tree was usually sugar. Until the invention of canning and the vacuum seal, there was no easy way to preserve syrup, whereas sugar was comparatively easy to store. Homemade maple sugar was a lot cheaper than cane sugar imported from the West Indies.

Traill lit a fire beside a stump and hung her kettle on what she called a crane, noting "any bush-boy can fix a crane of the kind." These bush-boys—not profiled in any more detail—clearly came in handy at the time. Traill first boiled the sap from sixteen pailfuls to two. Then she filtered the liquid twice. Next she beat an egg white and spread that over what she calls the liquor; before the liquid boiled she skimmed off the scum. The liquid first became yellow and frothy, and then thickened; when the drops fell ropy from the ladle, she continued to stir the liquid as it cooled. It became gritty and whitened into sugar. She later found it simpler to let the liquid harden into a sugary mass, then pierce its crust and drain the liquid through a colander. What remained was sugar.

Traill was in good company with family members in rural Ontario. Her sister Susanna Moodie also came to Canada in 1832 and gained fame with titles such as *Roughing It in the Bush*. She too waxed poetic about the sugar maple, and even wrote a song called "The Maple Tree": "When the snows of winter are melting fast, and the sap begins to rise; and the biting breath of the frozen blast yields to the Spring's soft sighs: then away to the wood for the maple, good, shall unlock its honeyed store."

A brother of Traill and Moodie, Samuel Strickland, immigrated to the same part of Ontario in the early 19th century. He stuck to the family business: writing books. Given that sugar maples grow in *eastern* Canada (from Nova Scotia to Ontario), you may wonder why Strickland—who immigrated to Canada from Suffolk, England, in 1825, preceding his sisters by seven years—titled his ribald bestseller of 1853 *Twenty-Seven Years in Canada West*. The answer lies in the terminology of the period: In Strickland's day, the British colony extended only as far west as Ontario. Ontario at that time was "Canada West."

Samuel Strickland was a gentleman known for a light touch with his pen. His 700-page epistle on the joys of the early years in Canada gains its droll humour from the contrast that arises as the British upper crust braves the forest. A commissioner of the Canada Company invites him and friends to dinner near Goderich on Lake Huron, which requires a journey on foot on a new road cut through the bush. "I wonder what our English friends would think of walking in their shirt-sleeves, with their coats and neckcloths thrown over their arms, eighteen miles to a dinner-party, with the thermometer ranging something like 90 degrees [Fahrenheit] in the shade."

At the same time there's discomfort in reading Strickland's book today. In his preface, he writes that "the subject of colonization is indeed one of vital importance for it is the wholesome channel through which the superfluous population of England and Ireland passes, from a state of poverty to one of comfort." Indigenous Peoples would differ with Strickland on the wholesomeness of colonization.

Long sections in Strickland's book instruct settlers on how to cut down the trees; it is a skill at which early settlers were expected to excel. "A good axe-man should be able, with fair chopping, to cut an acre in eight days," Strickland writes. "The regular price for chopping is five dollars per acre, with board, or six without." The settlers mostly came from places like Scotland. At one time, Scotland too had been covered in trees, but after they were cut down, the sheep were left to graze and the land was never able to reforest. In Canada, eager to grow crops, the settlers wanted open land.

There is a hint here that helps to explain Ontario's relatively small role in today's global maple syrup production: the settler obsession with clearing the forest. Strickland displays his colonist disdain for the forest when he writes that often the farmer intends to destroy the sugar bush within a few years, if it is near their house. If it is during syrup season they often prefer to gouge the maple tree with an axe to get its sap, since that technique not only is quicker but produces more sap while sacrificing the tree.

With all of this chopping, it is a small wonder the maple syrup industry waned in Ontario. That said, during Strickland's time sugar-making remained an important activity. He laces accounts of his adventures in the sugar bush with self-deprecating anecdotes that acknowledge he had a lot to learn: The first year, he hollowed out forty logs to make troughs for catching sap. He tapped his sugar maple trees and the troughs filled with sap, but when he went back to collect this bounty he discovered the troughs were half empty. A local said, "I see you have made your troughs of basswood, and they always leak." These troughs had other uses, however: They were found to be excellent cradles for babies.

Strickland titles a chapter in the second volume of his memoir "Sugar-Maple Sugar," with such subtitles as "Prince's Misadventure," "Succeeding Misfortunes," "Careless Sugar Sentinel" and "Cow-Pilferers." Among the travails of syrup-making is the ever-present risk that one might wipe out days of toil by burning the syrup. An equivalent feeling of despair comes when one works days on a piece of writing only to have the computer crash and somehow swallow the work whole. I know the feeling, having both lost writing and burned syrup. It's no fun. There is consolation in knowing that I am not the first to ruin great sap-gathering and boiling efforts in a charred molten mess. During one syrup season, Strickland teamed up with two companions. Exhausted from gathering sap all day, the trio decided to take turns sleeping while one of them stayed up as "sugar sentinel" to tend to the fire under the kettle of sap.

"My companion and myself then stretched ourselves in the camp before the fire, and were soon lost in pleasant forgetfulness. How long we had been in this comfortable state of somnolescence I know not, being awakened from my nap by a strong smell of burning, which, upon jumping up, I found to proceed from three large sugar-kettles, which were literally red-hot, every particle of sugar being literally burnt to a cinder," Strickland writes. "And where was the guardian of the kettles? Why, fast asleep in the camp, and totally unconscious of the misfortune his mistimed and faithless nap had occasioned." Some Quebec producers of that era created an innovation to prevent burned syrup: a one-legged stool for the sugarer. If the sugar-maker fell asleep on such a stool, they would fall on the ground—and surely wake up.

On another occasion three of Strickland's cows drank all his syrup. His efforts also attracted humans. He notes that "you are apt to receive manifold visits from young ladies and children, who, of course, only come to see the process; but who, somehow or another never make their appearance during the first part of the operation, but wait patiently until the sap is transformed into a more mellifluous substance, when spoons, tins, and ladles are in great requisition."

In the first half of the 19th century, even as Strickland struggled to make syrup, many Ontario sugar bushes fell to the axe. So busy were the settlers at cutting the forests that Upper Canada, now Ontario, had in the period more than 1,600 sawmills. Goodbye, sugar bush! Catharine Traill, writing in a later edition of *The Canadian Settler's Guide* in the late 1850s, notes that maple sugar-making had by that point waned: "The farmer, considering that his time can be more profitably employed in clearing his land, will not give his attention to it, for maple sugar is less an article of trade than it used to be. The West India sugars are now to be bought at 4d per lb, or if you pay a dollar, you can get 14 lbs of good soft sugar."

THERE IS NO record that the Strickland siblings—Catharine, Susanna or Samuel—have descendants that continue to make maple syrup today. But many families in Ontario, hard at making syrup in the 21st century, can trace their lineage and forest roots back to the immigrants of two centuries ago. One of these is the Shaw clan. While researching this book, I heard from Tom Shaw, a keen booster of the syrup business in Ontario. Tom's father, Ron, had served as chair of the North American Maple Syrup Council. One November I made a plan to visit the Shaw sugar bush. The weather had other ideas. The night before my trip was cold and rain soaked in Toronto. Shaw's farm, in the township of Oro-Medonte about 125 kilometres north of the city, is in the snow belt where our kids learned to ski. I had yet to install my winter tires. "Better not come," Shaw texted. "There's ice everywhere."

Come January, with winter tires installed, I made it to Shaw's. Highway 400 north from Toronto crosses endless suburbs and then vast tracts of farmland including the Holland Marsh, the source of most of Ontario's onions and carrots. Trees are scarce. But when I turned off Highway 11 and headed east on the 14th line in Oro-Medonte toward the shore of Lake Simcoe, I was quite suddenly plunged into a hardwood forest. Driving through the forest I eventually arrived at a clearing where a layer of fresh snow covered the parking lot in front of the Shaw pancake house, built in 1967. Shaw stood at the back by a woodshed, heaving chunks of stove wood into an outdoor furnace, which heats water to warm his workshop, sugar shack, garage and restaurant.

The Shaw clan came from Scotland two centuries ago. They initially raised pigs on a farm just down the road. In 1883, Tom's great-great-grandfather, also named Thomas, bought a 32-hectare, or 80-acre, forest in Oro-Medonte from the Grand Trunk Railway. They cut firewood in the forest, which they hauled by horse and sleigh to nearby Orillia to sell at the farmer's market. In 1904, Thomas's grandson, James, suggested they tap a few trees and sell syrup, too; thus began the Shaw's syrup business. Today the Shaws operate a thriving sugar bush and pancake house on land that is too rocky and hilly to profitably clear for a farm.

The Shaws are good at saving stuff; visitors to their sugar shack can see the evolution of maple syrup equipment. Behind the present-day evaporator is a display of spiles: more than one hundred gathered over the years and traded with other syrup-makers across the northeast. The first spiles are made of wood, later ones of steel, and the most modern of plastic. Nearby lies the old cast-iron cauldron in which the first Shaws, at the birth of the 20th century, boiled sap into maple syrup that first year when they put sixty taps in trees and collected the sap in buckets.

We walked on a trail to the back of the Shaw sugar bush, following the tracks that a coyote left in the fresh snow. We stopped at a hulking, rusted, crumbling rectangular iron box, listing on the forest floor. I could make out the words "The Grimm MFG CO Montreal" above the old firebox doors. This was the first Shaw evaporator; it had lived in a sugar shack built in 1906. The old shack collapsed after the family built a new sugar camp closer to the road in the 1960s. The iron hulk of the old boiler looks a bit like a beached whale; still, it lingers not as a tragedy but as a monument in a story of continuity and perseverance in the maple syrup industry, amid rapid deforestation in southern Ontario.

The Shaw family innovated over the generations. As a young couple, to make ends meet outside of syrup season, Shaw and his wife Teri-Lynn got into the catering business with pig roasts; in an average year they now cater 50 events and supply pigs and roasters for 250 do-it-yourself pig roasts. As we walked back through the forest alongside the leafless trees, Shaw told me that in a few weeks he would start tapping trees again, with the help of two friends.

I asked him what has kept him and his wife in the business of maple syrup. "What I see is continued interest in all things maple syrup," Shaw said. "The books and articles I read are all about the story. The story is what sells, and the maple story is incredible. The fact that the Indigenous Peoples started it, and as soon as settlers came over here, they joined in making maple syrup, because of the decadent, incredible flavour. And there was a time when that sugar was being taken back to England. It's incredible that the story still survives. They weren't taking grain back to Europe in 16th and 17th century, but they were taking maple sugar." And Tom's maple syrup story continues. He has a plan to sell the ancestral pig farm down the road and invest the proceeds in a $6-million sugar shack, above which he and his wife plan to live.

Despite the hardship of the era, Catharine Parr Traill concluded her first book on an upbeat note. "I love Canada," she wrote, adding that she was, "as happy in my humble log-house as if it were a courtly hall or bower; habit reconciles us to many things that at first were distasteful. It has ever been my way to extract the sweet rather than the bitter in the cup of life." The joy that she, her brother Samuel Strickland and sister Susanna Moodie found wallowing in the woods as winter gave way to spring lives today in Tom Shaw, me and all other syrup-makers who drink—and share—the sweet in the cup of life.

GIVE US THIS DAY
OUR DAILY SYRUP

n 1965, a fine morning in March found Prince, a Belgian workhorse, tromping through a sugar bush in Sainte-Clotilde-de-Beauce, Quebec. Prince, a blond gentle giant, pulled a sled and blew clouds of breath from his nose with a kind of whooshing sound; the steam dissipated into the crisp spring air. His harness jingled as his thick strong legs picked their way with confidence through the deep snow. Walking beside Prince was Aurélien Grenier.

The eldest of eighteen children, Aurélien grew up to become a farrier and a blacksmith. In late winter, in preparation for the upcoming maple syrup season, Aurélien was a busy man, shoeing the horses of St. Clotilde, a village in the Beauce, a forested region in the Appalachian Mountains that stretches south from Quebec City to the US border at Maine and New Hampshire that was, and remains, the biggest maple syrup-producing region on Earth. When the thaw came in spring, all the horses left to work in the sugar bush; Aurélien had nothing to do. So he bought a forest—to make maple syrup to feed his growing family, to earn extra cash and to make firewood to heat his home.

The people of St. Clotilde had much to do to prepare for the syrup season. Aurélien and his wife, Rose-Aimée, were blessed with eight children—seven sons and a daughter—and they all had jobs. In the fall they carried hay and oats to the stable in the sugar bush, more than a kilometre from the road. It was easier to get the horse's provisions into the forest before the snow fell. When winter came, the family went out with snow shovels to clear the trails in the sugar bush to make it easier on Prince.

The family did not own Prince; each spring they rented the horse from a merchant in the village. When the warming spring sun caused the sap to flow in the maple trees, Aurélien kept his children home from school to help. The great march of the sugar bush began. Wearing snowshoes, Aurélien led the way with a brace and bit (a hand-cranked drill). He stopped at a maple and, at about chest-height, drilled a hole. An elder son followed behind to tap in a tin spile. The younger children pulled a sled stacked with tin sap buckets. The children hung a bucket from each spile. The family could place 100 to 200 taps in the morning and another 200 in the afternoon. In three or four days, they finished hanging 1,500 buckets. When the sap began to flow into the buckets, Prince pulled a sled that held a tank, into which the Grenier clan poured the maple sap.

The global heart of the maple syrup industry is Quebec. In Ontario, where I live, I make a bit of syrup, as do lots of other people. Overall, though, Ontario produces a thimbleful of syrup compared to Quebec. It's hard to understand why.

We can't blame the forest: The Ontario Maple Syrup Producers Association proclaims that Ontario has the largest number of maple trees in Canada. I combed the written record and asked academics, syrup-makers and others across Quebec and Ontario to explain Quebec's ascendence to rule the world of maple syrup. No one offered a simple answer to this question. I believe the reason, as typified by the Grenier family syrup story, mixes geography, demography, climate, culture and, crucially, the Roman Catholic Church.

Maybe you, the reader of this book, are a maple syrup maker in Canada or the United States. There are eighty maple syrup producers in British Columbia. The government of Prince Edward Island listed four maple syrup makers there in 2020. New Brunswick's maple syrup industry merits its own chapter in this book. Nova Scotia has a small but proud industry that made more than 200,000 litres of maple syrup in 2020. We know of Vermont as a hotbed of maple syrup production, along with New York and Maine; Americans collect sap as far south as Virginia and as far west as Wisconsin to boil into syrup. That said, if you don't make your own, you may have bought syrup from a local producer on, say, St. Joseph Island, near Sault Ste. Marie, where Lake Superior flows into Lake Huron; that area is home to thirty maple syrup producers. Still, outside the northeast of North America, if you go to a grocery store anywhere on the planet, the maple syrup for sale most likely comes from Quebec, the source of about three-quarters of the global supply.

A few years ago a *National Post* photographer and I travelled deep into the boreal forest in northern Quebec to report a story about logging. At a logging camp on the Mistassibi River, a many-hour drive north of Quebec City, we joined the lumberjacks in their mess hall at 4 a.m. for breakfast, and I was impressed to see them drenching their crêpes in authentic maple syrup. Quebec loggers do not get out of bed for anything short of the real stuff. Québécois call table syrup made from cane or corn *sirop de poteau*, or fencepost syrup.

"I remember some restaurants served table syrup when I was a kid," Lynne Faubert, a food writer in Montreal, told me. "But these days every restaurant puts real maple syrup on the table." Something immutable in the culture, the psyche, the very pores of their bodies, bound up in history and pride and identity and mystique, causes the Québécois to feel a kind of kinship, a loyalty, almost a dependence on pure maple syrup. Meanwhile, in other provinces, only the best restaurants bring you maple syrup for pancakes.

In the settler days in the 1850s, leaf trees covered most of southern Canada. Ontario and Quebec produced comparable maple sugar before the use of metal cans to preserve syrup became widespread. Around Confederation, Quebec began to pull ahead in the maple sweetener game. According to the Census of Canada for 1870–71, Ontario produced 6.2 million pounds of maple sugar; Quebec made nearly twice as much: 10.5 million pounds. Ten years later Quebec nearly quadrupled Ontario's production. Portneuf, a region north of Quebec City, saw its maple sugar production more than double between 1870 and 1880. Meanwhile in 1880, Bruce County, a bountiful agricultural region northwest of Toronto, made just one-quarter of the maple sugar it had made a decade earlier. That decline continued steadily. By 2022, Ontario produced less sweetener from maple trees than the province had made 160 years earlier.

Ontario's farmers cut down their sugar bushes to clear land for other crops, including another agricultural product whose cultivation we learned from the First Peoples: tobacco. The 1901 census shows Ontario made one-third less maple sugar that year than ten years earlier; by contrast, in 1901 Ontario grew ten times its tobacco output of a decade earlier.

Much of southern Ontario is flat. Cut down the trees and you expose rich clay in which to grow crops; large stretches of Quebec, such as St. Clotilde where the Greniers grew up, are more rocky and mountainous, and so not suited for cultivation. Places in Ontario where syrup production persists more closely resemble Quebec's maple syrup heartland. Lanark County lies west of Ottawa on the southern edge of the Canadian Shield and is an expanse of rock with thin soil that extends north to the Arctic. Maple trees grow well, and it's not worth cutting them down since the stoney ground cannot be cultivated.

"It's not good farmland here in Lanark County," explains Karen Ennis, who makes maple syrup with her sons and grandchildren in Fallbrook, southwest of Ottawa. She grew up further north in a hamlet called Middleville. "My father plowed around all the stone piles. Maple syrup is a good way to supplement your income. You weren't making money farming." And she notes that, compared with parts of Ontario to the south, her county gets more snow and a later spring. "Maple syrup just kind of gets in your blood and you can't help it. For most people that was just what you did in the spring."

Elsewhere across Ontario, however, over the past two centuries, many sugar bushes fell to the axe. "This area had five people making maple syrup," Tom Shaw, the fifth-generation syrup-maker in Oro-Medonte, explained to me. "There's only two people left now." He said people stop making maple syrup because it's too hard a slog. "Because it's seasonal, because it's gut-slugging work, you already have a job you are working twelve months a year, now all of a sudden for two months in the spring you've got to dedicate yourself to making maple syrup. And it's hard to make. People eventually say 'Screw this. I'm not doing this anymore. I can't schedule my holidays during the time that sap is going to run. We are giving it away, and we are not making money.' Once you stop making syrup, the very first thing you do the next year is you sell off your bush." Sawmills are eager buyers of quality maple logs, for furniture and flooring, among other uses. "There's $20,000 to $40,000 in trees, in logs, sitting in the bush, so you sell that, they cut those trees off. It doesn't change the price of the property at all, and they grab that money." Once the trees are gone, whoever buys the land cannot make any maple syrup.

The United States' northeast has huge leaf forests, too. As the 20th century dawned, the US led Canada in maple syrup production. Whereas in 1901 Canada produced about $1.8 million worth of maple sugar, the United States produced $2.6 million, the equivalent of 26 million pounds of maple sugar. But, as in Ontario, US maple sugar production plummeted during the 20th century: from 40 million pounds in 1860 to less than 341,000 pounds by 1948. Syrup production stayed flat in the same period, even as the US population soared. A census in 1947 found that more than 80 percent of American households lived in urban areas and so did not gather sap in spring; besides, by then cane and beet sugar cost less. By 1950, maple accounted for less than 1 percent of the sugar consumed in the United States. Maple syrup went from being a staple on the dinner table to a niche, luxury food.

But there was one place where the maple tree—as sacred to the locals as a cow is to Hindus in India—did not get the axe. That place is Quebec. There are many reasons. While

France's colonies in Quebec were small and grew slowly compared to English colonies in New England, the early close contact of the French settlers, known as habitants, with the Indigenous Peoples gave them a head start in making maple sugar. The menu of the habitants was already a copy of the Indigenous diet: moose, porcupine, rabbit; and for starches, corn, oats, beans, peas and barley. For sweetener, the French used maple sugar.

Under Quebec's seigneurial system, created when Quebec was a colony of France, habitants received land from a seigneur, or lord, to whom they paid a tithe. In the 19th century, and up to about one hundred years ago, the Greniers' homeland in the Beauce region was criss-crossed with sugar bush trails, which the inhabitants of the seigneuries built together to get to the sugar bushes sprinkled across the region. These sugar bush paths were very narrow but would run 30 to 50 kilometres, or about 20 to 30 miles, into the heart of the forest. They were only passable when snow covered the stumps, tree trunks, branches, stones and roots.

Quebec's sugaring prowess relied on the workforce provided by big families like the Greniers of St. Clotilde. History and religion help to explain these vast broods. In 1759, in Quebec City, French forces lost to the English in the Battle of the Plains of Abraham. In 1763, with the Treaty of Paris, France ceded what is now Canada to Great Britain. Following the English victory, the most powerful force in Quebec became the Catholic Church. The Church's influence was clear to me as I criss-crossed Quebec to research this book, using my old-school road map of the province to guide me. On the map the S column dominates a list of place names: About half of Quebec municipalities begin with the word *saint.* As Quebec grew, every town got a church, every church got a priest, and the priests took control. The holy fathers enforced a policy now known as "the revenge of the cradle," obliging women to bear many children, to ensure the French would continue to dominate in Quebec. Quebec's very high fertility set it apart from the rest of Canada; married women in Quebec bore an average of seven children during the French and British colonial periods. Bolstered by these ground troops, the triumphant march of Quebec to global dominance in maple syrup had begun.

Quebec's big families persisted until the 1970s, the decade when I moved to rural Quebec. (You may recall that on the dirt road where I grew up, the farmers next door had nine children. They could dress an entire hockey team.) In each village in Quebec, once a year the priest would visit every farm on a parish tour. In each house, if there was not a new baby, he would ask the mother if there was a problem. Women needed a document from the priest to give the doctor permission to perform a hysterectomy. (The Church was not the only impetus to procreation; my mother had five children and my father, with a number of partners, sired ten. That's a story for another book.)

Big families were key to Quebec's maple syrup success. Back in the day, before plastic tubes sucked the sap from maple trees, making maple syrup, as Indigenous Peoples knew, was labour-intensive. It required a lot of bodies to fan out every spring afternoon and snowshoe through deep snow in the sugar bush, pour sap from each bucket that hung on a maple tree into a pail, haul it to the sled, and then empty the sap at the sugar shack. This put families like the Greniers at an advantage: They had the trees, the horses, and, critically, the children to gather the sap.

"The parish was a little nation, utterly absorbed in the work of the fields and the joy of watching grow, in the shadow of the bell tower of the old church, the number of those who, sons of solid peasants, kept alive the tradition of the soil, and defended it fiercely."

J.-EDOUARD FORTIN,
"The Benediction of the Maple Trees," *Le Terroir*, 1919

The influence of the Church extended beyond family size. Catholic rituals were tightly woven into the world of maple sugar. In the 19th century, benedictions of the sugar bush were common. In 1920, the Quebec artist Marc-Aurèle de Foy Suzor-Coté created the oil painting *La Bénédiction des Érables,* or *The Benediction of Maple Trees.* The painting hangs today in the Musée Nationale des Beaux-Arts de Québec, in Quebec City. It depicts a priest clad in a sparkling gold and embroidered cope leading the congregation into the sugar bush. An altar boy joins him, along with a man carrying a cross. The priest beseeches heaven for an abundance of sap.

In 1919, a priest went further in the newspaper *Le Terroir*, managing to compare the suffering of the stoic maple trees, as the farmers pierce them to extract sap, to the crucifixion of Jesus Christ: "Canadian, your soul is made of this wood, that we wound freely, that we tap and mutilate. How many times have we wanted to kill you? You always green back up. Their hatred is useless."

In the 1960s, when Aurélien and his many children worked their sugar bush with the horse Prince, they had just one iron-clad rule: They could not enter the sugar bush on Sunday. On this holy day, the devout would have to wring their hands as they watched maple sap drip from overflowing buckets and go to waste on the forest floor. This devotion even inspired a fable: the story of Felix the Obstinate, whose zeal for maple syrup led to his downfall.

On the Ile d'Orléans, an island in the St. Lawrence River east of Quebec City, lived Felix Pelchat; behind his house spread a wood that had been in the family two hundred years. Times were tough, until one spring when a merchant from Quebec City promised Felix he would buy all the syrup and sugar Felix could make. On Good Friday, Felix got up early and dressed quietly. Alas, his wife, a light sleeper, woke up. He said he was bound for his sugar shack. She told him he must come first to Mass. Felix ignored her, harnessed his old mare, Fan, to the wood sleigh and walked to his maple forest. But as he entered the sugar bush to gather the sap, Felix noticed that rather than sap, red drops flowed from the maple trees. He began to tremble. Blood, not sap, dripped into the buckets. Felix knelt in the snow, tore open his shirt, clutched his scapular—a necklace, often with a square of wool cloth, worn to show Catholic devotion—and begged God to forgive him. From that day on, Felix never missed a Good Friday Mass, and no one ever again set foot in his sugar bush.

In my research I have found no empirical evidence to prove that God contributed to the success of the maple syrup business in Quebec. But the Church certainly served as a unifying force for the syrup-makers and encouraged a veneration for the sugar maple that persists in Quebec, even as people have ceased to go to church.

Back in the day, syrup producers were among the thousands of Catholics who made an annual pilgrimage to a church in Sainte-Anne-de-Stukely, near Sherbrooke, Quebec, to thank Our Lady of the Maples for the syrup harvest. In 1951, at the request of syrup producers, the French sculptor Albert Chartier carved a life-size statue in Italian marble of Notre-Dame-des-Érables, or Our Lady of the Maple Trees: the Virgin Mary, standing in a floor-length robe. Upthrust in her hands is the

Baby Jesus, who holds aloft a maple leaf. At the request of a co-operative of Quebec syrup producers, Cardinal Paul-Émile Léger travelled to Rome in 1957 to meet Pope Pius XII. Léger, on his return to Quebec, announced, "I spoke to the Holy Father of your wish concerning devotion to Our Lady of the Maples. He welcomed my request. The image may be reproduced, and the invocation received 300 days of indulgences."

Reid Locklin, an associate professor of Christianity at the University of Toronto, explained to me this question of indulgences: If a Christian shows their devotion to the Church and attends confession, then when that person prays to Notre-Dame-des-Érables, they receive a benefit of 300 days off the time that they, or someone they designate, must wait after death in purgatory before ascending to heaven. "The Pope has access to the National Bank of Heaven," Dr. Locklin explained. "The currency of the bank is days in purgatory. The Pope is offering an incentive for the faithful to cultivate this devotion."

Petrucci et Carli, a studio in Montreal, made 5,000 copies of a Notre-Dame-des-Érables statuette in lead glass, which the syrup co-operative distributed to members who asked for one to put in their sugar shacks. Syrup producers believed that this figurine had the power to protect the sugar shack from fire.

Despite the occasional wastage of sap on a Sunday, the collective faith of Quebecers, knit together by the Church, may help explain their sugaring success. This collective mindset extends to the sugar bush, where government and the citizenry work together, in contrast to English Canada, which tends to be much more competitive and individualistic, says Randal Goodfellow. Goodfellow grew up in Quebec on a dairy farm east of Montreal. He worked for the Farm Credit Corporation and the Bank of Montreal, and later became a lobbyist for agribusiness and forestry. Like many English-speaking Quebecers, Goodfellow moved to Ontario after Quebec, in 1976, elected a government with a mandate to separate Quebec from Canada; today he lives in Lanark County, the centre of Ontario's maple syrup industry. He and his wife tap a sugar bush; he also heads the Ontario Maple Syrup Producers' Association. Why does his native province of Quebec produce so much more syrup? "In Quebec the government is an equal partner at the table," Goodfellow told me. "In Quebec it's a more collective mindset. A rising tide lifts all boats."

Quebecers also innovated in sugar shacks. Indigenous Peoples built the first lean-tos in the woods as shelter during maple syrup season; settlers copied these makeshift structures. By the era of Aurélien Grenier, most sugarers were tapping trees in their own forests, and gradually their structures became more permanent—and the sugar shack, or *cabane à sucre* in French, was born.

One of the main purposes of the sugar shack was to house the evaporator, which remains the tool to boil sap into syrup. The original evaporator was an invention from the United States. Gustave Henry Grimm, the son of a family of tin workers born in Baden, Germany, immigrated to the United States in the 1860s and settled in Ohio. In 1881, he innovated with an evaporator: a long series of pans with corrugated bottoms, a firebox below and a chimney at its rear, known as the "Champion" and marketed for the making of maple sugar, sorghum, cider and fruit jellies. The Grimm Company spread its reach through New England, and in 1892 Grimm's younger cousin, John H. Grimm, relocated from Vermont to Montreal to run the Quebec branch of the company, to support the maple syrup industry. By this point Grimm made over 1,000 evaporators a year. The company, now called Dominion & Grimm, to this day still makes Champion evaporators. In Dunham, Quebec, the Small brothers in 1889 patented the Lightning evaporator—another popular Quebec evaporator brand.

Quebec and Canadian government guidebooks and pamphlets produced in the first half of the 20th century for sugarmakers included several pages of drawings for a basic sugar shack: a concrete floor (to minimize fire risk), a cupola (to let out steam) and a raised butte beside the building, made of earth and stones (as a spot for the team of horses to climb and dump the sap into a reservoir above the shack so that the sap might flow by gravity into the evaporator). Some shacks even had a place to eat and sleep, for those long days and nights in the forest. And these shacks became the sites for the first sugaring-off celebrations, offering a chance for family and friends to get together after the sombre months of winter. Hidden as they were in the woods, these sugar shacks had other uses, too: During World War II, they became convenient hiding places for young conscripts who wanted to stay out of the war.

By the early 20th century, the improved efficiencies of sugar shacks and modern evaporators meant that sugarers could greatly increase their production. More and more farmers were making maple syrup not just for their own needs but also for export, and countries around the world were starting to notice.

The Pure Maple Sugar and Syrup Co-operative Agricultural Association held its fourth annual meeting at Rigaud, Quebec, just west of Montreal, in February 1916. The meeting was a watershed moment for Quebec's rapidly growing, and quickly evolving, maple syrup sector. Gustave Benjamin Boyer, the Rigaud Member of Parliament, told those present that a care package of maple products had been sent to the Canadian soldiers fighting for the Empire in the war that was raging across Europe at the time. Before delivering the maple products to soldiers on the front lines, the shippers displayed them at a department store in London. "Since then," Boyer said, "we received orders from this city, the most important in England, for several hundred tons of maple sugar. And not just from England—we received an order from a French merchant for 45 tons of maple sugar, or 90,000 pounds. I received an order from Chicago for 25,000 one-pound loaves of maple sugar, an order that I cannot fill."

At the Rigaud gathering, syrup enthusiasts exhorted participants to up their maple syrup game. Pure maple syrup, the crowd heard, was a money-maker. Charles Fisk, a sugarer in Abbotsford, Quebec, told the gathering that one needs 13 acres planted in oats to earn the same money as 10 acres of maple trees. Boyer echoed Fisk and asked the gathering: "Now frankly in the face of these figures taken from the statistics, are we not obliged to admit that the maple industry is the best paying industry on the farm without excepting the dairy industry?"

Quebec's dominance of the syrup industry would only continue to grow, with many farmers embracing Boyer's math, including Aurélien Grenier. Bolstered by the workforce of their huge families, Quebecers were now the undisputed world leaders of maple syrup.

In St. Clotilde, after the Grenier family and Prince spent a long day hauling barrels of sap on sleds through the sugar bush, Aurélien fed Prince hay for dinner and a bucket of oats for dessert. Prince got other treats, too. When the horse worked well, Aurélien rewarded him with a bit of maple sap in his water. Meanwhile, the family's matriarch Rose-Aimée worked in the sugar shack. The wood fire roaring in the evaporator kept Prince warm at night. Once the season ended, the children got to stay home again. By then the spring sun had chased the snow away and melted the ice from the creek.

Nelson, the fifth of Aurélien's eight children, recalled to me: "My father and Prince went to the stream with the same barrel we had used to pick up sap and filled it with water. My mom would make a fire outside to heat the water, and we would wash 2,000 buckets. It was beautiful weather. We had a picnic. We were happy to not be in school. I started when I was twelve or thirteen years old, and I worked that way until I got married."

Prince, at the beginning of sugaring-off season, had come to the forest with his ribs showing. But Aurélien loved horses and fed Prince well. When the snow melted and the buckets were washed and put away, Aurélien rolled the steel barrels of maple syrup onto a wagon and hitched up the horse. Prince had one last job: haul the syrup to the merchant, who both owned the horse and bought the syrup. The Grenier children mourned because they had to return to school to finish their year. But Prince left the forest a happy—and fatter—horse.

THE RISE AND FALL
OF THE MAPLE KING

The first person to get rich from the sweet products of maple trees was an American. George Clinton Cary was born in 1864 on a farm in Fort Fairfield, in eastern Maine on the border of New Brunswick. His father was a farmer and merchant; his mother was a school principal. As a boy of ten, Cary was already a budding farmer and had his own pair of steers. By age twenty-two, Cary was looking beyond the farming industry and became a travelling grocery salesman, moving goods by horse-and-buggy throughout Maine, Vermont and New Hampshire. The legend of Cary's start in the maple business began in the spring of 1886. Cary's wagon, pulled by a team of horses, got stuck in the mud on a road in Craftsbury, northern Vermont. The overnight low would refreeze the roads so the young salesman had to stop for the night. This unscheduled lull gave Cary lots of time to try to convince a local storekeeper to buy his wares. The grocer had no money but offered to place an order if Cary would take payment in maple sugar at 4.5 cents per pound. Cary agreed, and found himself with 1,500 pounds of maple sugar. On a train later that spring Cary met a tobacco salesman and learned that tobacco companies bought Barbados cane sugar to flavour plug chewing tobacco, and paid 5 cents per pound. Cary smelled an opportunity and finessed a deal to ship the maple sugar to a Virginia tobacco company. Then he went looking for more maple sugar. This lucrative partnership for tobacco flavoured with maple sugar from both the US and Canada would endure for decades, and it underpinned Cary's rise to omnipotence in the world of maple products.

Cary hedged his bets. In his early years he also sold cedar and pine shingles, milled in Maine and New Brunswick, to buyers across New England. Increasingly, however, his business was maple sugar, which Cary packed in wooden crates and loaded onto trains for shipment to tobacco companies. Cary was a fairly tall man, about six feet, and of solid build. A Boston newspaper compared him to the oxen that pulled the sap-gathering tanks on sleds through his sugar bush, and he demonstrated a similar determination. His business grew, and in 1898 he built a warehouse in Saint Johnsbury, Vermont, near the meeting of the Boston and Maine Railroad and the Saint Johnsbury and Lake Champlain Railroad. This turned into a chain of warehouses along Vermont railway lines. Cary hired hundreds of local sugar buyers.

Like a gluttonous dinner guest, Cary developed a voracious appetite. He wanted more sugar, and the best place to find it was across the border in Canada. The Cary Maple Sugar Company spread its sales force into Quebec. To corner the market, Cary made his buyers sign a contract to buy maple sugar and syrup for his company at prices named by Cary and "to buy no maple sugar or syrup for any other party." Cary paid his US and Quebec buyers a commission of one-quarter of 1 cent per pound of maple sugar, and 3 cents per gallon for maple syrup. By 1901, Cary reported that he had sold close to 1 million pounds of maple sugar. *The St. Johnsbury Caledonian* newspaper crowned Cary "Maple Sugar King." By 1904, The Cary Maple Sugar Company was the biggest maple sweetener company in North America.

In the first decades of the 20th century, up to two-thirds of the Beauce region's sugar went to Cary in Vermont. Cary set the price he paid for the maple sugar. In each Quebec village, Cary's buyer would meet the local farmers on the steps of their Catholic church after Mass in spring and offer a price; the farmers would discuss it and consult their priest. With Cary's clout, they usually said yes.

Flaunting his wealth, Cary hired an architect who worked for the Rockefellers, and spent some of his maple profits to build a home that befitted his stature, with laundry and central heating—rarities in 1902—plus three bathrooms and three fireplaces. His first wife and child had died in quick succession; Cary's second wife bore him three children. Cary's power grew. He bought a string of farms in North Danville, Vermont, and renamed them Highland Farms, becoming one of the largest landowners in the county. As packaging and taste evolved, Cary moved from buying sugar to buying maple syrup. Continuing to innovate, Cary pioneered the use of steel barrels as a more efficient way to move bulk syrup. Supplying the barrels to syrup-makers became a kind of informal contract to ensure some loyalty the next spring when the producers had more syrup to sell.

As Cary flexed his monopolistic power, his opulence and omnipotence grew. He was among the first Vermonters to drive a car, although when the dirt roads turned to mud in spring Cary often needed a team of horses to pull it out of the mire. (He obviously hadn't learned his lesson from the Craftsbury misadventure of his youth.) But Cary, a stubborn man, persevered. Having contracted scarlet fever as a child, Cary by his mid-forties had become deaf; he read lips and kept a pad and pencil in his pocket to communicate. Even so, he radiated self-confidence. By the 1920s, Cary controlled up to 80 percent of the world's bulk maple sugar and syrup market.

In 1927, the Sugar King produced a film to market the maple syrup business. For the film Cary hired members of the Penobscot Nation in Maine who, incongruously, put on headdresses worn by the Indigenous Peoples of the Great Plains, thousands of kilometres away. Their sugaring technique was a little more authentic: The Indigenous actors posed while boiling sap in a kettle over an open fire. To recreate the colonial era days, a man in a wide-brimmed straw hat and full beard carried a shoulder yoke and two wooden sap pails. Then, for the modern period, Cary's film showed off a company breakthrough: the Brower Sap Piping System, a pioneering effort to connect trees via steel pipelines.

With a flamboyance that matched his personality, Cary boarded the Vermont Maple Sugar Special in 1926, a train tour to promote maple products with nine sleeping cars and four cars to exhibit maple delicacies; each year from 1926 through 1929 the train visited Boston, New York, Washington, Philadelphia and Chicago. Cary rode the train with his secretary, his daughter and his niece. On its journey, the train

was met by the mayor in New York and US president Calvin
Coolidge in Washington, D.C.

Sugaring had been a bucolic springtime activity replete
with priests sprinkling the sugar bush with holy water to
help the run of sap, horse-drawn sleds to gather sap from the
maple trees, and eager families gathered in the sugar shack
around the billowing steam from the evaporator, happy to taste
the sweet elixir of spring. But as the maple syrup industry
evolved it crashed into the industrial realities of the 20th century, and here our story veers pell-mell into the world of big
business, market capitalism, razor-thin margins, predatory
monopolistic enterprises, technical innovation and industrial
expansion, arson, rebellion and theft—all set against the back-
drop of unpredictable weather. This is the story of the fall
of Cary and the rise in power of Quebec, Inc., to global dominance of the maple syrup business.

Maple syrup producers are farmers, not salespeople. Both
US and Canadian farmers initially welcomed George Cary: He
bought all their product and took away the hassle of haggling
with consumers, grocery stores or dealers. But his power also
rattled them. Cary called the shots: He paid Quebec farmers
4 cents per pound for maple sugar in the 1910s, but in 1923 he
cut the price to 2 cents and then a year later convinced the
US government to close the border, to force a further drop in
the price of Canadian maple sugar.

Syrup farmers on both sides of the border decided to organize, reasoning that unity would give them strength to bargain
with Cary and keep more maple money in their own pockets.
Vermont maple producers formed a co-operative in the early
1920s. Two things doomed that effort: the independent nature
for which Vermont farmers are famous, and the lack of capital

to get the enterprise underway. The Vermont co-op even had to rent syrup barrels from Cary. Not long after its birth the Vermont co-operative collapsed in bankruptcy, with Cary's company buying up its remaining products and equipment.

Predatory pricing that favours middlemen over farmers is an age-old story in agriculture. In a series called "The True Cost of Chocolate," *The Globe and Mail*'s Africa correspondent introduced us to Félicien Angui, whose family of five work a 4-hectare cacao farm in Ivory Coast. Even as profits for global chocolate giants—Hershey, Lindt, Mondelez and Nestlé—soared, the newspaper reported that the chocolate giants paid farmers less and less for cacao. The farmers isolated the problem: They had no connection to the consumer. The big cocoa buyers stockpiled cocoa and shifted their purchases to other farmers, buying wherever they got the cheapest price.

The plight of Africa's cacao farmers would sound familiar to generations of maple syrup producers. Before World War II, farmers in Canada who made maple sugar or maple syrup in larger quantities, whose main export market has always been, and remains, the United States, served at the mercy of a few buyers. Cary was the most famous: The Maple King was a kind of Hershey/Mondelez/Nestlé of his day, with the power to dictate the price of maple sugar and maple syrup.

This servitude lasted until Quebec farmers got organized. In their bid to unite and flex power, maple syrup farmers had one advantage over cacao-growers: Though cacao originated in Central America, farmers were now growing cacao in Africa, Indonesia and across Latin America and the Caribbean. In contrast, nobody has successfully established a sugar bush in Europe or Asia; the tree that makes maple syrup thrives only in the northeast of North America. Once

Quebec syrup farmers organized, they had a better chance to wrest control of the price.

The visionary, the Napoleonesque figure behind the move to unite Quebec maple farmers and take on the power of Cary, was Cyrille Vaillancourt. One of a family of fifteen children who grew up south of Quebec City long before the invention of the automobile, Vaillancourt is a founding father of the modern maple syrup industry in Quebec. Vaillancourt later led what is now North America's biggest credit union (Desjardins), sat in the Senate of Canada from 1944 to 1969 and was named to the Order of the British Empire. But his origins were in maple syrup.

Vaillancourt's story begins in the village of Saint-Anselme on the Etchemin River southeast of Quebec City, a place whose religious devotion and rural simplicity would shape the man Vaillancourt would become. In the 1820s, the Catholic Church commissioned Quebec architect Thomas Baillairgé to design a church for the town; the stone sanctuary opened its doors in 1850. During this period, Cyrille's grandfather built the village's first sawmill and flour mill. Cyrille's mother, Marie-Louise, married Cyrille-Émille Vaillancourt, a doctor. His father was later elected to Parliament as a Liberal. This fact would come back to haunt his son.

Marie-Louise gave birth to five children between 1872 and 1879; notwithstanding her husband's profession, all five died of croup. Undeterred, the couple produced nine more children. Joseph-Cyrille-Antoine, born and baptized in 1892, was then the youngest (a younger sister died as an infant). Vaillancourt later said that his mother and father ran a tight ship: They never punished or threatened their children; they simply told them how to behave and expected them to obey.

When Vaillancourt was eight his parents sent him to the Saint-Louis-de-Gonzague boarding school in Quebec City, where he played a bit of hockey. Later he attended university, majoring in philosophy. After a brief stint as a journalist, Cyrille returned home as a young man and applied for a job at the St. Anselme post office. The local MP was a Conservative; as the son of a Liberal, Vaillancourt couldn't get a federal job. He travelled quite a distance west along the St. Lawrence River and found work with the Trappist Fathers at their monastery in Oka, west of Montreal, a centre of agricultural research still renowned today for excellent cheese. The monks sought to design a chicken coop that would incite chickens to lay eggs in winter. Vaillancourt's job paid $10 a month but only required one hour's work a day; Vaillancourt spent the rest of the time in classes, including a course on beekeeping. His keen study of the industrious collective achievements of bees informed his later success assembling maple syrup producers for co-operative success. World War I hit and sugar was scarce; the Province of Quebec hired Vaillancourt to teach Quebec farmers to keep bees. His pay soared to $3 a day. He crisscrossed Quebec by train and horse-and-buggy to talk bees. Vaillancourt put a beehive in the window of a department store on St. Catherine Street, the principal shopping thoroughfare of Montreal; a thick throng of gawkers blocked the street and the police ordered him to remove the hive. Vaillancourt founded a newspaper, *L'abeille*, or *The Bee*, to help teach beekeeping, united the beekeepers, and helped them with classification and honey packaging.

Seeing Vaillancourt's success with honey, after the war the Government of Quebec gave him a new assignment: maple syrup. To raise the quality of the product and attract more sales, the Province had, in 1914, created the first sugaring school, or Sucrerie école, in Sainte-Louise, northeast of Quebec City. In 1918, Quebec's minister of agriculture enrolled Vaillancourt in the school. "Eating maple taffy and maple sugar is good," Vaillancourt told his biographer, Jacques Lamarche. "Making syrup is different. I found myself dressed like the sugar bush workers. With snowshoes on my feet, I hesitate, and learn to walk, and especially to fall down. I started picking up maple sap. I watched it boil and evaporate. I observed, and I learned."

At the time maple sugarers in Quebec had few standards and less regard for quality; those who made a lot of maple sugar sold most of it to American buyers, principally George Cary. Cary's buyers at the time paid the same price for any maple sugar or maple syrup, regardless of quality. In one sugar shack, a producer told Vaillancourt: "We're not going to travel 100 miles to sell our sugar. The American buyers come to us. They buy our nice sugar at the same price, whether it's brown, blond, black or not very nice." And the prices were low. One day a sugar buyer arrived by train at the station at Bras d'Apic, east of Quebec City, and offered farmers 5 cents a pound for their maple sugar, adding that he could just as well offer 2 cents since he was the only one there.

The Cary company in the early 20th century bought up to two-thirds of the sugar produced in Quebec's most prolific sugaring region, the Beauce. This particular maple sugar, known at the time as Beauce Sugar, was darker and had a stronger flavour, making it the preferred sweetener to blend with tobacco.

It was akin to a race to the bottom. Vaillancourt was not proud of the era's maple sugar. Producers, Vaillancourt said, made sugar in loaves of 10 to 18 pounds, of every shape and

> "Sugar makers: We are in the market for all you can produce of good, hard pure Maple Sugar packed in standard new wooden sugar pails or sugar tubs."

THE CARY MAPLE SUGAR CO.
Newspaper advertisement, 1912

colour, and packed them in empty bags that had contained bran, oats or even cement. The farmers brought their sugar to the train station, packed in torn and gutted bags, and carried on wagons that had been used for anything save for moving clean products. "If that's the national sugar produced by the French-Canadians, it was pretty hard to look at," Vaillancourt said later. But he saw a way out. "I thought, 'If this is really our national sweetener, we have to get out of this rut and present the product with more dignity.'"

Quebec's deputy minister of agriculture told Vaillancourt that to improve quality, he'd have to convince buyers to pay more for higher-grade syrup and sugar. The biggest buyer was Cary. In 1925, Vaillancourt decided to visit him. He had taken some English classes as a child but never mastered the language; Vaillancourt asked the deputy minister to join him for the trip. The train that carried the two men clattered past the warehouses where Cary stockpiled maple sugar on its way to the headquarters of the Cary Maple Sugar Company in St. Johnsbury. Sitting across from the Maple King in his spacious office, Vaillancourt asked Cary to pay producers more for higher-quality maple syrup and maple sugar. Cary refused. Vaillancourt then told Cary, to the deputy minister's surprise, that producers would form a co-operative to take control of syrup quality and to wrest better rates for their wares.

Cary laughed in his face. Then, with a sardonic grin, Cary dared Vaillancourt to try to gain control over the price of maple sugar and maple syrup. Cary told him that the people of Vermont had tried to form a co-operative but failed and went bankrupt, after which Cary bought their syrup barrels for pennies. According to Vaillancourt, Cary said: "Today they all bring me their products and they don't speak of their failed co-operative. You won't do any better, young man, and you will soon be happy to see me again. I am still the Maple King."

After his 1925 Vermont visit, Vaillancourt returned to Canada not defeated but rather determined. Gathering together seventeen maple syrup producers that year in the village of Plessisville southeast of Quebec City in the heart of sugar maple country, Vaillancourt founded the Company of Sugar and Pure Maple Syrup Producers, known in French as the Société coopérative des producteurs de sucre d'érable. To communicate with them, he renamed his newspaper *L'abeille et l'érable*, or *The Bee and the Maple*. Vaillancourt realized that the maple sweetener industry could never win a price war with cheaper cane sugar and corn syrup. For maple sugar and maple syrup to survive, they'd need to evolve them into a specialty or luxury product. But he faced a tall task: to prove that he could command a premium price for higher-quality maple syrup and sugar. He sent empty barrels to the seventeen producers and asked them to fill the containers with their finest syrup. "Put your black syrup in your old barrels and sell it to Mr. Cary," he added. Vaillancourt wasn't too sure how to sell the high-quality syrup, so he asked the producers to send it to his home in Lévis, on the south shore of the St. Lawrence River across from Quebec City.

Workers at the Lévis train station were a bit surprised to see the syrup barrels pile up on the platform. His wife may have raised an eyebrow when Vaillancourt took it all home and stored the syrup in his basement. Vaillancourt married twice: His first marriage in 1916 ended in tragedy two years later, when his wife and child both passed away. In 1920, he married Marie-Blanche Normandin, a miller's daughter from Kamouraska, east of Quebec City. The couple settled in Lévis.

They would go on to have eight children. Amidst that busy household, in 1925, during his lunch hour or when he got home from his government job, Vaillancourt went to see possible syrup or maple sugar clients: friends of his brothers, doctors, lawyers, government officials. Some ordered one gallon of syrup, some took two. Vaillancourt set up a stove in his basement, and at night, after a quick supper, he and Marie-Blanche boiled syrup for clients who had ordered maple sugar, which they stored in waxed paper.

The next day he wrapped his twenty little loaves of sugar to make a 20-pound package. With the package under his arm, and carrying two 1-gallon jugs of syrup in the other hand, he caught the streetcar that stopped in front of his house. At the port he boarded the ferry to cross the river to Quebec City. On the city side, he took another streetcar to deliver the sugar and syrup.

Somehow that year Vaillancourt managed to move 3,000 pounds of syrup on his own. The co-op began to grow. The co-op rented a room in the basement of the Plessisville City Hall, and expanded to the house next door a year later, but they couldn't fit all the syrup. One night an agronomist working with the group slept the night on top of a delivery of 5-gallon cans, to keep them safe, because people had heard about the quality of the syrup and everyone wanted some. Vaillancourt's promotional efforts met with success: Producers saw their payment for a gallon of syrup rise—and, most importantly, saw a pricing structure emerge that rewarded syrup quality with a better price.

Vaillancourt's efforts improved the quality of maple syrup and its appeal at home, but Cary was not defeated yet. Cary decided to expand his footprint northward: In 1929, on land purchased from the Canadian Pacific Railroad, the Cary Maple Sugar Company opened a three-storey plant in Lennoxville, in Quebec's Eastern Townships near the heart of maple syrup territory, with two elevators and a 38-metre smokestack. The plant featured the latest equipment to store, handle, cook and pack huge volumes of maple syrup. Cary opened the factory to produce exports of syrup for British markets, thus sidestepping British duties on US products.

Pride goeth before the fall: The meteoric rise of Cary's empire was surpassed only by its cataclysmic collapse—partly due to the syrup producers' collective action, and also due to the Great Depression of 1929, to which we must add Cary's own hubris. Cary had visited Washington, D.C., to call on the government to raise the tariff on maple sugar from Canada to 8 cents per pound, effective mid-1930. To avoid paying the higher tariff, Cary bought as much Quebec maple sugar as he could find. The American Tobacco Company knew Cary had lots of sugar and wanted to pay a lower price. Cary refused. He was left with a massive inventory of sugar and no buyer. With the global economy in freefall, bankers stopped loaning money to Cary. In the summer of 1931, he resigned as president of the Cary Maple Sugar Company. In September 1931, Cary declared bankruptcy, owing more than $3 million, much of it to Canadian banks. Suffering from stress, two months later Cary died of kidney failure.

"Maple Sugar King Is Dead" announced the headline on the front page of the *Brattleboro Daily Reformer* for November 23, 1931, adding "George C. Cary of St. Johnsbury Had World's Biggest Business at One Time—67 Years Old." One had to read the obituary to understand that, rather than the "world's biggest business," it was in fact the world's largest maple sugar company. An auction that year sold off Cary's nineteen Welsh ponies, as well as his tractors and car. Creditors took control of the Cary Company.

The repercussions were devastating: Maple prices plummeted and syrup-makers went bankrupt. Vaillancourt asked for help from Joseph-Léonide Perron, Quebec minister of agriculture. Perron told Vaillancourt that if syrup-makers put in 1 cent per pound of sugar to sustain the co-op, the province would double their money. Vaillancourt addressed a hall in Plessisville packed with 800 members of the nascent syrup co-operative, all of them frightened for the future of their industry. Though a deeply religious man, Vaillancourt on this occasion skipped the homily.

"When a little boy is drowning in a river," Vaillancourt told them, "when even his mother is shouting from the riverbank, 'Pray to Saint-Anne!' the boy needs to swim, not to pray. I don't think the saints can do anything for us; it's our turn to swim." More than 750 members signed on to pay a tithe to the co-operative. The group raised $32,000.

Even so, faith remained central to Vaillancourt and to his fledgling syrup co-operative. In 1934, in the dark days of the Great Depression, the syrup producers' co-operative, known today as Citadelle, coopérative de producteurs de sirop d'érable, asked a priest to compose for them a kind of prayer of consecration to the Sacred Heart, which the syrup-makers' newspaper, *L'abeille et l'érable,* published each June through 1970 so that syrup producers might recite the words as a family.

By the heat and the fire of our stoves, the water of our maples loses its impurities and becomes our delicious maple syrup. Is it not by the heat and the fire of our hearths, burning with the love of your divine heart, that our poor hearts, purified of their imperfections, will change into hearts that love you more? . . . Please ensure that our will be as strong as the hard wood of our maples, so that we always respect the laws of justice and Christian honesty in our work and our commercial transactions. . . . Be the loved and respected king in our sugar shacks. We promise to show Your image so that all our sugaring off parties take place under your protection.

Vaillancourt believed that faith mixed with teamwork would conquer all. In a 1934 edition of a Quebec government pamphlet for syrup-makers, Vaillancourt wrote: "According to the 1931 census, there are in Canada 46,639 cultivators tending 24.2 million maples; if all these sugar makers did a bit of promotion, either by themselves or by organizing co-operatives, imagine how far we could develop our industry! It's always the same thing: an isolated man is weak, but, linked to others through a co-operative, what a powerhouse he can become! A bee in a hive is nothing, but a whole swarm together, what strength!"

The swarm of which Vaillancourt spoke—the maple syrup makers' co-operative—helped the producers stay in business in the depths of the Dirty Thirties. The co-operative created testing labs and ensured standards for syrup and sugar from maple trees and packaged its members' sweet stuff for sale across the United States and Canada, and even to Europe.

The next challenge came in 1936. One day the phone rang at the young co-operative. On the line was a US Customs officer in Chicago. "Sir," the officer said, "you have sent us three rail cars of poison syrup. It's full of lead. I will not let it into the U.S.A. Keep your poison syrup in Canada."

Vaillancourt scrambled. A chemist at Laval University in Quebec City devised a way to solidify the lead and extract it from the syrup, allowing the sweet stuff to finally cross into the United States. But what about the recurrent problem of lead in syrup? Producers tracked the source to the sap buckets, made of tin, which had a seam along the side, soldered with lead. Many buckets also had a lead coating to reduce rust. Inspectors also found lead pipes in the sugar shacks, lead spiles and lead solder in the evaporators used to boil the sap.

Vaillancourt, by this point on the board of the local Lévis credit union, cut a deal with a Belgian beer barrel-maker, Georges-Armand L'Hoir, to make new syrup equipment. With loans from the credit union, the syrup co-operative built a factory and rented it to the steel-maker. The timing was off, however: The factory opened in 1939, the year Germany invaded Poland and Canada declared war. Canada rationed all metals to make guns, planes and ammunition to fight World War II; the factory could get no metal. In 1945, when Canada and its allies won the war, L'Hoir finally got the aluminum he needed.

L'Hoir's factory worked twenty years to produce the twenty million aluminum buckets needed to swap out the lead-soldered tin sap receptacles. Syrup-makers brought their old buckets to Plessisville to exchange for the new aluminum ones; photos show trucks piled high with thousands of old sap buckets, arriving for the swap. Governments and producers split the cost of the new buckets, with Canada and Quebec each paying one-third of the price and the syrup-maker the other third. The United States re-opened its borders to Quebec syrup after two years; it took until 1960 to replace all the buckets. Some of the old buckets kicked around, though; on the farm where I grew up, we collected sap in lead-soldered buckets.

Among the explanations for Quebec's success in the sugar bush was Vaillancourt's co-operative, which had made huge strides in uniting sugarers to produce great quantities of maple syrup and sugar, marketed under the co-op's brand name, Citadelle. Vaillancourt coined the name looking north out the window of the co-op's first office in Lévis. Across the St. Lawrence River on top of the cliff of Quebec City stood the Citadelle, the biggest British fortress in the Western Hemisphere, built after the war of 1812, its stone walls thrusting outward like the points of a star. The logo of Citadelle maple syrup combines the points of the fort with the points of a maple leaf. The co-op standardized the quality of maple syrup, requiring its producers to deliver their syrup at 66 Brix, that is to say, two-thirds sugar. Below 66 percent the syrup spoils; above 66 percent it crystallizes in the container.

In 1955, Abby Maurice Proulx, a Catholic priest, agronomist and trailblazer of documentary film-making in Quebec, released the colour film *Maple Sugar and Co-operation*, filmed at the Citadelle co-operative. By this point, the co-op had more than 5,000 members. The film, accompanied by a score of upbeat strings, depicts women in white lab coats—lab technicians supervised, in the rigid gender roles of the day, by male chemists—who pour syrup into test tubes to check its sugar level, its clarity, and the presence of lead.

"Thanks to co-operation and scientific methods," intones the narrator, "we offer to consumers a pure and uniform product, which commands a premium on the world market."

Long gone was the dark sugar wrapped in bags that had once contained cement, hauled to the train station on filthy wagons. Here was pure, clean, sparkling syrup and sugar of which its makers could be proud. Cary had traversed the

United States to promote maple syrup to the mayor of New York and the president of the United States; Citadelle found its own style in marketing; the co-operative gave gifts of maple syrup to King George VI, Queen Elizabeth II, French president Charles de Gaulle, and Pope Pius XII to boost its profile. The profits from sales of the syrup, known in English by the brand name Camp, now went back into the syrup-makers' pockets. Still, Vaillancourt's challenges in speaking English did present a recurring obstacle. Vaillancourt recalls a 1932 sales trip to a big grocery store in London, where he stood beside a pyramid of maple sugar. A woman approached and asked what kind of soap he had to sell. Vaillancourt, who did not know the English word "soap," replied, "the most natural one." The shopper hesitated because of the price. So Vaillancourt sliced off a piece and handed it to her. She asked, "What do you want me to do with it?" Rather than reply, Vaillancourt swallowed the sugar, licked his lips and handed her another piece. "Bloody foolish salesman," the woman said, as she fled.

Other marketing efforts met with more success. When British prime minister Winston Churchill met US president Franklin Roosevelt and Canadian prime minister William Lyon Mackenzie King at the Citadelle in Quebec City in August 1943 for a military conference as World War II raged, Vaillancourt saw an opportunity. He served maple products and gave out maple recipe booklets to journalists from far and wide, generating press for maple syrup around the world. Later Vaillancourt turned his focus to other forms of collective action, including leading what became the powerful Desjardins credit union. Even so, until his death in 1969, at age seventy-seven, Vaillancourt remained general manager of Citadelle. He always kept his sweet tooth.

OPEC IN THE SUGAR BUSH

I n June 1950, a thick petition arrived with a thump on the desk of the Department of Justice in Ottawa. The signatures on the petition came from producers of maple products in the Beauce district of Quebec. The farmers said that the larger buyers of that province's maple products had formed a combine to fix a common purchase price for syrup and cheat the producers. Ottawa ordered an investigation under the federal Combines Act.

One would imagine that the work of Cyrille Vaillancourt, to create a Quebec co-operative of maple syrup producers, would have solved this issue. He had formed that co-op to combat the power of the big syrup buyers, the most prominent being the Cary Maple Company of Vermont. Indeed, the Citadelle maple syrup and maple sugar co-op helped many syrup-makers work together to make a better product and get a decent price in the market. Still, maple syrup bottling and retailing giants in both Canada and the United States remained in control of the price farmers received for their syrup because, while thousands of syrup producers joined Citadelle, most producers in Quebec, as elsewhere, remained independent and sold syrup to whomever they chose. In poor seasons when producers made scant syrup, prices soared, but in years when the sap flowed freely and farmers made lots of syrup, the price cratered. "Syrup back then was a hobby, and people who made it lived on a roller coaster," sums up Jean-François Laplante, a New Brunswick syrup-maker.

Syrup-makers were convinced that the buyers plotted in secret to drive down the price. The Government of Canada appointed a commissioner, J.D. MacDonald, to investigate. Concerns about price fixing were rampant back then: Commissioners during the period also investigated possible collusion among bread bakers in western Canada, coarse paper producers in British Columbia, flat glass makers in Ontario and Quebec, and flour millers in every province, while Canada's Department of Justice also conducted an investigation into what it described as "an alleged combine in the manufacture, distribution and sale of matches." With maple syrup, the government found no collusion in 1953. MacDonald wrote: "It has not been proved that the parties have taken control of enough of the business nor exercised enough power over the market for us to say with certainty that their agreements hurt the public, in this case, the producers."

MacDonald's report illustrates Quebec's dominance of the maple syrup industry by that time. In 1941, of 39,000 producers of maple syrup in Canada, 25,000 were in Quebec. Meanwhile, yearly production of syrup in the United States fell from about 41 million pounds in 1920 to less than half that 30 years later. "Increasingly attractive prices for maple lumber have led to the cutting of many maple trees in the producing areas of the United States," the report notes, adding, "in Canada the rate of reduction of maple bushes by cutting does not appear to have exceeded the rate at which new trees have been brought into production."

Even as syrup production increased in Canada, the syrup price roller coaster continued for another half-century. Then syrup-makers came to understand that only by uniting could they control how much syrup entered the market in any year, and thus control its price.

The Beauce region took action first: In 1958, eight out of every ten syrup producers of Quebec-Sud approved a plan to market all their syrup collectively. In 1966, syrup-makers created a new branch within the Catholic Cultivators' Union: the Fédération des producteurs de sucre et de sirop d'érable du Québec, or Quebec Maple Sugar and Syrup Producers Federation. As the Federation has evolved, so too has its name. In 2018, the organization became the Producteurs et productrices acéricoles du Québec (PPAQ), for the first time specifically acknowledging women who make maple syrup: the "productrices."

The Federation had a simple proposition: Let's pool all the province's syrup and sell it together. Every few years, we will sit down with the bottling companies and agree on a price. Rather than pay farmers individually, bottlers pay the Federation; the Federation distributes the proceeds to the syrup-makers. And the Federation stockpiles surplus syrup.

But many Quebec farmers balked at the Federation and its threat to their independence. In 1983, two-thirds of syrup-makers voted against the creation of a single sales agency for syrup. Seven years later, in a new vote, most supported the idea. But the vote did not seal the deal. One key problem: The bottling companies didn't want to deal with the sole sales agent and refused to pay 4 cents per pound of syrup to the Federation.

Backers of the Federation pressed ahead. The road proved rocky, but Mother Nature helped the Federation's argument. In 1987 came a small harvest. The price of maple syrup shot up to $2.40 per pound. The next year was a very, very big syrup season. Syrup-makers found that, even at $1 per pound, nobody wanted it. There was a surplus of about 2 million pounds. Producers were heading for bankruptcy. The buyers were in trouble too, because they'd bought syrup at $2.40 per pound and, with $1 syrup around, their markets were getting undercut.

The federal government gave the Federation $5 million to buy the excess syrup. That took the syrup off the market. The buyers were happy, and the makers got their price. That started the reserve of maple syrup. Then 1989 brought another abundant syrup year. The government stepped in with another loan for maple syrup, but then told the syrup-makers to figure it out among themselves. The producers created the Federation and the sales agency, and agreed with the buyers on a price. The syrup price roller coaster briefly halted. But then it started up again. In 1992, the Federation declared bankruptcy. The governments of Quebec and Canada rode to the rescue, bailing out the sales agency.

Some farmers, who wanted freedom to cut their own deals for their own syrup, got mad. Gatherings of syrup-makers erupted into screaming matches. Then came March 2000: a bad month for the leaders of the Federation of Maple Syrup Producers. And for once the problems had nothing to do with the sugaring weather. First the sugar shack of Rolland Urbain, who had a leadership role in the Federation, caught fire and

"It would be tough if the Americans or people from New Brunswick made as much syrup as the people in Quebec. They could cut the price in good years. But we produce 75 percent of the world. We establish the price."

ALAIN GAUTHIER,
president, Québec-Rive-Nord section,
Quebec Maple Syrup Producers, 2023

burned to the ground. A week later the sap-pumping station of syrup producer Éric Lampron, an administrator of the Federation, also burned down. Two weeks after that, the sugar shack of Pierre and Monique Lemieux, where their family had made maple syrup for seventy-five years, also caught fire. Lemieux was president of the Federation.

The headline in the newspaper *La Presse* read "The Syrup Mafia Strikes." The Quebec City correspondent reported: "Sugar shacks burnt, harvest sabotaged, vandalism—the fight against the black market of maple syrup, led by the Agricultural Producers' Union, has started to face the kind of resistance expected of biker gangs."

"For three administrators of the Federation to suffer fire damage in the same year, that's hard to believe," Lemieux told a reporter. "Sugar shacks burn down every year, but three? I don't want to be paranoid, but let's just say it's a lot."

Undeterred, the Federation of Maple Syrup Producers continued its crusade for a cartel that could set the price of the sweet liquid. Syrup producers, with government help, rented a warehouse to stockpile unsold syrup. The Federation set a price for syrup, but some syrup-makers didn't want to wait to get paid through the system; about one in six syrup-makers in 2000 sold their syrup on what the Federation called the black market. In the same year the sugar shacks burned down (2000), a big syrup harvest produced a surplus of almost 20 million pounds of syrup that the Federation did not have the money to buy. Many buyers seized the chance to offer producers just 85 cents per pound for maple syrup, even though the minimum price fixed by the joint plan was $1.56 a pound.

The syrup producers got together and asked members to kick in an extra 4 cents per pound, to pay the interest on a

$40-million loan they sought from the government to buy up surplus syrup. Eleven regional syrup syndicates held meetings to discuss the idea. The producers agreed to double their contribution on each pound of syrup sold to 8 cents. Still, the government stayed quiet. In September 2020, four hundred syrup producers gathered in Rivière du Loup to put pressure on the government. Quebec City finally agreed to help. This allowed syrup-makers to stockpile unsold syrup, to protect it from being sold at a discount and causing a syrup price collapse. The Federation now had control of the syrup market.

The system, called a joint marketing plan, governs all maple syrup producers (aside from hobby farms) in Quebec. Other than syrup sold at the farm gate, in farmers' markets and in direct deals with local grocers, syrup producers agree with syrup bottlers on one syrup price. Farmers ship their syrup to bottling companies or to the Federation, and receive payment from the Federation on a schedule set by the Federation, who then store the excess syrup until buyers want it; producers get paid in full for that syrup once it is sold. The Federation also decides how much syrup each producer may make, and allocates any new taps in sugar bushes in Quebec.

Speaking to *The New York Times* in 2012, Simon Trépanier, then acting general manager of the Federation, or PPAQ, compared his group to the Organization of the Petroleum Exporting Countries: "It's like OPEC," he said. He added that by producing 70 to 78 percent of the world's syrup, the PPAQ can adjust the quantity of syrup in the market. Thus, Quebec controls the price.

Tom Shaw, the Ontario maple syrup producer, praises the Quebec plan. "It has absolutely made the Quebec maple syrup business," he said. "It has absolutely made all those producers money. It has absolutely raised the profile of maple syrup worldwide, because they've got the marketing budget to market syrup globally. Sure, there is always whispers in the back: 'Why did he get quota and why didn't I get quota?' There's lots of room for corruption in that type of system. You know there's producers making extra syrup that magically ends up in Ontario or other places. It's not perfect, but the system itself has been extremely good for maple syrup."

Shaw also commented that Quebec's Federation proved its worth during the COVID-19 pandemic. Because everyone stayed home and cooked, demand for luxury goods such as maple syrup skyrocketed. At the same time, 2021 was a poor syrup year.

"There was a bad season," Shaw recalled. "But all of a sudden there was tons of syrup being sold. Back in the olden days before the Quebec marketing board, nobody in North America could have had the syrup to meet that kind of demand. They would have sold out of syrup there. But Quebec's got five- and six-year-old syrup sitting there. They started pulling syrup out of the strategic reserve." It's remarkable, he adds, for "a little niche commodity like that to have that much power and that much syrup in stock where they could handle this huge spike. And it wasn't even that bad of a year. It could have been worse, and they still could have swallowed it."

Even so, when I asked Shaw whether he wants a syrup cartel in Ontario, his answer was instant and emphatic: "No!" But then he qualified it a bit. "I shouldn't say that. I guess it would be okay to have it here. I do like free markets; I do like those things."

On the other hand, David Briggs, a syrup bottler I met in

New Brunswick, added, "It's created a black market. Producers will sell ten barrels on the black market for cash."

The most recent Marketing Agreement for Maple Syrup, signed in April 2023 between the PPAQ and the Buyers of the Product Identified by the Joint Plan of Quebec Syrup Producers, represented by the Quebec Maple Industry, is a 56-page document with annexes A through P. As per the deal, producers are to receive $3.20 per pound for the best-quality maple syrup, defined as syrup that lets through at least 75 percent light; the price for this top grade rose to $3.40 in 2024. Very dark syrup, which transmits less than 25 percent of light, sold for $2.75 per pound in 2023. Organic syrup gets a markup of $0.22 per pound. The Federation takes a cut of $0.10 to $0.50 per pound to classify, stockpile, pasteurize and otherwise manage syrup. There is a lot of fine print.

Not everyone likes the rules: My first foray as a journalist into the maple syrup industry, in 2015, involved maple rebels who tried to buck the system. The story of those who call themselves "recalcitrants" comes a bit later on.

For many years, the biggest challenge syrup producers faced was that, in years when they made bountiful syrup, the price of syrup would crash. To smooth out these highs and lows, the Federation now stockpiles all syrup that does not sell in any given year in drums in one of three vast Quebec warehouses. The decision to fill a warehouse with thousands of barrels of a highly lucrative product—maple syrup—to sell in lean syrup years turned one storage depot along a rural stretch of a Quebec highway into a sort of Ali Baba's cave: too tempting for a group of enterprising, and to some extent amateurish, criminals to resist.

THE GREAT
MAPLE SYRUP HEIST

O n a sunny afternoon in August 2011, several cars and trucks arrived at a warehouse on busy Highway 20 between Montreal and Quebec City. They parked in the back where they were not visible to anyone driving by. Men emerged into the stark sunlight of the day and entered the warehouse. These men were about to pull off the most valuable theft in the history of Canada.

This crime was not undertaken in the heat of the moment. Stealing from Quebec's largest maple syrup reserve required detailed planning and a solid technique. These warehouses contained thousands of barrels of maple syrup, each weighing about 225 kilograms, or 496 pounds (about the size of a standard barrel of crude oil). To pull off a theft of this scale, these criminals needed a lot of equipment: a transport truck, a truck driver, forklift trucks, forklift drivers, a key to the warehouse, extra barrels that look just like the barrels of syrup that you want to steal (so nobody notices that barrels are missing) and somebody who wants to buy lots of syrup and not ask questions. In short, stealing maple syrup at scale is logistically a massive task. But these thieves had everything they needed, including burner cellphones and, crucially, help on the inside. And they succeeded, at least for a time.

As discussed in the previous chapter, the Quebec Maple Syrup Producers had a policy of stockpiling maple syrup in years when production was high, thanks to the right weather conditions. In 2011, the Federation, having filled its existing storage space with syrup, sought a new warehouse to stockpile overflow syrup in anticipation of the coming harvest.

Enter Avik Caron, a former insurance salesman and main ringleader of the heist. He and two partners had bought the warehouses along Highway 20 in July 2010. Caron put his stake in the warehouse in the name of his girlfriend. The warehouse, a former hardwood flooring factory, stretches several football fields, lines up east to west, has a red brick front and is sheathed in steel on all other sides.

In spring 2011, the Federation signed a deal with Caron to rent space in this warehouse so they could stockpile excess syrup. The producers calculated that they would not need this syrup for two to four years. At the rear of the warehouse was an 18,000-square-foot annex that was informally called "the Bertha." The Federation contracted the warehouse owners to supply forklifts and forklift drivers to unload trucks and stack the heavy barrels of syrup. Once the process of moving the syrup began, workers spent all day every day loading maple syrup into the Bertha. At 4 p.m. on this afternoon in August, the workers called it quits and went home.

Soon after, the other guys pulled up to the Bertha. They did not need to wear masks because the syrup bank had no security cameras. Caron had spent weeks planning the details of the syrup theft. He knew the syrup's value: a 205-litre, or 53-gallon, barrel of syrup at that time was worth about $1,800, about eighteen times the price of a barrel of crude oil. But Caron needed help because a Great Lake's worth of maple syrup is a tricky product to sell. He knew no one in the world of maple syrup. But he did know a truck driver: Sébastien Jutras. Years earlier, Caron had sold an insurance policy to a teenaged Jutras, and the pair had remained friends. Caron called Jutras to ask for help.

Jutras, a trucker who was usually on the road, suggested a meeting. He needed a spot where he could park his eighteen-wheeler. He picked a truck stop along the highway west of the syrup warehouse, with the unlikely name Le Madrid. The setting adds an element of mystery, if not to say kitsch, to the plot. The Le Madrid truck stop featured a restaurant and hotel housed in a kind of castle with a turreted tower, painted white, and a sloped red-tiled roof, in someone's whimsical interpretation of Spanish architecture. Even more improbably, surrounding the turreted restaurant stood thirty life-size dinosaurs made of fibreglass, along with a number of monster trucks.

The meeting took place in June 2011. Jutras, the truck driver, invited a third person to the table: Richard Vallières. Vallières was the perfect partner in crime. Not only had he grown up in the maple syrup industry, he also had a serious bone to pick with the Federation.

Richard Vallières had produced maple syrup as a child with his father, at his sugar bush south of Quebec City, and, before the age of thirty, made his own mark in the syrup business. In Quebec, any maple syrup sold in bulk must pass through the hands of the Federation. But some syrup producers balked at this straitjacket. Vallières became what a court document called a *rouleux de barils*, or "barrel roller," the term for a shadowy character who will come to your sugar shack by night and load the syrup onto a truck for secretive transport to a buyer, and pay you cash for the sweet stuff, with no need to wait for payment in instalments—as the system dictates—and no need to give a cut to the powerful Federation. It's all highly illegal under Quebec's maple syrup supply management system, but he styled himself as a hero, not a criminal.

The Federation got wise to Vallières. An investigator working for the Federation posed as a syrup-maker and sold syrup to Vallières outside of official channels in 2004. Prosecutors working for the agriculture board later charged Vallières with trading in contraband syrup. In 2007, Quebec's powerful Régie des marchés agricoles et alimentaires, the board that regulates Quebec farm products, ordered Vallières to pay a $1.8-million fine.

"I had run-ins with the Federation, and one day I'm being offered maple syrup and I knew it was stolen," Vallières told a parole board hearing in 2022. "I really wanted revenge. I wanted revenge because I had been pursued by the Federation. . . . I wanted revenge because they pursued me and had my house seized." With extensive contacts in the world of maple syrup and chafing with resentment, Vallières was the perfect person to enlist in a brazen syrup theft.

Making maple syrup is a lot of work. Stealing maple syrup, in very large quantities of steel barrels, can pose challenges, too. One tricky detail for the thieves: In the spring and summer of 2011, the Federation added barrels to the warehouse stock every day. When the Federation arrived in the morning with a syrup shipment, there could be no sign of missing barrels.

At Le Madrid, Caron, Jutras and Vallières plotted their crime. A 16-metre, or 53-foot, transport truck can haul 104 barrels. To remove 104 barrels of syrup, Caron needed 104 other identical barrels to fill the hole in the stockpile. As they finished their meal, the three men—witnessed that spring day by fibreglass dinosaurs and monster trucks—shook hands and agreed to go into business together.

When the thieves arrived at the warehouse that late afternoon in August, Jutras drove a truck loaded with 104 barrels painted off-white with a faint blue tinge, identical to the hue of the barrels belonging to the syrup federation. When authorized buyers receive delivery of maple syrup from the Federation, the barrels are supposed to be recycled rather than reused. Caron had combed the province and managed to buy barrels that had been emptied but not yet recycled. Some were rusty. He found a company that matches paint colour and got them to copy the official colours. Caron then filled these barrels with water.

Forklift drivers working for Caron, operating the same forklifts that the Federation used during the day, removed 104 full barrels of syrup from the front and put them to one side. They then took another 104 barrels of syrup from the next row, loaded them onto a truck, and replaced the hole with their barrels of water. They then put the barrels of syrup back in the front. No trace of any change remained. A truck hauled the stolen syrup to the sugar shack of Vallières' father, Raymond, in Saint-Adalbert. The thieves transferred the syrup into other containers and refilled the original syrup barrels with water from a nearby pond. From then on, the thieves always had a rolling inventory of 104 barrels filled with water to replace barrels they stole from the warehouse.

During the day, the Federation continued to fill the warehouse with barrels of syrup, completely oblivious to the crime that was taking place. After they left for the evening, the thieves showed up again and repeated the pattern. This went on for about five months.

The foreman of the forklift drivers was Sylvain Bourassa, a friend of Avik Caron, and he was able to assist them from the inside. Bourassa would manage the day shift and then at 4:00 or 4:30 p.m., once everybody had left, Bourassa came back and aided the theft.

Another of the forklift drivers was Pascal Patry. Patry was an honest guy, at first. One day, moving barrels in the warehouse, Patry noticed that several of the syrup barrels were sweating. On a glass of cold water, droplets of condensation form on the outside of the glass, which can leave a ring on the table. The same was happening to the barrels filled with water. The condensation on these barrels was causing rust, which was not normal because a barrel of maple syrup doesn't sweat. Patry knew something funny was going on. He mentioned the sweating barrels to Bourassa. Bourassa told Caron. Then the pair went back to Patry and said, "How much for your silence?" They gave him $1,000 and asked him to work for them. During the day Patry worked his shift, went home and ate supper, and then on evenings when they needed him, he went back to the warehouse and operated a forklift for the thieves.

Another accomplice was Steve Picard. He too started honest. Picard was the warehouse handyman who lived on

"I needed a big budget and a lot of police officers, because nobody had ever seen a theft like that."

MICHEL COMEAU,
detective, Sûreté du Québec,
in *La Terre de chez nous*, 2015

a rural route nearby. Driving from his house to the highway, Picard had to pass the warehouse. One night he noticed activity. He drove up. Caron was parked at the Tim Hortons near the warehouse, and he saw Picard. Caron asked him where he was going, to which Picard replied, "I have to go the warehouse." Caron told him not to go, which Picard found strange, so Caron let him in on the theft and implicated him. After that Picard worked as a sentry and also a wiper. He had to wipe the barrels if they sweated to get rid of any traces of water, and wipe up any evidence of the theft from the floor of the warehouse.

The best way to get rid of a lot of syrup is to spirit it out of Quebec. One good destination is New Brunswick, the next province east, which has a growing maple syrup industry. Quebec syrup production and sales rules do not apply outside the province. Vallières, during his earlier incarnation as a "barrel roller," had often sold syrup to Étienne St-Pierre, a major syrup buyer in New Brunswick who exports syrup to the United States and overseas.

Once the Saint-Louis-de-Blandford theft began, Vallières told St-Pierre that he had a lot of syrup to sell him. On October 11, 2011, St-Pierre travelled to Quebec and met Vallières in a vacant lot in Saint-Nicholas, west of Quebec City, to see the syrup. St-Pierre agreed to become a buyer.

The truck driver Sébastien Jutras or his father, Gaetan Jutras, drove their long-haul transport trucks to the warehouse at night, picked up loads of syrup and ferried the stuff to their buyers in New Brunswick, Ontario, Vermont and New Hampshire. According to court documents, each truck load leaving the warehouse contained about 45,000 pounds of maple syrup. Vallières paid Caron between $75,000 and

$100,000 for each load of maple syrup, sometimes handing over a shoe box full of cash. The government estimates that overall Vallières bought between 90 and 110 transport-truck loads of stolen syrup in 2011–2012. Caron paid the truckers, according to bank drafts, more than $500,000 for their service.

The caper was too good to last. In July 2012, the Federation began a routine inventory of the syrup in its warehouse on Highway 20. An accountant named Michel Gauvreau arrived at the warehouse, which on paper contained 16,000 barrels of syrup. Gauvreau, in an impressive act of thoroughness, climbed the barrels, stacked six high. One barrel on top rocked with his weight. He almost fell. When he regained his balance, he shook the barrel. It was empty. The thieves had gotten sloppy, leaving evidence of the heist. The Federation called the police.

One of the lead detectives put in charge of the investigation was Luc Briand. Briand grew up in the Saguenay region of Quebec, a verdant land of lakes and forests known for a bounty of blueberries. As a kid, Briand dreamed of becoming a police officer. His first job was with the Sûreté du Québec (SQ), or Quebec Provincial Police, in Saint-Anne-de-la-Pérade; he later won a promotion to the detachment at Trois-Rivières. Briand joined the team of detectives who investigated major crimes throughout the centre of Quebec.

Briand had a number of successful major crime investigations on his résumé. In one case, Briand tracked a gang of bank robbers who held up twenty-one Quebec credit unions, known as *caisses populaires*, while wearing masks with the faces of US presidents.

Briand had busted many bank robbers, but he had never tracked syrup thieves. It was a whole new challenge, and while it seemed funny to some, to the authorities this was a very serious crime. After all, the sums of money involved dwarfed any bank job in the history of the country. Briand bristles at the memory of the late-night US talk-show hosts who had such fun joking about the great Canadian theft of maple syrup.

"People thought it was really funny," Briand, now retired, recalled when we sat down for supper in Trois-Rivières where he lives. "There was so much work in this file," Briand said of the syrup heist investigation. "Sure, it's unusual. A theft of maple syrup. But often, the commentary we heard was 'Oh, it's just maple syrup.' It bothered us a bit, honestly. Because it's a lot of money. We're talking about $18 million. And it wasn't a one-shot deal. They worked for more than a year. This was an established organization. They were not career criminals, and they made a lot of mistakes. But we put so much into this. The first weeks, I put in 110 hours a week. And then after that, 60 to 75 hours a week. For the two years after that, I didn't have a life."

Police assembled a team to investigate and called their probe Projet Luisance (Project Lustre). The police shuttle through the letters of the alphabet to name their probes; investigations started in 2012 all began with the letter "L." Briand first learned of the syrup crime in August 2012, almost exactly a year after the heist had begun, and headed straight to the warehouse, about an hour's drive from his station. "Then I did a double take, because I asked myself, how are we going to treat this scene? There were 16,224 barrels there, piled six high. Supposing we take down the barrels and on one barrel we find a fingerprint and a hair. We are going to have to be able to say where that barrel was. What row, what level. We had to number the rows. We found a system. Then we started. It took us two weeks. The guy on the forklift from the Federation, under our supervision, took them off the pile, took them to the scale, weighed them. If we found barrels that were empty or that had water in them, then we put them aside."

Since the warehouse had no security cameras, police had to use other means to try to identify the thieves. "Our technicians were powdering, powdering, powdering, trying to find fingerprints. If they were on the top row, some had footprints on them. That was the biggest crime scene of my career. A crime scene, in almost all cases, has one crime scene technician." On some days, the warehouse in Saint-Louis-de-Blandford had nine crime scene technicians. The investigators determined that, all told, the thieves emptied more than half the syrup, making off with a total of 9,571 of the 16,224 barrels in the warehouse.

Until then, the Federation and police had kept the theft out of the news. Enter Yves Charlebois, a journalist. Charlebois lives in the little town of Saint-Ferdinand in Quebec's Chaudières-Appalaches region. Charlebois covered agricultural news. His stories don't usually end up as headlines in big international newspapers. But Charlebois's scoop of 2012 soon bounced around the world.

One August Sunday, Charlebois went to a family lunch in Montreal. Leaving Saint-Ferdinand, he drove winding roads through the forested mountainous terrain onto Highway 20. The route took him past the maple syrup warehouse. "I see the police forensics truck—a white truck—next to the warehouse," he recalls. "I see a police dog. So I think it's the canine squad practising. I go to my lunch, I come back at night, and there were still police cars there.

"Then on Tuesday, I had to go to a cultivators' gala. I slept in Saint-Hyacinthe. The next morning, I went home and saw police still there, so I pulled over and they told me the news."

Since the theft, Charlebois has been elected mayor of Saint-Ferdinand. I asked him to meet me at Le Madrid because I had heard the dinosaurs were still there. Alas, a few years ago Le Madrid went out of business. The new owners demolished the old castle-style restaurant and hotel, and built a new restaurant, Le Madrid 2.0. To my delight, the new owners kept the dinosaurs; they stared at us from outside the windows as we ate.

Charlebois has written many articles about the syrup industry. In his village, many people make maple syrup and big local bottling companies buy it up. When he heard of the theft, he struggled to wrap his head around the logistics of the crime. "*Ça n'avait pas de bon sens,*" he told me. ("It makes no sense.") "I said to myself, 'Come on. This is impossible. You need trucks to get maple syrup out of there.'" Charlebois called a buddy who buys bulk syrup, who told him it would take about 150 truckloads to move that much syrup.

The next day, Charlebois broke the news of the maple syrup theft in the farmers' union's weekly newspaper, *La Terre de chez nous*, and the Montreal newspaper *Le Journal de Montréal.* "Big Maple Syrup Theft from a Warehouse," read the headline. Lower down in his story Charlebois wrote, "It's worth noting that it takes audacity to steal barrels of maple syrup. A tractor-trailer can contain 90 barrels of 45 gallons, worth about $1,800 each. You need a lot of time, and a forklift, to load a truck."

News of the syrup theft spread around the world. *The New York Times* reported: "In $18 Million Theft, Victim Was a Canadian Maple Syrup Cartel." *Vanity Fair* magazine looked "Inside Quebec's Great, Multi-Million-Dollar Maple-Syrup Heist." The UK's *Guardian* newspaper reported: "Maple Syrup Heist: Quebec Producers Bounce Back From Sticky Situation."

Once Quebec's police got a sense of the scale of the syrup theft, they set up a command post in Victoriaville to begin their investigation. I asked Briand how much the police investigation of the syrup theft had cost.

"It was very, very expensive," Briand replied. Switching to English, he added, "*The sky is the limit.* There was crazy interest from the press. Quickly, this went up to the top of the command of the SQ. Our team leaders were saying, 'We need this, we need more detectives. Do you give us the green light?' and the bosses said, 'Do what you need to do. We are going to pay what it costs. We have all the authorizations.' I don't know the final cost, but it was extremely expensive."

The police began to look for suspects. "If I became a criminal tomorrow, I couldn't get rid of those quantities of syrup," Briand said. "I don't know anyone in that world. We asked the Federation: Do you know anyone with the knowledge and the contacts necessary to get rid of those quantities of maple syrup? And the first name that came up was Richard Vallières."

Police sources led them to a warehouse in Beauceville about 100 kilometres south of Quebec City. Police learned that the Beauceville warehouse belonged to a relative of Vallières. They got a warrant to search the warehouse. They found no syrup but did find traces of round barrels and a sticky floor. "It supported our suspicions that Vallières was becoming a serious suspect in the investigation," said Briand.

Vallières liked to live well. He changed his car often and liked to buy drinks for his friends at nightclubs in Quebec City, such as Beaugarte, a discotheque that was famed as a hangout for everyone from politicians to musicians to hockey players.

In fall 2012, flush with the proceeds of the syrup caper, Vallières went on vacation. The timing was interesting: He left just after reporters broke news of the syrup theft. A court document later said that he had "fled the country." On September 9, Vallières, his girlfriend and their young daughter flew to the Caribbean. After a cruise to Jamaica, they visited Fort Lauderdale, Florida, then Puerto Rico, before finishing their holiday back in Florida. Then the girlfriend and the child returned to their home in Loretteville, in the north suburbs of Quebec City. Vallières followed a few days later. It had been a nice vacation—more than a month. Clearly, money was not a problem for Vallières. But his jet-setting life of luxury was about to come screeching to a halt.

While Vallières was out of the country, the SQ searched his house in Quebec City. They seized electronic equipment and documents, and left him a note saying that they had searched the house, as is required by the Criminal Code.

Near the end of the month, Vallières, then aged thirty-four, flew from Philadelphia to his home in Quebec City. At Jean Lesage International Airport, detectives awaited the plane. They did not greet Vallières; the police made sure that he never saw them. But they watched him and, armed with a general warrant and a search warrant, pursued the plan they had come up with to investigate Vallières' activities. What the police really wanted was access to Vallières' cellphone.

"Sometimes when you go through customs," Briand explained, "they pull you aside at random for a secondary search. That day, it happened that Richard Vallières had to go through a secondary search, with the judge's order." Police arranged that Vallières be pulled from the line of travellers at the Quebec City airport, making it seem random. "Sometimes, when border guards do searches, they ask to check the cellphone, looking for child pornography, for example. The guards asked Vallières, 'Do you have a cellphone?' 'Yes.' 'Is it locked?' 'Yes.' 'We will ask you to please unlock it.' When it was unlocked, a customs officer said, 'Just a minute sir, we are going to check it.' They took Vallières' phone to a room and gave it to our technicians. Our technicians made a copy of everything on his cellphone. When they were done, they gave it back and said, 'Okay, we checked. Everything looks good. Have a good day.' He never suspected anything."

Briand then got search warrants to read text exchanges between Vallières and all the contacts on his phone. The phone led police to a treasure trove of detail about Vallières, his activities and the people in his circle.

Police became interested in a second man, Avik Caron. It was tough to prove anything about Caron, who was careful in how he communicated. But one day in July 2011, Vallières had sent a text message to a number that the police did not recognize in which he expressed congratulations on the birth of a baby and asked whether the birth had gone well. The Quebec police checked with the civil birth registry and discovered that, on the same date Vallières had sent that text, Caron and his girlfriend had welcomed their second child.

For the next two months, Briand and his team combed through the texts of seventy-five cellphones. Caron had tried to be careful. He regularly switched out everybody's cellphone, Briand said. But the thieves left clues anyway. On September 9, 2011, Vallières texted one acquaintance, writing, "*Ok jai de quoi pour toi pour faire bcp* [short for "beaucoup"] *argent,"* or "Ok, I have something for you to make a lot of money."

"It was organized crime done by disorganized guys," said Briand. "They tried to be careful, but they would text someone and say 'If you want to contact me here is my new cellphone number.' One of the thieves texted 'Come and meet me at my dad's garage. It's got a red roof. Exit 200 on Highway 20.' So we drive over and find a garage with a red roof."

The police also looked for the stolen syrup. Documents found suggested that much of the syrup had gone east, across the border to Kegdwick, New Brunswick, to SK Exports, the business of Étienne St-Pierre. Quebec police, aided by the Royal Canadian Mounted Police, raided SK Exports in September 2012.

For the thieves, one tricky detail had been finding containers to hold all of the syrup. The brigands landed on totes: 1,000 litre (264-gallon) plastic cubes, about chest-height, usually translucent white in colour, the plastic protected by a wire cage, which are typically transported on shipping pallets. At St-Pierre's business, police found many totes filled with syrup. Some totes had a red sticker, and some had a green sticker. The stickers read "Mercier." Briand remembered seeing a kind of junk yard called Mercier, near where he'd driven a patrol car earlier in his career, filled with pipes and metal and used totes and wood pallets. They confirmed that this had been a source of totes for the syrup thieves. More troubling was the information about the stickers: A tote with a green sticker means the previous owner washed it out with a water jet before selling it. "Red sticker is a tote so dirty that they sell it as is, not even washed," Briand said. "At Étienne St-Pierre's we found totes that had green stickers and red stickers. Mercier told us that at the beginning they only wanted green totes, but they wanted so many that at some point they just said 'Give us anything.'"

Detectives also tracked a great deal of the syrup to the United States. It now appears that many thousands of litres of stolen syrup ended up drizzled on pancakes on breakfast tables in the US, with consumers quite unsuspecting that the condiment was, if you'll pardon the pun, hot. The police, during their investigation in September–October of 2012, visited three US maple syrup buyers: Bascom Maple Farms Inc. in New Hampshire, an eighth-generation family business that is the biggest syrup distributor in the United States, along with Highland Sugar Works and Maple Grove in Vermont. From weigh bills and documents they seized from Vallières, Briand said police were able to prove that the thieves had sold $3.2 million worth of syrup into the United Sates. Barrels of syrup that police found at Bascom had the number 155 written on them, a number connected to Richard Vallières in the accounting methods of SK Exports, he said. So Vallières' gang had taken the syrup to New Brunswick, and St-Pierre then sold it to Bascom in New Hampshire.

Police decided not to try to bring the syrup home. Seizing that quantity of syrup risked pushing the US syrup companies out of business, Briand said, so they left that syrup stateside. Prosecutors also decided that while the US buyers had paid less for the stolen syrup than they would have paid through official channels, the price difference was not enough to prove that the buyers had displayed "wilful blindness" that they were buying stolen goods.

The police also found rental contracts for forklifts, among other evidence. Just before Christmas, on December 18, 2012, at 6:15 a.m., police entered Vallières' house in Quebec City and placed him under arrest. The same day, locksmiths opened the houses of Sébastien Jutras and his father Gaetan, and police armed with search warrants seized materials from Jutras. All told, the police raid of the maple syrup gang lasted three days, December 18 to 20, and involved eighty-five police, including constables, detectives, analysts, IT technicians, police locksmiths and command post officers. Police charged thirty-six suspects in all.

FOLLOWING THE RAIDS and arrests, and as the details of the crime emerged, it was clear to the public that the maple syrup industry was not the cottage industry depicted on the syrup container labels, of grandparents in checkered shirts leading horses through the snow to collect the buckets of sap. Maple syrup, the crime showed us, was a world of steel drums, vast warehouses, forklifts and diesel-belching transport trucks moving syrup up and down the highways of North America.

It took four years for the case to reach court. Richard Vallières was tried by jury during fall 2016 in the Palais de justice, an imposing grey stone edifice in Trois-Rivières. Police in testimony described every aspect of the theft, plus other details: It transpires that, confident in their success, Vallières, Jutras and others went to Mexico's Yucatan Peninsula to celebrate their newfound riches. At the Congobar in Cancún, the thieves posed for a photograph that the bartender glued to a bottle of beer as if it were a label and gave the gang as a souvenir.

Richard Vallières argued in his defence that he committed the theft under duress. He told the jury that when he realized the syrup he was buying came from the Federation warehouse, he tried to back out, but Caron threatened him at gunpoint. Vallières said his wife and young daughter also faced threats. But the jury also heard of friendly text messages between him and Caron. When the Federation discovered the theft and it made global headlines, Vallières texted a contact "The party's over." Vallières later tried to present himself as a kind of Robin Hood, portraying the Federation as the criminals. "Stealing from thieves is not stealing," he said.

Also facing trial was one of the biggest buyers of the stolen syrup, Étienne St-Pierre. St-Pierre pleaded not guilty, arguing that he had been buying syrup from Vallières for many years and could not know it was stolen. Prosecutors anticipated this argument and showed the jury a chart that compared the amount of syrup St-Pierre had bought in 2010 to the amount he bought a year later. In 2010, Richard Vallières had sold about a two-storey house's worth of syrup to SK Exports, and the next year he sold a CN Tower's worth. In 2011 and 2012, Vallières had sold more than $2 million worth of syrup to St-Pierre. The jury later agreed that St-Pierre had been willfully blind to the fact that the syrup was stolen.

After a three-week trial, in November 2016 the jury found Richard Vallières guilty of theft, fraud and traffic of stolen syrup. Étienne St-Pierre was convicted of fraud and trafficking; sentenced to two years less a day, to be served in the community; and ordered to pay a $1-million fine. The jury found Raymond Vallières, Richard's father, guilty of possession of stolen syrup. He also got two years less a day and a $10,000 fine.

Two months later, Caron pleaded guilty to two counts of fraud over $5,000: one for the maple syrup and the other for insurance fraud. The court sentenced Caron to five years in prison for the syrup theft and a consecutive one-year sentence for insurance fraud, along with $1.25 million worth of fines.

Others who pleaded guilty included Sylvain Bourassa, a ringleader, who pleaded guilty to theft over $5,000 and was sentenced to three years and a $145,000 fine; Sébastien Jutras pleaded guilty to conspiring to commit theft, to theft, and to trafficking in stolen goods and received a 42-month sentence; his father Gaetan Jutras also pleaded guilty to one count of theft and one count of trafficking and received an 18-month sentence, to be served in the community. Pascal Patry pleaded guilty to one count of theft over $5,000 and received a sentence of 12 months, to be served in the community; Steve Picard pleaded guilty to one count of theft over $5,000 and got 18 months, also to be served in the community.

Richard Vallières got the stiffest sentence: eight years in prison and a fine of $10 million. He later appealed; Quebec's appeals court reduced the fine to $1 million. The Crown appealed the case to the Supreme Court of Canada. In March 2022, nearly ten years after the discovery of the theft, the Supreme Court upheld the fine from the original trial and ordered Vallières, who had recently been freed on day parole, to pay back the full $10 million that had passed through his hands during the year-long theft. If he can't pay it back, he must serve another six years in prison. Briand told me that Vallières has not repaid the money and has declared bankruptcy.

I later asked Joël Vaudeville, a spokesperson for the syrup producers' cartel, whether he believes the Global Strategic Maple Syrup Reserve is currently safe. He pointed out that the syrup producers now own three warehouses with the combined capacity to store up to $500 million of maple syrup and do not rent any space from third parties. The syrup is secure, he confirmed.

"Following those sad events of more than ten years ago, the producers have taken steps to make sure it doesn't happen again. I can't talk about it because I don't want to tell you about the security measures of the strategic reserve, but we are confident that it won't happen again. Every dollar of stolen syrup was reimbursed to the producers. Our insurance took care of us, the thieves went to prison, and we are very satisfied with the end of all this. This is all ancient history to us. And it all happened during a period of more skepticism about the collective system for maple syrup. The growth, the new businesses that are being born every year, the effervescence in the maple business, shows that the producers—who were visionary twenty or thirty years ago when we decided to get together and work collectively—were right. I think things are seen differently now by the producers."

Most producers support the system. Others . . . not so much.

REBELLION

A ngèle Grenier came into the world in 1957, into a Quebec controlled by the iron grip of the Catholic Church. She was born a rebel.

Fernande Grenier, Angèle's mother, gave birth to her in Sainte-Clotilde-de-Beauce, a little village of about 600 people, comprising a church, a garage and a few houses. The doctors of that era recommended that after childbirth a woman stay in bed for two or three days. At the same time, Catholic rules dictated that the child be baptized within twenty-four hours of birth, lest the infant die and end up in limbo, without ascending to heaven. And so, typically, an aunt would take the newborn to the baptism.

Fernande handed the baby girl to her sister Cécile for the trip to church and told her the baby's name was Marilyn (Marilyn Monroe was a big star at the time). Once they arrived, the priest, Curé Hébert, who was very severe, decreed that "Marilyn" was an indecent, impure name. The priest wrote

Angèle in the registry. There was no phone in the church or in the birthing centre, so the aunt acquiesced to the priest's decision. "When my aunt brought me back to the hospital with my new name my mom was so mad," Grenier told me, during one of our many interviews over the years at her home, her sugar shack and her sugar bush. "At school kids constantly teased me, mispronouncing my first name. And then I vowed, when I was just five or six years old, that I would grow up and have a daughter and name her Marilyn. Which I did."

It was not to be Grenier's only act of defiance. The Beaucerons are a tough and independent people. Back in 1775, early in the American Revolution, the people of the Beauce helped Benedict Arnold, a US general who led a force of revolutionary soldiers up from Maine in an ill-fated plan to capture Quebec City, by that point under British control. That Beauce fighting spirit lives in Angèle. She is no angel— at least to her enemies. And over time, her enemies grew to include the entire infrastructure of Quebec's officially sanctioned maple syrup cartel.

Sometimes a story lands in your lap like a brace of Cornish game hens on a silver platter. In 2015, I worked as a journalist in the *Financial Post*, a subsection of the *National Post*. As winter turned to spring that year, I had yearned to write something about maple syrup. I stumbled upon the drama of the maple syrup rebels. These syrup-makers included a couple named Steve Côté and Caroline Morin as well as Angèle Grenier, who defiantly insisted on what she felt was her constitutional right to make maple syrup and sell it to whomever she damn well pleased. The story had it all: maple syrup, Canada's iconic elixir; security guards; deep snow; roaring fires; big sums of cash; sheriffs; and a quixotic crusade for liberty from the iron rules of supply management, a system that also regulates production of milk, eggs and poultry across Canada, and against which the *Post*, champion of unfettered free enterprise, has railed for decades. Best of all, the story featured a rebellious snowshoe-clad grandmother with curly red hair.

The *National Post* illustrated the story, "Maple Syrup Rebels," with a drawing of a hand raised in a gesture of defiance, in the style of Chinese propaganda posters from the 1960s, clutching a bottle of maple syrup. The story played perfectly into the *National Post*'s conservative tropes of the little guy, the David, fighting against the Goliath of Big Government—in this case bureaucrats and inspectors in the service of Big Maple. To report this story, a photographer and I drove from Toronto, through Montreal, and kept heading east as the snowbanks alongside the roads rose higher and higher, until we got to Sainte-Clotilde-de-Beauce.

One arrives in Sainte-Clotilde to find the inevitable tall, needlelike spire of the local Catholic Church—the only structure that dares to rise above the sugar maples. Or at least that was the case for centuries. These days wind turbines poke out of the forests on the ridges of many of the rounded mountaintops, taller than the trees or even the steeples.

The photographer and I drove snow-covered dirt roads to the sugar shack of Angèle Grenier, which was attached to the house she had built with her husband, Nelson Grenier.

Like many Beauce families, Angèle grew up in the maple syrup business. Angèle's father and mother, Rosario and Fernande, had four children, who all helped with the syrup in spring. "When I was a kid, my father hooked up an ox to a sleigh, and we picked up the syrup," recalls Angèle. "We got out of school and we went to the sugar shack. We lay on the

"The sun must shine again on the sugar bush in Quebec so that in our sugar shacks, our assemblies and our meetings, the laughter takes the lead again over the bitter fights of the past and the worries of the present."

PIERRE LEMIEUX,
president, Producteurs et productrices
acéricoles du Québec, 2000

ox's back to ride home." She spoke as she laid out a seasonal lunch for her visitors: white bread and buckwheat bread, hot from her oven; pea soup, deep-fried smoked pork jowls, ham baked in syrup, baked beans, new potatoes, sausages, coffee; and for dessert, maple syrup pie, maple ice cream, whipped cream and *des grand-père en sirop*—dough balls fried in syrup. Beside the spread rested a bottle of the first syrup of 2015.

Angèle's parents owned two sugar bushes. When they died they left one maple forest to each of their sons, Alain and Denis. The daughters separately acquired sugar bushes; Francine, the eldest, has a forest nearby.

In 1975, Angèle married Nelson; his surname is also Grenier. The pair are short in stature and brim with energy and determination. Angèle and Nelson Grenier had three children. It almost seems foretold that they would make maple syrup. They bought their first sugar bush in 1988. Then they heard about a bigger maple forest for sale on the same dirt road as the sugar bush of Angèle's childhood; they bought it in 1993. The forest was overgrown; the pair spent the first year cutting out alder that had filled in everywhere. The next year they built the sugar shack and installed the tubing and made the road. Attached to one end of their sugar shack, the Greniers built a house. Angèle led the operation; Nelson and four of his brothers worked full time at the family company building components for trucks. In 1995, the Greniers started making maple syrup. They joined Citadelle, the co-operative that grew from Vaillancourt's pioneering organizational work for the syrup industry in the 1920s. Angèle said that the Citadelle co-op at that time paid more quickly: "You got paid everything by fall. You had to become a member, pay $200. If there was a surplus of money, they paid us a dividend."

But as the new century dawned, Citadelle joined forces with the Quebec Maple Syrup Producers—now the Producteurs et productrices acéricoles du Québec (PPAQ). This group decides how many maples its members may tap to extract the sap that becomes syrup, which is called "quota"; a similar system exists for milk in Canada. The PPAQ also negotiates a price with syrup bottlers and retailers, and passes payment from the buyers to the syrup farmers. They also maintain the strategic syrup reserve. The system works, say its defenders, because it ensures that farmers receive a steady, predictable price for their syrup.

Angèle and Nelson say they never agreed to this system; they insist that no one asked them. They did not like to be told how much syrup to make, what price they would get, and then have to wait a year or more to get fully paid. And yet the rules governed them, too. The regimentation and the punishment for disobedience reminded Angèle of nothing so much as the Catholic Church, that hated temple of orthodoxy that had forced her name upon her.

Indeed, the PPAQ's connection to the Church is fairly direct. In 1924, Quebec farmers formed the Union Catholique des cultivateurs, or the Catholic Cultivators' Union. Fifty years later the organization adopted a more inclusive name: the Union des producteurs agricoles (UPA), or Agricultural Producers' Union. The PPAQ is a branch of this union.

Not everyone supports the syrup marketing system. "I didn't want to get into the Federation," Angèle said. She wanted freedom. "So I decided 'I am going to export.'" She had an export permit from the Canadian Food Inspection Agency, which she said gave her the right to sell syrup as she wanted outside Quebec. She found a buyer in New Brunswick: Étienne

St-Pierre, later convicted in the syrup heist. She got the best of both worlds: the same price as the Federation, but instead of waiting a year, she received her money by the beginning of July. Angèle believed that she was in the right, but the PPAQ disagreed; this battle would later end up before the courts.

Angèle Grenier compared the PPAQ to the Church. "It's a spinoff of religion," she said. "Religion got weaker, so they created a system that is just like religion. The cultivators were not resourceful enough to be able to manage the business themselves. That's how they got the farmers together."

One of the sticking points in the cartel system, if you will pardon the pun, has to do with the unpredictable nature of the weather: Some years the heat comes too early, and there is scant sap to boil into syrup; then there are good springs, with lots of cold nights and warm days, when sap flows abundantly. In a good year, a farmer might produce more syrup than their quota specifies. Angèle balked at getting paid in instalments and at only getting paid for what they produced inside the quota. If they sent overstock syrup to the PPAQ, she said, it might take them fifteen years to get paid. "We went to all the meetings and we saw what was happening. A lot of buyers didn't want to get involved in the system. Citadelle got into it."

For many years Citadelle had paid its members directly for their syrup. Jean-Marie Chouinard, a longtime corporate secretary of Citadelle, later explained that the PPAQ now sets the syrup price and quotas, and transmits payment to the syrup-makers; Citadelle continues to market its members' maple syrup and provide its members with insurance, technical support and syrup barrels.

The PPAQ says its system provides producers with predictable, steady revenue. In 2020, they published a book on a century of syrup-making in Quebec, titled *Si l'érable m'était conté*, in which they paint a negative caricature of "barrel rollers"—traders who buy syrup outside the regulated system—depicting them as villains worthy of a Pink Panther film. The syrup farmers sound pretty gullible.

> They show up in pickup trucks, threading their way along the rural routes, lined with maple trees, to get to the little sugar shack. With a flourish, they pull from their pockets rolls of bills held together with a big elastic band. With a well-moistened thumb, they pull out and spread the bills as they negotiate the price: "Here, I'll give you a dollar a pound for your barrel, it's a good price, my friend." The cultivator will use these few precious dollars to fix the leaky roof of the barn or to buy seeds to sow in spring. The money changes hands, neither seen nor known (and well hidden from the tax collector), the visitor drops the gate of his pickup and rolls in the barrels, and drives off to the next sugar shack, in a cloud of dust.

It's not quite like that in real life. Still, in one detail the depiction is accurate: Sales of syrup outside the official system do give farmers quicker access to cash. Angèle and the other rebels liked that a lot. The rebels thought they could beat the system and forged ahead in defiance of the rules.

From 2002 to 2014, Angèle exported hundreds of barrels of maple syrup to New Brunswick. The Federation, however, didn't like it one bit. A team of syrup producer agents keeps a close watch on producers to try to stem any leaks from its system. The PPAQ went to court. The Federation laid dozens of charges against the Greniers and other syrup rebels at an administrative tribunal that enforces the laws on sales of foods produced in Quebec. Under those rules, Quebec syrup producers may only sell to buyers authorized by the Federation.

In the mid-2010s, syrup-makers who opposed the Federation organized and held protests. One spring, the syrup rebels met at the Chutes de la Chaudière, across the St. Lawrence River from Quebec City, and drove to Boulevard Charest, a key artery in the provincial capital's downtown, blocking two lanes of the road.

In April 2014, as the syrup season drew to its end, Angèle knew the Federation's enforcement division had her in its sights. She needed to move her syrup and move it quickly. Angèle's brother and her neighbour each showed up on tractors. Her cousin and her son helped, too. In under an hour, with three tractors, the team loaded dozens of barrels, including syrup from other rebel producers—forty barrels in all— on a transport truck. "All the children came, and we did it quick, quick," she recalls. The truck sped off down her dirt road, headed east across the Quebec–New Brunswick border to maple syrup freedom. It was to be her final sale of syrup to the buyer of her choice.

After that, the Federation shut down Grenier's exports. In March 2015, a Quebec judge wrote an order permitting "a sheriff to penetrate into the sugar shack of [Grenier], without notice, at any time judged reasonable and as frequently as they judge appropriate . . . to verify the inventory of maple syrup, take photos and videos of the locale and the inventory, and put a mark, a seal, a tag or any other necessary identifying label on every maple syrup container."

That spring I visited Angèle's sugar shack for the *National Post* to shoot footage for a video. While we were there,

Mathieu Audy, an inspector from the Federation, pulled up. He entered the sugar shack and began to take notes and snap photos. Then the questioning began: "Did you change your press?" Audy asked Angèle. "How much maple syrup have you made? What size are those barrels? Thirty-two gallons? Thirty-four? Did the sap run on Good Friday? Is it just running from gravity? Do you have a production registry?"

A second rebel syrup producer was in the Grenier sugar shack that morning: Gilles Marois, who, with his wife Ghyslaine Fortin, had racked up fines of over $1 million from the Federation.

Audy, the inspector, said, "In the case of Madame Grenier, the Superior Court ruled that you are wrong."

"We are at the appeals court," Angèle shot back.

"Yes, we are in appeals court," Audy said. "You say that you are right. But I tell you that for us, right now, under the law, you are not right, under the laws of Quebec."

"Laws made by whom?" asked Marois.

"Laws made by the producers," replied Audy, standing next to a plastic barrel of syrup with his back against the Greniers' evaporator.

"Not true," shot back Marois, the angry syrup producer. "The delegates only made those laws. They have never had a general assembly of syrup producers."

Two days later the photographer and I drove to Saint-Mathias-de-Bonneterre in southeastern Quebec, on a dirt road high in the Appalachian Mountains, where we met Steve Côté and Caroline Morin at their sugar shack. Four-wheelers were parked outside; inside the place bustled with activity. Clouds of steam billowed up from an evaporator as big as a sailboat. Morin, wearing a lab coat, opened a spigot to pour molten syrup from the evaporator into a steel barrel. She had taken a month off from her job at a daycare to help with sugaring off. The couple's four daughters were there too, to help.

In that spring of 2015, Côté and Morin were in their own battle with the Federation. The couple had, like Grenier, sold their syrup to whomever they pleased, in defiance of Quebec rules. In April 2013, the Federation had shown up at their sugar shack with sheriffs, a truck, a loader and two police cruisers. They took 100 barrels of Côté and Morin's syrup, and about 1,500 cans to their warehouse in Laurierville. Investigators also searched his bank accounts and questioned staff at the local IGA, to whom he sold syrup. To escape another seizure, in 2014 Côté loaded his production on trucks at night and sold it in the United States.

At the time of our visit, the Federation had counter-attacked Côté and Morin in spectacular fashion. When we arrived at their sugar shack, we found it under guard. Out front sat a sedan with the Garda Security logo. In the boiling room, Côté, wearing fireproof gloves, used a hand truck to roll a barrel of fresh syrup, too hot to touch, to a storage room. A security guard followed and affixed to the barrel's spout a tamperproof seal: "Sticker 19057 of the FPAQ. Barrel 4094, produced 08/04/15, sealed 08/04/2015." A court had issued a "seizure before judgement" of Côté's 2015 syrup, before the season even began. If he broke these seals, a judge could find Côté in contempt of court. The guard's job: to make sure that every drop of maple syrup made in this sugar shack flowed only to the cartel. The cartel did not trust Côté with his own maple syrup. This was one of three sugar shacks to which the Federation had posted guards that year: three shifts of eight hours each—twenty-four hours a day, seven days a week. The Federation sent the bill—$1,000 a day for each guard—to the maple syrup producers themselves.

Among the treats made from maple syrup are small cones, like ice cream cones, filled with soft maple sugar. Côté handed me such a cone, the size of a plum. "Hide it under your coat when you leave," he said. "I'm not joking. If the guard sees that leaving the shack, I will be in trouble."

Côté said he was being treated like a criminal for doing what Quebecers have done for generations: sell maple syrup. Attending a court date that spring, Côté ran into an old friend. The friend said he was in on a marijuana charge. (Canada legalized cannabis three years later.) "Later I saw him and asked, 'What did you get?' He said he got a $150 fine. And for selling maple syrup, I have a $424,000 fine. There is something wrong with this picture." Angèle Grenier escaped the indignity of having security guards at her shack because she signed an agreement to send her syrup to the Federation while her opposition to the system worked its way through the courts.

Our *National Post* story on the maple syrup rebels produced quite a ripple effect. Throughout the rest of 2015, everyone from the BBC to *The New York Times* to the *Weather Network* matched the piece with their own accounts of the maple syrup cartel and the insurrection. The British magazine *The Economist*, in its version titled "A Sticky Situation," suggested that the province's tree-tappers were "ripping off pancake-lovers."

After the *Post* story appeared, the Government of Quebec picked Florent Gagné, a retired senior civil servant, to study Quebec's maple syrup supply management system. Gagné's sixty-nine-page report appeared in December 2015. He called Quebec's system to control maple syrup makers "autocratic."

He noted that New York State alone boasts more maple trees than Quebec, and warned that if the system endured, the United States could become self-sufficient in maple syrup in ten years, destroying the province's biggest syrup export market.

Gagné wrote at length about my story "Maple Syrup Rebellion," observing that, in the maple syrup sector in Quebec "the malaise is much bigger than the federation cares to admit. Many producers feel a profound frustration with 'their' union, which they see as a distant and authoritarian bureaucracy, which defends a rigid system and its own corporate interests rather than its members." The words sounded a lot like criticisms that many have levelled at the Catholic Church in the past.

Gagné worried that the system encouraged producers to leave the province. "Producers outside Quebec benefit from the fixed Quebec price but have no quotas and needn't contribute to marketing costs," Gagné noted. He added, "We should abandon the syrup quota system."

At a news conference after the report came out, Pierre Paradis, Quebec's minister of agriculture, warned syrup producers, "We had 80 percent of the market, we went to 70 percent, and now we're heading to 60 percent. Is that the direction we want to go?" It was not an idle warning. Researchers in the United States suggest that their country, which now relies on Quebec for most of its maple syrup, could become self-sufficient, since the US right now only taps 1 to 3 percent of its available sugar maple trees. Gagné added that Quebec should allow producers to sell bulk syrup to whomever they wish, and that the Federation should worry about syrup quality, not just quantity.

The Federation greeted Gagné's report with apoplexy. A few days after Paradis's remarks, dozens of buses braved a snowstorm to roar into Quebec City. The buses disgorged up to 1,200 syrup producers, who crammed onto Quebec's Parliament Hill waving placards and shouting their support for the syrup single-market system.

After the protest, efforts to reform the Quebec syrup cartel began to unravel. The Federation hired dozens of lobbyists to pressure Quebec City to keep its cartel in place. Paradis wavered in his confidence in the Gagné report. In 2017, Paradis stepped down as agriculture minister.

The Quebec government decided to leave the syrup supply management system intact, with one change: the Federation agreed to permit syrup-makers to tap a great deal more maple trees. The Federation authorized producers to put seven million additional spiles in maple trees in 2021, and another seven million spiles in 2023 to 2026. The logic is that with more trees tapped to produce syrup, Quebec will continue to maintain its dominant share of the global supply.

I stayed in touch with the rebels. In 2016, Quebec's Court of Appeal ruled against Angèle Grenier, prompting her husband, Nelson, to suffer a heart attack, he said. In June 2017, the Supreme Court of Canada declined to hear Angèle Grenier's appeal on her conviction for selling syrup outside Quebec's supply management system. The Greniers had two options: (1) settle with the Federation, pay their fines over a number of years and work within the system or (2) sell. That year, they sold their forest, house, sugar shack—everything that they had built and loved.

In the first years of Angèle's rebellion against the Federation, in the early 2000s, her siblings joined her protest. But as Angèle lost in court, all her siblings became compliant with the syrup control system.

Denis Grenier, Angèle's youngest brother, had inherited the family farm, including the main sugar bush and sugaring operation that all four children had worked in as kids. Denis converted the operation from buckets to tubes to gather the sap and bought a new evaporator, though he still boils his sap with wood, as his parents did. Today he has 3,500 spiles in sugar maple trees. Originally, he refused to follow the Federation's syrup rules.

"I never stopped supporting her," Denis Grenier told me. As for his own decision, "We didn't have the choice but to stop." Denis, who also keeps a herd of beef cattle, said that he has a lot of money invested in his farm. To continue to fight the PPAQ would have put him at risk of losing it all, he said.

I asked Denis whether there was any benefit to membership in the PPAQ. Isn't it true, I asked, that the PPAQ system has stabilized prices, whereas in the past farmers would get wildly varying prices for their syrup? Denis shrugged.

"My father told me the buyers used to come by the house. He said, 'One year I'd get more for my syrup than my neighbour, and the next year it was the opposite.'" Under the PPAQ rules it takes a while to get paid for one's syrup, Denis said, but "We make do with it."

Maple syrup for Denis is less a business and more of an addiction, he said, and a kind of touchstone that connects him to generations of Greniers. His own son Gabriel is a registered professional forester and plans to take over the family sugar bush.

"It's a sickness to go into the woods," he said. "It's my vacation, when I go to my sugar bush. The sun comes out, you are working outside. When you are in the forest, you relax. We have a little wood stove. We eat in the woods. On Sunday nights, we make ourselves toast in the sugar shack."

IN 2023, I went back to visit Angèle and Nelson Grenier for the first time in eight years. Having sold their sugar bush, which included their home, the Greniers moved to the tiny main street of Sainte-Clotilde-de-Beauce, to a split-level bungalow that had belonged to the family. As is her custom, Angèle laid out a sumptuous lunch: pork, chicken, fresh-baked bread and cake for dessert with maple syrup icing. Then we drove out to her old sugar shack. It was the start of maple syrup season.

The house the Greniers had built in the 1990s adjacent to their sugar bush, where the couple raised their three children, still stands. Absent were the immense corded stacks of stove wood to fire the evaporator. Angèle's evaporator is gone, too. The maples in what was Grenier's forest remain connected by tubes to a sap-extraction system; the sap from these 9,000 spiles flows into a holding tank in her old sugar shack. But then the sap departs again. The new owner installed a second pipe that sends the maple sap down the hill, under the road and into his sugar shack. There he mixes this sap with sap from his other forest to boil for syrup.

On my 2015 visit Angèle had been boiling sap—heaving big logs into the raging fire in the evaporator. She was defiant that night, and even opened a bottle of white wine to celebrate the season's first syrup. Eight years later the sugar shack stood as cold and silent as a tomb, with its evaporator gone. Angèle and I watched the crystal-clear maple sap gush into a holding tank in the building and then depart to its new owner by a second big black plastic pipe. We looked at graffiti on the wooden door. In felt pen, Angèle's granddaughters—the daughters of her eldest child, Marilyn—had written the date that the syrup season began each year from 1995 (March 14) to 2016 (February 4). Angèle stared out into her old forest.

"I love to boil," she said. "I also love to walk in the woods. It makes us sad because we loved this. But we would still be paying our fines. It was all just too difficult."

There is a silver lining to this arrangement. Angèle is on great terms with the new owner. During maple syrup season Angèle gets to put on her snowshoes and tramp through the woods to look for leaks in the sap tubing. In exchange for her help, the new owner gives Angèle enough maple syrup to meet her family's needs. And Angèle's son lives in their old house, so she can visit the property whenever she wants.

The Greniers have abandoned their fight for syrup freedom. Even so there will probably always be syrup producers who seek to skirt the rigid controls of the Quebec syrup system. "*Là où il y a de l'homme, il y a de l'hommerie,*" said Joël Vaudeville, a PPAQ spokesman, using an old French expression that loosely translates to "Where there are men, there is corruption."

Eight months later I visited the Greniers a third time. I wanted to make sure I had my facts straight. Did I seek another of Angèle's fabulous meals? Perhaps. I arrived at lunchtime to find the Grenier house festooned with jack-o-lanterns, spiders and scarecrows for Halloween. Angèle took from the oven a deep baking dish filled with a harvest feast of chicken, pork and roasted root vegetables, including carrots she had pulled from her garden that morning.

After lunch the Greniers had a surprise for me. In Nelson's SUV we drove north and turned onto a logging trail on which we bounced and rolled. For the third time in their almost fifty years of marriage, the Greniers have bought a sugar bush: They now own the forest that had belonged to

Nelson's parents, where Nelson and his many siblings gathered sap as kids. The old sugar shack fell down years ago, but the old stable for the horse still stands. Angèle picked up an old spile, made of tin; some silver paint is chipped off and the metal is bent from where a hammer banged the spile into a maple tree. She gave it to me as a souvenir.

Nelson told me that this forest has enough sugar maple trees for 2,500 spiles. But the Greniers do not plan to make syrup here.

"We have tasted the pleasures of the Federation," Nelson said. "To have them again as a close friend, I am not sure. For seventy-six years our family made maple syrup here. We have been expropriated from the maple syrup business. We would have to apply for a quota, for syrup. But last time, it gave me a heart attack. We understand that fighting a monopoly can't work."

Just owning some forest seems to lift the Greniers' spirits. Nelson busies himself here making stove wood. He gives seven cords to his brother René and eight cords to his brother Hermann, who is partially paralyzed.

As we bumped along the trail back to the main road, I noted the success of Nelson and Angèle's fifty-year marriage. Nelson recited a philosophical French homily, related to marriage, that perhaps equally applies to a relationship with Quebec's syrup Federation.

The rough translation of Nelson's words: "The beginning of wisdom for a husband [or sugarer] comes when he realizes that he is as well-off having peace as being right."

SHOWDOWN IN
NEW BRUNSWICK

Saint-Quentin, which lies in northern New Brunswick, turned one hundred in 2010. To mark the occasion the town erected a three-storey high, sculpture of a giant maple leaf in its Centennial Park. A fundraising campaign gathered $150,000 for the statue. The project also received government money and funding from Groupe Savoie Inc., which owns two sawmills in the town. A Quebec artist sculpted the leaf in copper, a metal that oxidizes naturally to a lovely shade of green.

People in St. Quentin agree on the pivotal place of the maple tree to their culture and to their economy. What people don't necessarily agree on in this French-speaking community, known both for its rodeo and its maple syrup festival, is the best use for a maple tree. Groupe Savoie, which is the town's biggest employer, cuts the maple trees to supply its mills. But a growing number of locals have another use for the stately giants in the woods that surround the town: making maple syrup.

In January 2022, about sixty protesters gathered at the big maple leaf in St. Quentin. The crowd wore coats and toques and mittens and boots to protect them from the cold, and masks to protect them from one another, given the COVID-19 pandemic that raged at the time. Placards read "Crown land belongs to all!" and "*Le gouvernement reste muet*" ("The government is mute"). That sign added: "Forest companies aren't the only ones that pay taxes: The maple syrup industry wants equitable access to Crown land." The protesters accused their provincial government of favouring the logging industry at the expense of the maple syrup sector. One syrup-maker, Denis Côté, told a newspaper: "They're logging everything." Another syrup-maker said that as soon as he identified a piece of Crown forest suitable for expansion of his sugar bush, loggers went in and cut the trees down. Once a forest is logged, the syrup-makers say they must wait at least fifty years for new maple trees to grow to the girth where they can be tapped for sap. To tap the trees rather than felling them, say the syrup-makers, is better for the forest, for the economy and for the planet. Syrup producers in Quebec are locked in similar battles with loggers for access to public hardwood forests. The New Brunswick syrup-makers demanded access to more Crown land, asking for additional forest, about twice the size of Manhattan, to make maple syrup.

This kind of dispute is relatively recent in New Brunswick, whose economy has been historically dominated by the timber industry. For example, J.D. Irving, a branch of the powerful Irving family, controls about half the forest products sector in New Brunswick. The Irvings' reach is legendary. As a student at the University of New Brunswick, I borrowed books from the Harriet Irving Library, named for a matriarch of the family, and got my first job in journalism writing reviews for the *Daily Gleaner*, an afternoon newspaper owned, like every other New Brunswick daily newspaper at that time, by the Irving family. Logging and wood-processing, in part to make paper to print the newspapers, was, and remains, a very big deal. Historically, the government was in charge of handing out licences to the forest products sector to cut down the trees on Crown land. Most of New Brunswick's hardwood trees end up as writing paper and toilet paper; some become shipping pallets, parquet flooring, furniture or wood pellets for furnaces.

New Brunswick's forest industry did not take kindly to the syrup protest. Kim Allen is executive director of Forest NB, a lobby group for the forest products industry. She called the maple syrup sector tiny compared to her sector. Allen told me the forest sector had revenue of $4.6 billion in 2022, compared to just $35.8 million for the province's maple syrup industry.

"Our position is there are ways we can work together and collaborate," Allen said. "But what occurred a couple of years ago was that the pressure that the maple syrup industry was putting on the Department of Natural Resources also became very targeted toward certain industry participants, because they are hardwood users, and it just became unsavoury, with accusations back and forth. They used terminology like 'ravaging the land' and things like that, and it became . . . it just became very challenging. And so, my role was to speak on behalf of our maple users in the province, and our industry at large, because industry tends to get a lot of criticism here in

New Brunswick, which is ironic, since the forest sector is one of the leading industries in the province and has been for many, many years."

Jean-Claude Savoie is owner of Groupe Savoie. Using maple and other species, the company's 600 employees make lumber, fibreboard (used, for example, in kitchen cabinets), wood pellets for heating, wood for guitars, and shipping pallets. Savoie is displeased with the New Brunswick government's allocation of forests for maple syrup.

"The government started giving out land to the syrup-makers left and right," he told me. He said he has nothing against maple syrup; he even has his own sugar bush, with 1,200 taps. "We think there's room for everyone. But they're pushing us out of the bed."

I suggested to Savoie that he faces a tough public relations battle since the syrup industry wants to keep the forests standing and he wants to selectively harvest the trees. A soaring maple tree has more appeal than a plank of maple flooring.

"A cute little lamb in the field is much more sexy than a rack of lamb," he admitted. "But both are good."

That said, the maple syrup industry in New Brunswick has the wind in its sails. I spoke to brothers Éric and Sylvain Caron, two professional foresters who grew up in Madawaska County in French-speaking northwestern New Brunswick. The area is the ancestral home of the Maliseet and the Wolastoqiyik First Peoples; today just about everyone speaks French. For years, the Caron brothers have logged the Crown forests of the province. They also plant about four million trees annually. They never thought they would get into the maple syrup business, Éric said. Whereas many kids in rural Quebec grow up next to the evaporator in the sugar shack, perched on the knee of a grandparent, Éric said that, in contrast, "We weren't born in a cauldron."

Even so, the brothers are now maple syrup producers. The job complements their other businesses, Éric said. They plant trees in summer and fell trees in fall and winter; spring thaw is a dead time in the forest sector—you can't operate heavy equipment because the machines chew up the soft forest floor and threaten breeding birds and mammals. Crews are idle. The Caron brothers can redirect the workers to tap sugar maple trees. In 2016, with a bank loan, the Carons sank $4 million into a sizable organic maple syrup operation on Crown land. They dubbed their company Sylvacer, a combination of the words *silviculture* and *acer*. They built a sugar shack about an hour's drive north of their house, deep in the bush at a place called Summit Depot, where they now, each spring, put 80,000 spiles in maple trees.

New Brunswick has Canada's fastest-growing syrup industry. The number of taps, or spiles, in maple trees in Quebec grew by about 20 percent from 2011 to 2021. In New Brunswick in that period the number of taps almost doubled. Historically many New Brunswick farmers made some maple syrup in spring; today big players tapping Crown forests in the province's north dominate New Brunswick's syrup sector. New Brunswick now makes almost two times more maple syrup than Ontario, which is quite a feat considering it is less than a tenth of the size of Ontario and has one-twentieth of Ontario's population. Ontario has far more maple trees. So how come, over just the past few years, New Brunswick has begun to put spiles in its sugar maple trees with such fervour?

The plot thickens, so to speak, when we consider that maple syrup is one of the most fickle of farm products because it is so dependent on the weather. A grain farmer in Saskatchewan, for example, has four or five months to play with—drought may be an issue, but there is a good chance that rain will come. By contrast, syrup producers have a tiny window: You can extract sap from maple trees for about four to six weeks in a good year, sometime between February and April, depending on the latitude of the sugar bush. Unless conditions are favourable in that short period, you will have a problem. Walk into a bank, Caron said, and ask for a loan for a syrup enterprise, and the banker will likely say that the business is ridiculously unpredictable. The banker will wonder, if they lend the client money, how probable it is that they will get it back.

Quebec's syrup cartel has changed that equation. Éric thanks Quebec policy for the rapid growth of the syrup industry in New Brunswick. Consistently in the 21st century, Quebec syrup producers have negotiated a fixed price with the main syrup buyers. Producers in New Brunswick, unlike their Quebec counterparts, can produce as much syrup as they want. There's no quota/limit. That said, the New Brunswick producers sell their syrup at the price set by Quebec, year in, year out. And that is a predictability that they can take to the bank.

"We have an expansion project now," Éric said. "If we didn't have a predictable price, we could not expand." The New Brunswick producers get the best of both worlds: They can count on the Quebec price, plus when they sell their syrup they get payment right away, unlike in Quebec. The Caron brothers sell up to 90 percent of the syrup they make to big bottling companies in Quebec.

This mixture of maple syrup freedom and steady market demand have combined to cause a bit of a maple syrup gold rush in New Brunswick, says David Briggs of Moncton, New Brunswick, whose family has produced syrup in the province for five generations. "A lot of Quebec producers have migrated across the border to freedom, to tap as much as you want, produce and sell as much as you want. It's always been free in New Brunswick, and we hope it stays that way. It's easier. There's no Federation to restrict the amount of syrup you are able to sell."

Briggs lives next to the Bay of Fundy, an inlet in the Atlantic Ocean that separates New Brunswick from Nova Scotia. This bay is a wonder of the world, featuring the biggest tidal shift on Earth. Tourists flock from everywhere to witness this marvel at Fundy National Park of Canada. Every year about 1,500 buses filled with visitors drive past Briggs Maple, the family's shop in Hillsborough, on their way to the bay. Many of those buses stop at their shop to buy New Brunswick maple syrup.

On a shelf at Briggs Maple sits an old empty glass bottle that once contained Gordon's Dry Gin. Pasted over the gin label is the sticker of A.M. Briggs & Son, Stilesville, New Brunswick. Arthur McNutt Briggs died in 1936, and this bottle serves as evidence that the Briggs family has made and bottled maple syrup for five generations. Briggs Maple has expanded over the years; these days the family employs up to five cashiers and keeps others busy in its bottling plant and confectionary kitchen, which makes maple-flavoured cotton candy and maple lollipops in shapes that represent local wildlife, such as moose and lobster. Much of the Briggs syrup heads to the ports across Atlantic Canada: Passengers who disembark from cruise ships in Halifax and Sydney, Nova Scotia; Saint John, New Brunswick; and Charlottetown, P.E.I., love to buy maple candy and maple syrup.

Maple syrup was just one of the products from the family farm when David Briggs was a boy growing up in Stilesville. The family also raised beef cattle, pigs and chickens for eggs. "Maple was always part of your income in spring," David said. "Everybody made maple products. That's what people used to cook with." But as the growing city of Moncton encroached on the farm, David's father, Lea Briggs, moved west to Albert County, where he bought 80 hectares, or 200 acres, for sugar bush. He later expanded, also tapping trees in Crown forests nearby.

In recent years the Briggs family has weathered good times and bad. The good: Business is booming. The bad: at the end of 2023, David's father, Lea, died suddenly at the age of seventy-seven. For David's whole life his father had been a reliable supplier of maple syrup while David and Sherry grew the bottling and the retail business. They expanded their source of supply to ten local syrup producers. Even so, they always counted on their original partner: Lea Briggs.

Still, the show must go on. David's younger brother Jason works seasonally driving a cement truck; there is not much demand for cement in early spring. Now Jason intends to take over his father's sugar bush, with about 13,000 taps in sugar maple trees.

Among other challenges for the Briggs, David Briggs lists the unpredictable weather. "Mother Nature is very hard on us. Many windstorms and ice storms." Every snowstorm now changes to freezing rain, he said. In 2023, an ice storm snapped tree branches all over the province. Limbs fell on sap lines.

And what of the next generation of Briggs? Sherry and David have a daughter, Ashley. Sherry is a diabetic and rarely eats maple syrup, but Ashley is a huge fan, who, as a

"Maple syrup, maple taffy, jam, jelly, granulated sugar, candy, maple butter, and even maple vinaigrette or barbecue sauce—plus, many New Brunswick craft alcohol producers create delicious special edition maple-based drinks. You'll want to bring it all home with you!"

TOURISM NEW BRUNSWICK WEBSITE, 2024

child, ate maple syrup on everything: carrots, squash, turnips. Ashley is studying commerce at St. Mary's University in Halifax; her parents hope that she will one day take over the Briggs Maple business.

Other people in the province are expanding their operations. One recent January in the meeting room at his sugar shack near Saint-Quentin, New Brunswick, Jean-François Laplante assembled his team of twenty workers. To each he issued an orange-and-black tapping apron, a drill with a sharp drill bit and two charged-up drill batteries. Each apron contained supplies for tapping, such as tapping hammers and extra 5/16-inch tubing. Among the team was the eldest of Laplante's three children, his son William, age twenty. William was back after spending a year studying at the Centre de formation en acériculture, a maple syrup-making training centre in eastern Quebec. Several of the others in the sugar shack that morning were retirees, men who have tapped sugar maple trees their whole lives and who enjoy the forest. And for the first time the Laplantes had hired temporary foreign workers: four men from Guatemala, who spoke only Spanish. Those workers had arrived a few days earlier. Laplante drove the Guatemalans to a workwear store to buy long underwear, snow pants, shirts, fleeces, winter jackets, gloves, toques and winter boots good to minus forty degrees. "You have to dress like an onion peel," Laplante told me, because it can be cold in the morning, then warm up, then cool off. Laplante had set up a screen so the Guatemalans could watch some online training, produced by the Quebec Ministry of Agriculture in Spanish, to help the workers learn the techniques of tapping trees.

The weather was mild for this part of Canada in January, with a daytime high of -10°C, or 14°F. The locals had seen something rare: a green Christmas. By mid-January the snow cover was about a third of what is typical. In many areas, the workers didn't need to wear snowshoes to tap sugar maples. Laplante spent the morning going over the rules of tapping. "If you don't train your guys you can't complain if they do a bad job," he said. He divided his workers into teams, splitting them among seven pickup trucks for the tapping job.

As a teen, Laplante had enrolled in the Royal Canadian Navy, where he trained as an electrician. After three-and-a-half years in the service, he returned to northern New Brunswick and worked four years for a maple syrup producer, Denis Côté. "I got hooked," he says. Laplante had no background in making maple syrup; his father was a truck driver. But as a kid he'd worked on a local dairy farm, which taught him the kind of hard work and sacrifices necessary to succeed in agriculture.

Then Laplante set up his own syrup business. The first year he put in 20,000 spiles. By 2024, after he bought several of his competitors, his business had grown to 165,000 spiles, making him one of the biggest syrup producers around. Things have gone well for him. He says the key is to have the right attitude. "We often walk in a hallway where the doors are open, but you still have to walk through them," he said.

A COUPLE OF years after that snowy protest by syrup-makers in St. Quentin, Pierre-Marcel Desjardins, a professor of economics at the Université de Moncton, joined about 150 New Brunswick maple syrup producers at the industry's annual meeting in the provincial capital. The syrup producers had hired Desjardins to write a report on the syrup industry. "There were a lot of young people in the room," Desjardins said. "People in their thirties and forties. Not a lot of grey hair like mine. It's a new group that wants to professionalize and mechanize the syrup sector."

Desjardins, the economics professor, argued in his report that the syrup sector is better than logging for the economy. His research found that leasing forest to the syrup sector would create more than six times more jobs than a lease for forest harvest. The syrup sector also generates double the economic impact and tax revenue, compared with logging, he found. Plus, the syrup-makers argue, in an era of climate change it is preferable to preserve the maple trees and the carbon they are capturing rather than cutting them down, which would release much of that carbon. "The syrup sector is more labour-intensive," Desjardins said. "The sawmills and pulp mills are already built, but the syrup sector is making investments. For politicians it's a tricky decision to choose between the syrup business and the loggers."

In 2023, the New Brunswick government granted syrup producers access to over 5,000 hectares, or 12,000 acres, of additional Crown forest over five years, the first increase since 2015. Syrup producers cheered, but eight Mi'kmaw communities in New Brunswick, represented by the Mi'gmawe'l Tplu'taqnn Inc., said in a statement that the Province acted without consulting them. Kim Allen, executive director of Forest NB, noted that because most of the land along the St. John River, home to the Indigenous Peoples, is now in private hands, the remaining Crown land is precious to them.

Loggers in New Brunswick are also unhappy. They warn that setting aside Crown land as sugar bushes will cut the

wood supply to the province's mills. Allen says syrup producers are spreading misinformation about her industry, which
already has to protect some stands of sugar maples under
provincial policy. She says maple producers in the northwest
identified lands for expansion that were already under lease
to a forestry operation. Allen also notes that the syrup sector
sometimes uses roads to get into the sugar bush built and
paid for by her members.

Syrup producers such as Caron and Laplante point out
that the sugar bush they seek to tap represents less than
1 percent of the Crown forest in New Brunswick. "The sun
shines for everyone," Laplante said. "I don't think the forest
sector is thinking ahead. We hear them say that if they don't
get access to forests, they'll have to shut the mills." But, he
noted, that kind of frailty on the part of the lumber industry
suggests they have done a poor job managing forests for the
long term, given that the syrup industry only operates in a
tiny fraction of Crown forests. He called it David vs.
Goliath. "The forest industry always got 100 percent of the
forest. But they are working on Crown land. They are going
to have to share."

If the maple syrup industry right now uses 1 percent of
New Brunswick's forests and wants access to 2 percent,
doesn't that leave 98 percent of the forest to the loggers? Not
so, said Allen, who pointed out that 30 percent of Crown
lands are under conservation, with a planned expansion by
5 percent. "It does not leave 98 percent for the forest sector. It
leaves 98 percent for all other users of Crown land."

It seems likely the debate will persist for the foreseeable
future. Éric Caron is optimistic but troubled by one detail:
interest rates. A bank loaned the Caron brothers money to

expand their maple syrup operations. "We have some equity, and the rest is a debt that we don't like right now because interest rates are very high," Éric said. His fellow syrup-maker, Laplante, has a more fundamental concern. In 2024, Quebec saw a shortage of maple syrup; a bad syrup year in 2021 prompted the sale of a whopping 50 million pounds, about half of the province's reserve. Buyers snap up all the syrup that New Brunswick can make, at the Quebec price. But what happens in a year of surplus syrup? New Brunswick has no price guarantee. "It's not written down in a book that we have those advantages," Laplante said. "This could turn against us one day, and we would have nothing to protect us. I'd like us to have our own federation in New Brunswick."

For its part, Groupe Savoie—the St. Quentin-based hardwood lumber company that helped pay for the giant maple leaf at the entrance to town—is talking tough. On its website the company promises lumber buyers: "And don't worry about production capacity! You need it—we've got it." The company recently spent $25 million on a machine to automate decision-making for each hardwood log that comes into its facilities: to see inside the log and determine its best use. As is standard for harvest of hardwood forests in eastern Canada, loggers cut the forest in such a way that the trees will grow back—a result vital to the company's future since mills need a guarantee of future logs. The Sustainable Forestry Initiative certifies Groupe Savoie's operations. But the sugar bush may not grow back quickly enough to satisfy the syrup-makers.

Meanwhile, Laplante faces a slightly more subtle challenge: He named his business Laplante and Sons Sugar Bush. His daughter Léa, eighteen, is right now studying business at the Université de Moncton. She has spoken about joining the family syrup business after graduation and has hinted that her dad might want to come up with a more inclusive corporate identity.

BIG MAPLE

Nestled in the valley of the Sainte-Anne River, north-west of Quebec City, Saint-Raymond is the nearest village to one of the world's bigger maple syrup pro-ducers. In mid-March when it looks like the sap might start to run, I take a 10-hour road trip from Toronto to Saint-Raymond.

The First Peoples' early techniques for making maple sweeteners, using buckets and a wood fire, are still in use by hobbyists today, including myself. But producers who want to make syrup in volume have long since mechanized every aspect of the job. My goal for this trip: to meet the maple syrup barons, the industry leaders using the latest technology to make syrup at scale. Thanks to these innovators, maple syrup production in Canada has increased sevenfold over the past half-century. I seek the people pushing the syrup indus-try into the future. I want to meet Big Maple.

En route I stop at a Tim Hortons and see for sale by the cash register maple syrup in a bottle as big as a hotel ration of shampoo. For $10 you get 100 millilitres. This works out to $100 per litre. There's money in the sticky stuff. Back on the road, I head east of the Island of Montreal; the temperature, oddly, begins to rise. The snowbanks, taller than the cars and tinted grey and black from the soot of the traffic, are beginning to melt and recede. Planted spruce and pine line Highway 40. On the historic houses built between the road and the river, the snow clings to the overhanging curved eaves, designed to shed snow and icicles beyond the doorway and footpath. Irrigators parked in fields suggest intensive agriculture. As I pass through Trois-Rivières I see snow piled in hills the size of hockey arenas in parking lots beside the highway—they may still be melting in June. It is warmer than in Toronto, with the temperature to hit a high of 4°C, or 39°F.

One of my original intentions for this trip was to attend the inauguration of a new addition to the grandly named Strategic Maple Syrup Reserve: another warehouse to store excess maple syrup. The launch, which coincided with the start of another maple syrup season, was to be a glittering affair, with media, guests and members of the first women's professional hockey club in Quebec in attendance. Unfortunately, a bout of COVID-19 delayed my travels, and I missed the launch. Still, the scale of the press conference sums up how the Quebec syrup industry sees itself now. This picture is a little different from how things were over a century ago, when a newspaper called *Le Terroir* reported on a ceremony to launch the sugaring-off season in Beauceville, Quebec. On a March day in 1919, after Mass in a packed Catholic Church, the priest led his parishioners into the sugar bush, joined by the sexton carrying the cross and two children from the choir wearing robes "whiter than the snow."

The priest stopped at the biggest maple tree, sprinkled it with holy water, and then put his hand on the foreheads of the faithful and offered them benediction and the "Peace of the Lord." Fast forward a century and the launch of the season takes place not in the sugar bush with a church choir, but in a warehouse large enough to hold 85,000 barrels of maple syrup. Quebec produces maple syrup the way James Cameron shoots a movie: at scale. The big leagues. The throngs, once drawn to the church now pack the syrup warehouse.

Everything about maple syrup in Quebec is big. Like the country mouse who gawks at the splendour upon arrival in the city, Ontario syrup-makers like me stare in mute astonishment at the scale of these sugaring operations. The flagship syrup warehouse in Laurierville stretches five football fields and serves as a potent symbol of the influence of Big Maple. The new warehouse, equal in size, came together thanks to a $14-million investment by the Producteurs et productrices acéricoles du Québec (PPAQ). They now own three warehouses with room to store 216,000 barrels: the equivalent of fifty-three Olympic-size swimming pools full of maple syrup.

The other goal of my trip is to visit the syrup farmers leading these large-scale operations. I have written in newspapers for years about the clout of Quebec's maple syrup cartel and spent time with the rebels who fought them. Now it is time to meet the visionaries who built and defend Quebec's maple syrup supply management orthodoxy.

Alain Gauthier is my first stop. He is the PPAQ's president for the Quebec City region, and a grandfather of the maple syrup cartel: a veteran who fought in all the battles that led to the creation of the system that is of great benefit to his family business. Despite the scale of his operation, Gauthier is still very much hands on and regularly puts on his snowshoes to go out into the forest to tap the trees. When I call him to organize the logistics of my visit, the call drops out. "Sorry, I was on the mountaintop—the reception isn't the best," he apologizes.

When I finally make it to St. Raymond, I am struck by what a cultured spot it is, a place where the people take great pride in what they create. The local Hôtel Roquemont exudes rustic local charm, with a worn plank floor, faux log walls, birch forest wallpaper and a brewery on site. At suppertime, two couples at the next table laugh in loud Québécois; one man wears a Skidoo T-shirt. Screens suspended above the dining room play videos of snowmobiles flying over impossible cliffs and soaring through blue skies as they disappear into clouds of white powder. My burger is made up of locally grown produce: beef from Syldia farm, cheese from des Grondines creamery, bun from Le Soleil Levain bakery and mayonnaise made with the brewery's own Charlotte Milker beer.

The next morning at 6 a.m. a thin layer of fresh snow coats the parking lot. It's right around the freezing mark. I slip through the dark to my car and turn north, into the mountains. As dawn breaks in light snow, I follow a road that curves along the base of a forested mountain. Gauthier, my host, had sent me an email in French a few days before, with directions to his family's sugaring operation: "Hello. The season has begun and I have moved to the sugar shack. So when you get to my house on St. Paul, just continue on the same road for 15 kilometres. Then, turn right on the ZEC Bastican Nelson. We are 3 kilometres into the ZEC. I'll be

"Are we proud of what we do? Producing the best sugar in the world? Are we as proud as the Italians when they speak of their pizzas, focaccias or pastas? Often we take for granted that maple syrup is 'just' maple syrup. Let's stop being too humble and be proud of what we produce!"

NATACHA LAGARDE,
InfoSirop magazine, 2023

there regardless of what time you arrive." ZEC stands for *zone d'exploitation contrôlée*, or "controlled harvesting zone"—publicly owned forests leased out for commercial use.

The road hugs the base of the mountains. Thick blue and black plastic pipes run about chest-height along the edge of the road, held aloft by wires fastened to trees. Insulating plastic housing on the wire protects the tree bark. Thin blue plastic tubes, about the thickness of a pencil, climb the snow-covered mountainside in a webwork connecting these pipes to each tree.

Someone has been hard at work snowplowing. I pass a windowless barn-scale structure clad in aluminum. Snow has been cleared from the parking pad between the building and the road. On the front of the structure—a pumping station for maple sap—is a big billboard with a maple leaf and the words *L'Incroyable Érable* (Incredible Maple). This road is busy with tourists in summer; the PPAQ wants them to know that this is a syrup-making area. Mechanical pumps inside these stations maintain vacuum pressure in the lines to suck the sap from the maple trees into vast vats in each pumphouse. Then a truck empties the tank and hauls the sap to the sugar shack.

After a half-hour drive I turn north on a rutted dirt road—two tire tracks, with snow clumps and mud puddles, that wind up the mountain to a clearing in the forest. Here stands a long aluminum-sided building, some sections wider and with more roof than others, but all stuck together, evidence that the building has grown over time. There is a satellite dish for internet but no smokestacks. Snow that had slid off the roof has met the snowbanks, covering the windows.

Fresh tire tracks appear in the thin layer of the morning snow. The front door does not get much use; beside it a sign announces *Érablière les 5 Zef*, or 5 Zefs Sugar Bush. Several backhoes, tractors and snowblowers sit buried in snowdrifts. Near the side entrance of the shack, six snow-covered snow-mobiles are parked in a jumble on a snowbank. Affixed behind the seat of each snowmobile is a battered old ply-wood box spraypainted with a stencil of "5 Zef" to carry snowshoes, tubing and other supplies. Six black sap trunk pipelines, leading from the woods into the sugar shack, cross just behind the machines, high enough off the snow that a snowmobile can pass underneath. I park by a snowbank.

From a kind of barn door at the side entrance of the sugar shack emerges a slight, smiling gentleman with curly grey hair wearing blue long-sleeved overalls and tall insulated black rubber boots: Alain Gauthier. From behind him comes the roar of machinery.

"The first few days of the season we run around like luna-tics," Gauthier says. He is alone. He arose at 5 a.m. to get to work. "The season came on suddenly. The rest of the family have gone home to get their clothes and groceries."

Welcome to Les 5 Zef, the future of Canada's maple syrup industry. It's not what you'd expect. In his book *Meanings of Maple*, Michael Lange, a professor of anthropology and folk-lore in Vermont, notes, "The red-checked coats, horses, and buckets of the maple bottle imagery speaks of 'the way we've always done it', and that narrative is constantly reinforced in many marketing and other communications between sugaring and the public." But the buckets and the horses are long gone. Today's sugar shacks are marvels of technological innovation that rely on microwave signals, vacuum pumps, reverse osmosis, electric evaporators and temporary foreign workers.

Yet even this contemporary sugar shack retains comforting vestiges of the historic underpinnings of maple syrup production, relying as it does on the sweat of the extended Gauthier family, and their ingenuity and endurance, to weather the long hours and the relative isolation involved in making maple syrup. Despite all of the changes, one constant endures: you can only boil sap into syrup for maybe five or, if you are lucky, six weeks of the year. You had better have a committed group of people on hand, ready to stay up late in the forest to make the most of nature's fleeting bounty.

Alain Gauthier grew up with four brothers and two sisters on a farm in Saint-Basile-de-Portneuf a bit south of here. Their father was Joseph; locals abbreviated his first name to Zef, which came to form the collective nickname for his children: the Zefs. Growing up, the family made maple syrup on their dairy farm. "When we were kids, we did the rounds with the horses and the buckets and everything," Alain recalls. That operation required the manual labour of the classic big Catholic Quebec family, since it was itself a sizable operation for its era: about 3,800 spiles. The family made maple butter—made by heating syrup to 112°C, or 233°F, and then beating it rapidly as it cools—plus hard maple sugar and soft sugar. They sold it to friends and family, and at the farm gate.

When Alain was a kid the mountains north of his house were off limits to farm families like the Gauthiers; the government leased the public land to the wealthy, who came to private chalets in the area to summer, fish and hunt. "During the time of Duplessis," Alain went on, referring to Maurice Duplessis, the famed arch-conservative premier of Quebec in the 1950s, "Americans used to come by airplane to the nicest lakes in Quebec. They had private clubs, and the Québécois did not have permission to go there. There was a gate and we couldn't go through. There was a lot of protest. The citizens were really upset: 'How come we can't go into the public forests?' So, the government opened it up to all Quebecers. It became really public land."

In the 1970s these areas became ZECs—controlled management zones. In 1982, Alain and his four brothers—Renald, Roméo, Laurier and Mario—leased a mountainside to tap maples. Quebec charged them 1 cent per spile. They called their company "Les 5 Zef." Their two sisters, Jocelyne and Réjeane, chose not to get involved, Alain says. The brothers boiled their sap in a wood-fired evaporator.

The next year the brothers grew their business. They just kept stringing tubes on mountainsides. Each time they tapped a mountain, they painted a sheet of plywood to map the layout: red lines for roads and black lines for tubes. These maps hang on the sugar shack walls. The business grew some more. In 1989, when the famed Molson brewery of Montreal took over its rival, O'Keefe, the Zef brothers bought the O'Keefe beer tanks, cleaned them, and repurposed them to store maple sap. By 1990, with 40,000 taps in maple trees, Les 5 Zef was the biggest maple syrup producer on Earth.

Over the years, the brothers tapped more trees and bought out their neighbours' sugaring equipment and leases on public land. Today twelve sap-line maps adorn walls in the sugar shack—mountains 0 through 11. The pumping stations each have a name, such as "Merisier" (Cherry) and "Grizzly." They now have 125,000 spiles in maple trees, about 80 percent of them on Crown land, connected by over 1,000 kilometres, or 620 miles, of tubes. The family pays the province $50,000 a year for the right to tap these sugar maple trees. Total production: about 1,000 barrels, for a total value of about $2 million.

At 8 a.m. Alain switches on the big pumps, some of which have operated for forty years. These pumps suck sap from the sugar maple trees (if the tubing is sound). The scale of the equipment—motors, hoses, pipes, switches, all slightly dated and hard at work—dwarfs Alain.

Beginning in January, staff in snowshoes drilled holes in thousands of maple trees. In each hole they put a spile connected to a tube. When Alain flicks the switch on the mechanical extractors, pressure in the lines begins to draw sap from the thawing maple trees into the lines. The sap flows to the vats in pump houses at the base of each mountain. Three mountains' worth of trees' sap flows directly into the sugar shack; a tank truck driver hauls over the rest of the sap.

"The sap ran all night," Gauthier says. On a desk three monitors display rows of names and numbers in blue and green. Each line offers information about the air pressure in each tube, on each mountain. From a box Alain pulls devices that look like oversized decks of playing cards with antennae jutting from them. These are the battery-powered vacuum sensors that his crew installs along the tubing up the side of each mountain. Each box costs $800. The sensors' job is to measure and relay to the producers information about the vacuum pressure in the tubes.

Sensors on Mountain 4 bring Alain bad news: much lower pressure than normal. Somewhere on the mountain are leaks in the tubing. Branches can fall on tubes and cause a leak; a ferocious storm walloped the region in December. Even one hole in a tube can have a dramatic effect on the sap flowing from the trees. "I've already lost five barrels of syrup," Alain says. "At $2,000 a barrel, that's $10,000." He needs to wait for a crew to arrive to send them up the mountain and find the leak.

Following Alain around is his dog, Zac, a friendly border collie–golden retriever mix. Zac earns his keep, Alain says. The dog's job: hunting squirrels. There is something comic about these titans of the syrup sector with millions of dollars sunk into technology whose sleek systems can be laid low by a mammal no taller than a coffee cup.

"Zac is a squirrel-chaser," Alain says. "We have a big problem with squirrels—they eat our tubing. We probably killed 500 squirrels last year. We shot them. Zac is a great hunter. He'll chase a squirrel up a tree, and the employee knows where it is and can shoot it."

A cat also lives at the sugar shack; I ask Alain the cat's name. "No name," he says. "It's just a cat." A friend's mother had to go into a retirement residence and could not keep her cat, so Alain adopted it.

Once the sap arrives at the sugar shack, pipes send it through a machine called a reverse osmosis concentrator. Sap straight from the tree contains about 2 percent sugar; syrup is 66 percent sugar. For centuries, the transformation required a great deal of boiling. Reverse osmosis, invented in the 1970s, sucks much of the water out of the sap.

The inventors of this technique copied equipment long in use on ships, which filters salt water to make it potable. But whereas the ships keep the water, the syrup-makers want the sweetened sap concentrate. Pumps send the sap through a semi-permeable membrane that retains the sugar molecules and expels a demineralized water. These machines can remove up to 75 percent of the water from the sap, thus dramatically

REVERSE OSMOSIS (R.O.) SYSTEM

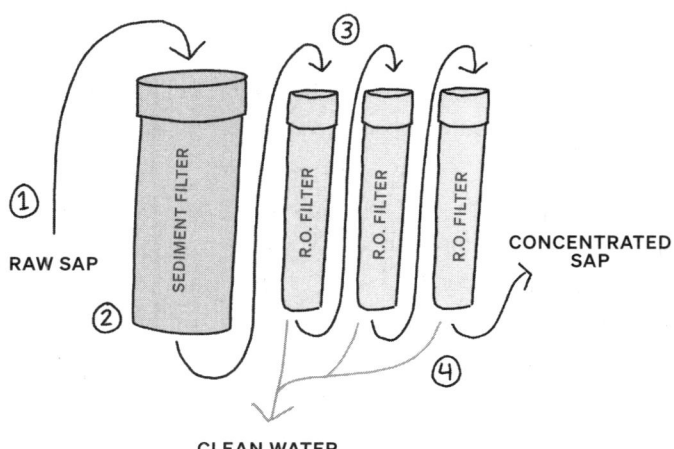

1. The raw maple sap is pumped through an R.O. system. Sap is a solution of two percent sugar and 98 percent water, along with small amounts of vitamins and minerals.

2. The sap then runs through a sediment filter, which removes dirt and debris.

3. The sap flows through one or more R.O. filters, which removes up to 90 percent of the water from the sap.

4. Most of what exits the R.O. is clean water. The remaining 10 to 20 percent flows out as concentrated sap, containing far more sugar than it had going into the system. Reducing the liquid volume means less fuel is needed to boil the concentrate into maple syrup.

reducing the amount of time you need to boil the liquid to make maple syrup. The *Crown Maple Guide to Maple Syrup* calls reverse osmosis "the biggest shift in maple technology in the 20th century." Syrup-makers use the pure water that the process emits to clean their equipment.

At the sugar shack this fine March morning, workers begin to arrive. Even though mechanization has shrunk the number of people needed to make maple syrup, most families today aren't large enough to staff the sugar bush. The 5 Zef employs five temporary foreign workers from Guatemala. They show up first: Sergio José Menez Arias, Estuardo Mexicanos, brothers Osman and Brandon Cruz and Jonathan Marroquin. They hail from Aldea Tenedores, a town in the municipality of Morales, near Guatemala's Atlantic coast on the border with Belize.

For generations, Guatemalans descended from the Mayans have supplied manual labour to farms that they do not own. In university, two fellow students and I wrote a term paper about the Guatemalan peasant uprising against the US-owned United Fruit Company. I became so invested in these struggles for economic justice that I pooled my pennies and spent a summer of my undergrad traipsing around Central America, including weeks in Guatemala. And here we cross paths again, the tireless Guatemalans and I, only this time in the snow.

Communication can be a challenge. Looking out the back of the shack Alain is puzzled to see two snowmobiles driven by Guatemalan crew members rumble down the mountain and stop beside the building. He pushes a button and speaks into his walkie-talkie: "Sylvain, where are you?"

"I am at the bridge, where you told me to go," answers Sylvain, who has worked twenty-five years for the 5 Zef and is Alain's right-hand man.

"Yeah, but the guys [the Guatemalan workers] have come back here."

"Yet I told them to follow me."

"You should have told them in Spanish!"

A car arrives and backs into the loading bay of the sugar shack. The driver is Anne Gauthier, Alain's niece. In 2020, she bought out her father, Roméo—the next generation has begun to take over the big sugar bush. Three of Anne's daughters, Maryse, Éliane and Diana, emerge and begin to unload the car: boots, snowpants, suitcases and groceries (tubs of crudités, potato chips, croissants). The family, who live about an hour away in Sainte-Catherine-de-la-Jacques-Cartier, is moving in for a month.

I join Anne as she pulls supplies from the car. Among them are cases of unrefined canola oil. This is not for cooking but rather for the syrup. As molten sap concentrate nears the 66 percent sugar mark that defines maple syrup, the boiling liquid tends to bubble and overflow. When we were kids my stepfather put a dab of butter on the frothing liquid, which caused the bubbles to recede; the evaporators here dispense minuscule amounts of organic vegetable oil, which produces the same bubble-calming effect.

The sugar shack in front of me is not one you would conjure in your mind's eye; you won't find children pouring out of school buses to eat maple taffy from the snow, or tables filled with big plates of beans, eggs and pancakes laid out for visitors. These are industrial buildings, designed only for large-scale production of maple syrup.

Rooms at the 5 Zef hold pumps and huge vats of sap. After the sap is concentrated through reverse osmosis, it heads to the evaporator. The boiler room at the 5 Zef has a painted wooden staircase at one end that leads up to a second floor. It's a sort of a loft area with a railing that looks out over the boiling room. Upstairs is a kitchen and several bedrooms, where the extended Gauthier clan sleeps during maple syrup season. The kitchen area has a table, chairs, sofas and microwaves: strictly for staff. As Alain heats a slice of pizza for lunch and I heat a sandwich, he jokes, "There are so many microwaves in this building that it can sound like a symphony at lunchtime when everyone heats their food."

In the boiling room, two of the remaining Guatemalan men, dressed in the dark blue sweatshirts embroidered with the logo of Les 5 Zef, listen as Anne, who took some Spanish in college, explains with halting words and a lot of sign language how to fit paper filters the size of a bar fridge door into the filter press. Maple syrup, while it is still hot, flows through this machine to filter out impurities.

A sign on the sugar shack wall advertises in French: "For sale: organic maple syrup, $8 a can [just over a half-litre], $55 a gallon; maple butter, $7 for 250g." A poster from the Union des producteurs agricoles, Quebec's powerful farmers' union, reads: "UPA: We are all part of the recipe. Power to feed, power to grow."

As has been true for centuries in maple syrup country in spring, here at Les 5 Zef success comes because the whole extended family pulls together at the critical moment when the sap starts to run. Anne's daughter Maryse-Noël, dressed in a headscarf, earrings and waterproof steel-toe boots, represents the next generation of this trend. When she finished high school she didn't know what to do with her life. Her grandfather Roméo showed her a newspaper ad that promoted a new program to learn the maple syrup trade at a college in Témiscuouata, Quebec.

"I figured 'Why not?' I am in the first cohort," she says. "I like making maple syrup. It's fun. We get here and there is snow everywhere and when we leave it will all be grass."

They have left their youngest sister, Alice, at home for the night. She is in grade eight. She assured the family she would be fine alone: She plans to eat Pogos and join the family at the shack on the weekend.

The girls' mom, Anne, stands by one of the two evaporators: sleek, stainless-steel beasts that look more like speedboats than stoves. It emits a kind of high-pitched grinding hum. This is a bewildering innovation. For centuries the sign of syrup-making has been the steam rising—at one time from the Indigenous Peoples' clay pots, later from cauldrons suspended from tripods of poles in the forest, and, still later, from the stainless-steel rectangular pans of the evaporator—as one boils the water from the sap to concentrate the sugar. Once sugar-makers moved their boiling efforts indoors, the steam that billows from the evaporator and pours forth from the cupola of the sugar shack became synonymous with spring in the sugar bush. This iconic image graces maple syrup labels.

The Gauthier brothers started boiling syrup with stove wood. In 1990, they switched to an oil-fired evaporator; by 2016, the 5 Zef operation burned more than 50,000 litres, or about 13,000 gallons, of heating oil each spring. That year the Government of Quebec gave Les 5 Zef a $172,000 grant to subsidize the conversion of their three oil-fired evaporators to electricity. This saved them $30,000 a year in fuel costs and reduced the company's annual greenhouse gas emissions by 138 tons.

The new evaporators at Les 5 Zef are an invention of Michel Bochud, an immigrant from France who worked as a physics professor at a Quebec college. Bochud noticed the huge losses of energy, in the form of water vapour, that escaped evaporators when sap was boiled to make maple syrup, so he developed a way to recuperate this vapour.

Working with one of his former students, David Bédard, of Tôle Inox, a maker of stainless-steel equipment, they developed EcoVAP, which captures steam during the boiling process and recirculates it through the evaporator. This new machine uses up to twenty times less energy.

Alain just has one minor regret about this innovation. "People would drive by the sugar shack," he says. "When they saw the steam pouring out from the roof, they knew you were boiling, and they came in to buy some syrup. Now there is no steam, so people assume that you are not making any syrup."

Beside the evaporator, Anne holds a wooden paddle the length of an oar. Molten maple syrup pours from the evaporator into a vat. Anne mixes a fine white powder into the syrup. This is diatomaceous earth, made from the sediment of fossilized algae; it helps extract a mineral called niter or sugar sand from the syrup to increase its purity. Filters used next in the process remove the sugar sand and the diatomaceous earth from the syrup. She uses a hydrometer to check the syrup sugar content; it's slightly too high, so she adds a bit of water to the syrup.

Before the colonization of Canada, Indigenous women took responsibility for the maple sugar harvest in spring; settler women did much of the work in the sugar bush as well. These days, about three-quarters of maple syrup producers are men. Anne Gauthier actually started her career far from the forest. Her mom's family is in the fur business, so she studied fashion. "I said, 'I can work in furs in the fall and maple syrup in the spring.' She enrolled in truck-driving school so she could drive a maple sap truck, and there she met her husband. The couple now have four daughters. Anne stayed home to raise the girls while her husband drove a truck. When their youngest entered kindergarten, she bought her father's share of Les 5 Zef and came to work here.

"So you have a degree in fashion design?" I ask.

"Yes," Anne says with a smile. "Can't you tell?"

I look more closely. She exhibits a kind of sugar shack chic: blue cargo-style work pants with black patches on the knee, black rubber steel-toe work boots, and a black fleece; her hair is pulled back in a pony tail. I ask about her clothing. Her "multi-pocket" pants come from Pilote et Filles. Quebec City fashion designer Marie-Lise Pilote makes work clothes for women, including steel-toed boots that zip up at the back. The knee patches of Anne's pants are pockets tailored to hold knee pads.

A car pulls up. We go outside to greet Claude-Noël, Anne's husband: a mechanic. Claude-Noël in his spare time helps repair the 5 Zef snowmobiles, four-wheelers, sap trucks and other vehicles. This operation requires 15 snowmobiles. The Gauthiers buy them used for about $3,000 each; Claude-Noël keeps them running.

"The Skandik is acting up," Alain tells the new arrival. "I think there might be a problem with the carburetor." Claude turns and walks toward a snowbank, and pops the hood on the defective machine.

After lunch I volunteer to join the brothers from Guatemala, Osman and Brandon, on the mountainside to inspect for leaks in the vacuum system that sucks sap. Everyone packs snowshoes. We set out in a truck for the sector christened "Vachon" in the 5 Zef lexicon.

The Vachon sector derives its name from the iconic bakery brand in Quebec that makes chocolate-dipped spongey creme-filled cakes such as Jos Louis and May West. Years ago, a driver totalled a Vachon cake truck. The truck's box, emblazoned with the Vachon logo, survived; the Gauthier brothers bought the truck box from a wrecking yard and installed it at the base of Mountain 6.

Vachon trucks have insulated boxes to keep the chocolate coating from melting off the cakes; temperature control is also vital in the maple syrup business. The 5 Zef installed a heater to maintain the temperature in the Vachon box just above the freezing point of water. Tubes on Mountain 6 flow sap into a tank in the old Vachon cake box. A cistern truck hauls the sap to the sugar shack.

Osman Cruz has worked five years at the 5 Zef. His kid brother Brandon, head crowned with a mop of curly black hair and dressed today in a grey snow jacket with reflective stripes across the chest along with high-viz orange knitted gloves, is a more recent arrival. They both don snowshoes and scramble up the mountain. In a funny way they seem at home here; their homeland is mountainous. In Guatemala years ago I tried to scale an emerald-green, forested volcano along the shore of Lago de Atitlán. I set out early, but the volcano proved too big for me. The Guatemalans in that region, who wore homemade leather huaraches with soles fashioned from recycled car tires, scampered past me, running up and down the volcano sides with as much ease as their goats.

Scaling a mountain in snowshoes, the Guatemalans again prove more adept than me. Huffing, I catch up to Brandon. The equipment had detected an air leak in this sector of the mountain. Brandon does not know where. The trick is stealth; in the still early spring air, amid the leafless maples on the steep mountain slope, keen ears can hear the hiss of air getting sucked into the tubing.

Brandon stops. He has found the hole. From a bag on his shoulder, he begins to pull tools. He first clamps the tube to prevent vacuum loss downstream. Then he uses pliers to cut the tube. He removes the tube section with a leak in it and pulls from his bag a fresh section of tube, which he cuts to length and clamps to the line. Finally, he removes the clamp, and the sap flow in the tube returns to normal. Bubbles moving slowly in the line indicates normal flow of sap; a quicker movement of bubbles denotes a leak.

"Last year," says Brandon, "was the hardest work year of my life. We inspected the entire operation."

A FEW DAYS later, I am far to the west in a region called Montérégie-Est. Otherwise known as the Eastern Townships, it is a verdant region speckled with lakes, ski hills, dairy farms, craft breweries and pastry shops that stretches south from Montreal. The Townships is a wealthy part of the province where quite a few of the old families speak English. In 1908, Montreal judge Robert Stanley Weir wrote the English words to "O Canada," the national anthem, while sitting at the piano in his summer home here, looking out over Lake Memphremagog. Not far from there, in Cowansville, another sugar shack is roaring to life. This one, on the Chemin d'Iron Hill, houses that rarest of breeds, with whom I had until then never crossed paths: an English-speaking Quebec farmer. Along with raising sheep, David "Fish" Hall is president of the Montérégie-Est region of the PPAQ. He is also one of Alain Gauthier's friends.

Gauthier and Hall are unlikely pals: one slight, the other large; one French, the other English; one buttoned down, the other bombastic; one tapping maple trees on public land, the other working forests that have been in the family for generations. But the two men share much in common: They enlist family and locals in spring to make large quantities of maple syrup, and they agree on the supply management regime that controls the Quebec syrup industry.

Wet snow clings to the dirt roads as I drive to the Hall farm. It's mid-March, and sugaring-off operations are in full swing. Compared to the organized 5 Zef, this place is jumbled. The melting snowbanks around the sugar shack are slowly receding to reveal the top of a ladder, hoses, tubing, a generator, a snow shovel, mud, rocks, gas canisters, shipping pallets, totes, and bulk tanks filled with sap concentrate.

From the building emerges David Hall. Loud, pugnacious, bearded, larger than life, Hall wears a baggy checked shirt, sweater vest, olive green work pants and running shoes, and a black ball cap with the logo of CDL, a syrup equipment maker. He lives with his wife, Sandra Smith, on Hallacres farm, where he raises sheep and makes maple syrup. Sandra and I know one another; I was a year ahead of her at Laurentian Regional High School in Lachute, Quebec. English-speaking Quebec is a pretty small club.

"It's by no means killing itself," Hall says of the sap volume when I arrive. "I've seen it run much faster. But you take what you can get." We climb into Hall's pickup truck with his dog, Tilley, to take stock of his syrup-making kingdom. Part way along the gravel road from his sugar shack to his home, we stop; Hall lowers his window to talk to a man wearing overalls and insulated camouflage rubber boots who is about to board an all-terrain vehicle.

"Larry is going to go up the mountain to check Line 5," Hall explains as we drive off. "He's retired. He did pretty well. He's a workaholic. He helps us out. We give him some lamb or we give him some syrup."

A few minutes later a call comes from the mountain and Hall punches a button on his console. Larry's voice fills the cab of the pickup truck: He's disconnected one spile that was leaking and patched the sap tube to bypass the problem. He commits to coming back to replace the broken spile.

Hall checks his phone, which offers him real-time information about the pressure in his sap lines. "Don't kill yourself," he says to Larry. "That one has popped it up like hell."

Hall's father, Grant, farmed this area before him. "My father loved the woods more than anything," he tells me.

These days Hall has a lot going on. In the cup holder of his pickup truck is a box of Castrator Aseptic Rubber Rings, "for castration and tailing of lambs." Today, alongside his sugar bush work, he is welcoming two sheepshearers. He discusses the holidays for which his sheep are in demand: Christian Easter, Greek Orthodox Easter, the end of Ramadan. "Eid is the big one . . ."

Sugaring is more complex than raising sheep or other farm pursuits, Hall says. "If you are growing corn and you have a bad July—well, you had June and August and September and October. In sugaring, if you have a bad month, you're fucked. Sugaring is organized chaos."

On his truck phone he calls Brome, a village a bit east of here, and speaks to Bob Derby, a fellow syrup farmer.

"I don't think we are going to get rich at the end of today," Hall tells Derby. "I've got some leaks somewhere. Sean is going to come and walk the bush for me. It's always the same every fucking year. Until we get one of those leaks tended to. You never know: You can hunt and hunt." He rants about the drawbacks of stainless-steel hydraulic clamps and other hose connectors.

As he speaks Hall turns the wheel. We careen off the dirt road and onto a farm lane along a tree line. He puts the truck gear in low to plow through the soggy, wet snow. "If we get over 60 centimetres [23 inches] of snow they'll pay us to shovel our main lines on our crop insurance," he says.

That was not the case this year. The truck churns and heaves and bucks and rocks like we're crossing a giant bowl of oatmeal. At last we arrive at a pump house that collects sap from another part of the sugar bush. Hall climbs a ladder to peer into a stainless-steel tank whose top is covered with melting snow. A blue hose the diameter of his arm feeds sap into the tank. Hall keeps an eye on the sap level to plan the collection of sap, for which he relies on a tanker truck driver named Tony. He wants to make sure Tony hauls the sap on time, and he has a gauge in his house that tells him the level of sap in this tank.

"His wife is not going to be happy if I call him at five o'clock in the morning because I get up to have a piss and I see that the tank is full," Hall explains.

On our drive back to the sugar shack we pass neighbour Joe on a tractor pulling a wagon loaded with three plastic totes each the size of an all-terrain vehicle, filled with maple sap, en route to his own shack. The men exchange syrup-season pleasantries.

As we make our way, Hall intersperses the drive with his soliloquies on the day's sap production ("It would be better if it started to rain. We've got so much snow."); sheep-shearing; his son Andrew ("Andrew has cabbaged onto a girlfriend.") and his various helpers, with philosophical musings about the clout of the PPAQ.

"We are not price takers," he says. "We set the price. We go out, we promote our product to try to sell more of it. Does it work 100 percent of the time? Probably not. But in the States, they are competing with each other. The UPA is notably a very nationalist organization [by "nationalist" he means dedicated to Quebec sovereignty]. But I've never been treated with anything but respect.

"Our costs have gone up. The syrup buyers think we are the Antichrist. We negotiated. We didn't pull the figure out of our ass. We came to an agreement." He is ambitious for the sector's future, noting, "The town of Brome Lake [in this region] has potential of just under one million taps."

At the sugar shack David's son Andrew is busy boiling sap. Fuel oil powers the Hall evaporator. The boiling room feels like the engine room of a ship, with the steam and the heat and the repetitive thumping, the growls of the pumps and everyone walking around like sailors in rubber boots and waterproof clothing—mostly men with lots of facial hair. David's wife, Sandra, arrives, stopping at the sugar shack on her way home from work—it's probably the only place where she will see her husband and her son at this time of year. The sap is running; there is excitement in the air. A computer screen displays the pressure of lines pulling sap into the sugarhouse: "Brook Top 3, 26.60; Brook Top 4, 26.57; Brook Top Shithole Lefty, 26.47; Brook Top Shithole Righty, 26.37." Syrup-making equipment measures vacuum in inches of mercury; a perfect vacuum seal is 30 inches. Giving names to sectors in the sugar bush is an age-old custom.

"Why is it called 'Shithole?'" I ask.

"If you go up there, you'll know," David says.

Here at Hallacres, as at the 5 Zef, I am struck by a constant that links today's big sugaring operations to their sugaring ancestors: the teamwork of family. A few days earlier at the 5 Zef, brothers Alain and Mario had sat hunched over the banks of monitors on an old wooden desk in a drafty room with a once-green cement floor and the persistent background hum of the pumps sucking sap from the sugar maples on Mountains No. 1, 2 and 3, the first three mountains that the Gauthier brothers tapped in 1981. It's a similar picture to the one seen at sugar shacks up and down the province: family pitching in to keep the operation going.

Despite some recent declines in global syrup demand, Quebec's maple syrup makers feel bullish about the future. The PPAQ at present counts 13,300 producers. It's a fraction of the 50,000 maple syrup producers of a century ago. Even so, Joël Vaudeville, spokesman for the PPAQ, tells me when I stop by at his office in Longueuil, a suburb of Montreal, that "If it weren't for maple syrup, there would be a drop in the total number of farms in Quebec. It's because of the syrup business that the number of farms in Quebec is actually growing, and that agricultural production is on the rise. Since 2021, 1,200 new producers have joined the Federation. That said, we expect to see in the next few years a consolidation of the syrup business."

Quebec's syrup producers want 200,000 hectares, or about half a million acres, of public land reserved for maple syrup production over the next sixty years. These additional forests alone would permit the industry to nearly double the amount of syrup currently made in the province. They point to the boon that the syrup industry has meant for innovation in technology, and for manufacturing, in Quebec. While loggers, paper mills and sawmills in Canada use harvesting equipment and mill machinery made in Europe and Asia, much of the innovation and fabrication in the syrup industry takes place in Quebec and finds buyers across eastern North America. Lapierre boasts on its website that it exports syrup-making equipment to Mexico, Haiti and Russia.

Alain Gauthier is optimistic for the future. "Fifty years ago in Quebec we were in the Stone Age with horses and buckets; now we are in the digital age and we have a better syrup. Last year [2022] we at 5 Zef made $1.5 million worth of maple syrup in twenty-five days. We expect to produce 10 million pounds of syrup this year. We produced a can of syrup for every Québécois. And there aren't many days I wasn't there to make it."

PROTECT THE
GOLDEN GOOSE

E very winter, once the weather in Toronto, Ontario, gets
frosty enough, I skate on Grenadier Pond in High
Park, west of my house. The pond is where our children learned to skate. In December every morning I look
with expectation, like a kid counting down the days to
Christmas, at the thermometer outside the kitchen window,
hoping the mercury falls below freezing. In 2022–23, for the
first time in my twenty-five years in Toronto, the pond never
froze. The same year the world's largest skating rink, Ottawa's
8-kilometre, or 5-mile, Rideau Canal, remained out of bounds
for the first time since 1971—the ice never got thick enough.
This was particularly distressing for Ottawans, some of whom
commute to work on skates in winter.

Climate change represents an existential threat to the
maple syrup industry. The freeze–thaw cycle of our typical
eastern Canadian spring works as a kind of pumping

mechanism, which allows us to extract sap from maple trees. Without it, the sap won't flow. Global warming also brings drought. If the planet heats up too much, the maple syrup industry, an iconic sector that employs thousands and connects Canadians to our forests, could be wiped out.

A researcher who spends a lot of time thinking about maple trees and climate change, and how global warming might affect one of our country's most iconic industries, is Dr. Christian Messier, a professor of forestry at the Université du Québec en Outaouais. Messier lives his maple passion on a personal level. He and his wife own a small sugar bush near Lac-des-Plages in west Quebec. The Messier family uses buckets and a wood-fired evaporator to make enough syrup for family and friends.

I first spoke to Dr. Messier a few years ago for an article in *The Globe and Mail* about global warming and its impact on maple syrup. That year the weather warmed too early. Producers had only a tiny window during which the sap ran. As days and nights warm up, buds start to swell on the maples' branches and the sap becomes yellow or milky as it begins to ferment; syrup made from this sap is black and has a very strong flavour. One old saw goes: "A successful preacher and a successful sugar-maker are alike. They both know when to stop." To compensate for the poor season, Quebec syrup producers announced the sale of 50 million pounds of maple syrup from the Global Strategic Reserve that year. *The Globe* asked me to weigh in on the threat of climate change to maple syrup, so I spoke to Messier. He told me that we should beware of how global warming, and other human-caused change, will impact the providential sugar bush. Drought stresses maple trees more than oaks or pines, he says, which are better adapted to dry periods. The weakened maples will become more vulnerable to insects or disease. As the planet warms, we may eventually no longer be able to extract sap from the maple trees, and this important tradition and way of life, begun by Indigenous Peoples centuries ago, will be lost.

Messier and I met in person at the annual conference of Forests Canada, a non-profit that has planted over forty-five million trees in the past couple of decades in a valiant effort at reforestation—I've worked with them for years. During a lunch break, I shook hands with Messier. He is a big, hearty man with tousled brown hair, a moustache, glasses and a ready smile. I brought the scientist to sit with Ken Jewett and me. Jewett made his money in the prepared foods industry, such as making chili for Tim Hortons. Jewett used some of his wealth to create a charity, Maple Leaves Forever, which subsidizes landowners to plant native Canadian maple trees along laneways, fence lines and the roadside of their properties. The word "native" is crucial here because many years ago municipalities from New York City to Montreal introduced a hardy non-native maple, the Norway maple, as a street tree. Norway maples have become an invasive blight, taking over the forests on Mount Royal in Montreal, for example, and seizing control of the ravines of Toronto. Among Norway maples' drawbacks: Their leaves turn spotted and yellow in autumn, not red and orange; many insects and birds shun them; they live comparatively short lives; and their sap is not very sweet.

Maple Leaves Forever has so far helped to plant more than 130,000 native maple trees in Ontario. Messier listened politely as Jewett introduced himself and his work. Then he had a question for Jewett, one that perhaps no one had thought to ask.

"Why only maple trees?" Dr. Messier asked.

At the time, Jewett responded with a similar line to that found on the Maple Leaves Forever website: the maple leaf is the country's symbol; maples provide "glorious fall colours"; and maples adapt to the local climate, are relatively resistant to severe weather, suffer from minimal pest problems, provide food and shelter for wildlife, add beauty and shade, control erosion, intercept dust, soak up excess water, and provide us with forest products.

But other native Canadian tree species, such as oak, birch, poplar, basswood, hickory, pine or spruce (to name a few) provide many of these same benefits. Dr. Messier and others worry about the impact of efforts to favour maples at the expense of other native trees, a form of preferential treatment in which Maple Leaves Forever has plenty of company. Maple syrup makers have simplified their sugar bushes to a risky extent, Dr. Messier argues, by cutting down everything that isn't a sugar maple tree. They just want to keep the maples, since maples yield revenue, but mixed forests with many tree species are more resilient, Dr. Messier's research shows. As an example, tent caterpillars prefer to eat poplar rather than maple leaves; allow some poplar trees to thrive in a maple forest, and the caterpillars will leave maples to grow. "Instead of looking at our sugar bushes as a milk cow," he told me, "we now need to reinvest." And yet, when he told Quebec maple producers at a conference that it is "criminal to have pure maple sugar bushes," he said "they weren't happy to hear that."

The removal of other tree species from the sugar bush, to leave only maple trees, is hardly new. Helen and Scott Nearing, role models for generations of sugarers, decided to cut down all but the maples in their Vermont sugar bush in the 1930s. In the Nearings' *Maple Sugar Book*, published in 1950, the couple write that many farmers have replaced monoculture with crop rotation. But with maple trees, which live a century or longer, crop rotation is not an option. The farmer must choose between a clear maple stand or a mixed forest. The Nearings chose to keep only the maples. That said, climate change was not a known worry back then.

This discussion—cut all trees other than maples or leave some variety in your sugar bush—has raged for a long time, and will continue to divide sugarers. Agriculture Biologique Québec specifies that, to be considered organic, maple syrup must come from a forest where at least 15 percent of the forest is "companion species," which means trees and shrubs other than maple. Considering that, naturally, a forest contains at best about 60 percent maple trees, this allows the removal of quite a few competing species. In practice, many sugarers in Quebec and elsewhere have managed their forests by cutting out just about everything else but the maple trees, as the Nearings did. Dr. Messier and others worry about the weakened ability of these forests to bounce back from disruptions.

My own thinking on mixed forests versus clear maple stands has evolved over time. In 2016, a forester wrote me a managed forest plan for the property we own near Madoc, Ontario. He recommended removal of the ironwood trees to give light and nutrients to the sugar maples. I took this counsel to heart. When I take the dogs for a morning walk, I carry a bow saw; for several years I would cut out a few ironwood saplings every day. But then I reconsidered, especially after I learned that ironwood trees produce small nuts that are food for squirrels, woodpeckers and nuthatches. Now as I thin my forest, I still cut some ironwood poles, but I also cut maples because I want to protect diversity. Even so, I empathize with

"Increased temperatures, changes in growing season length, more frequent ice storms, and a greater frequency of extreme precipitation events (droughts and downpours) have been observed over the past several decades throughout the maple-producing region of North America."

NORTH AMERICAN MAPLE SYRUP PRODUCERS MANUAL
"Future Climate and Its Impact on Sugarbush Management," 2022

the sugarers who need to maximize maple trees in order to make a living and pay off the debt they racked up to buy all their syrup-making equipment.

In 2022, Dr. Messier teamed up with other researchers to further investigate the connection between climate change and maple syrup. The scientists note that maple syrup production has surged over the past half-century, but they worry that the trees will struggle as the planet warms. They suggested that "assisted migration," as foresters call it, offered the opportunity, in a warming climate, to help maple trees, for example, move north to places that in the past were too cold but that may in the future be an appropriate climate for the trees to thrive.

The northern range of sugar maples in Quebec right now is Chicoutimi, about two hours' drive north of Quebec City. In Ontario, people make maple syrup as far north as Thunder Bay. Some researchers suggest we could help sugar maples thrive north of there, in what is now the conifer-dominated boreal forest. Other researchers have worried that the sugar content of maple sap will decrease as the planet heats up.

Dr. Messier told me that Canadian producers can gather maple tree seeds from New York to plant in Quebec and Ontario. He believes that these trees will have the genes to better withstand warmer weather. "People say, 'Let nature be,'" Dr. Messier says. "But we have already changed our natural environment. We need to start adapting our forests."

Will climate change destroy the maple syrup industry? In 2023, delegates at a climate summit in Dubai agreed to phase out the use of petroleum in a bid to curb climate change. Will these efforts come in time to save our syrup? Sugar bushes are most productive after a long winter with lots of snow, but there are many factors at play. Deep snow takes longer to melt, which keeps the forest cooler and prolongs the syrup season. The freeze–thaw cycle I described in the chapter *Acer saccharum* is key to the flow of maple sap in spring.

Canada may be in a better position to adapt its sugar bush to a warming climate compared to the United States. *Modern Farmer*, a US magazine, reported on the travails of John and Bonnie Hall, whose family has made maple syrup at Maple Breeze Farm in Westbrook, Connecticut, for four centuries. For the Halls, 2023 was disastrous. The weather was so warm that the syrup season ended on March 4, weeks before normal. "Sugaring is very weather dependent," Hall told *Modern Farmer*. "And this year, we didn't have any winter."

Can we move our maple trees farther north and keep making syrup? Maxence Soubeyrand and Fabio Gennaretti of the Université du Québec en Abitibi-Témiscamingue note one piece of good news: A more mixed forest in the boreal region, with more leaf trees, would be hardier against insects such as the destructive spruce budworm and would be more resistant to forest fires since leaf trees burn much less readily than evergreens.

A more contentious debate in the syrup sector of late concerns the minimum girth of a tree that syrup producers may tap on public land. To grasp this debate, it's worth learning an acronym that foresters toss around: DBH. Foresters measure tree diameter at breast height, or DBH. This indicator, applied to sugar maple trees, became central to a showdown between Quebec's syrup producers and their government.

In the early 2020s, Quebec's Ministry of Agriculture commissioned Dr. Messier to write a report on how to ensure the health of the sugar bush. His report on sustainable tapping recommended that, to maximize tree health, producers tap maple trees only when their DBH reached 23.1 centimetres, or 9 inches. Dr. Messier pointed out that Quebec's rule—to permit a tap in a tree that is 20 centimetres, or 8 inches, DBH—was the most permissive in the industry. In Ontario the rule says that a tree must measure at least 25 centimetres, or 10 inches, DBH to receive a tap, a rule intended to limit the stress and damage that tapping causes to maple trees. The North American Maple Syrup Producers Manual, meanwhile, recommends a minimum girth of 22 centimetres, or 8.5 inches, DBH. The Nearings, in *The Maple Sugar Book*, suggest that one never tap a tree below 30 centimetres, or 12 inches, DBH because young trees need all possible nourishment to grow, and the sap one gains in tapping too young a tree is lost in later years.

In 2022, Quebec announced that all trees on public land must have a minimum girth of 23 centimetres, or 9 inches, to receive a spile. The syrup producers warned that this new policy would require syrup farmers to withdraw close to two million spiles already installed on public land across the province. Eventually the province climbed down and announced that its new minimum DBH for tapping would only apply to new spiles on Crown land. Syrup-makers insist that their techniques (tapping at 20 centimetres, or 8 inches, DBH, vacuum pressure on tubes, and the like) will ensure a healthy sugar bush going forward. "The revenue is in the forest," said Alain Gauthier. "If the forest is unhealthy, we won't get any sap."

Syrup-makers, big and small, have plenty to grapple with down the road. Should we be risking weakening the resilience of the forest when the challenges of climate change are only just beginning? And while we're on the topic of syrup self-reflection, what about the maple syrup industry's own contribution to global warming?

Quebecers get most of their electricity from carbon-neutral hydro-electric dams, yet they need to face facts: Their syrup business is a big polluter. One internal study by the syrup-makers concluded that during the average twenty-day syrup season, the half of the province's syrup-makers who burn fuel oil to boil sap generate the same pollution as about ten thousand SUVs driving for a year. The syrup producers have a plan to switch the evaporators over to electricity or wood pellets, and hope that by 2030 just one-third of syrup-makers will burn fuel oil.

One syrup season the neighbour at my maple farm in Madoc, Ontario, Gunter Vierich, teased me about my own carbon footprint after he read in the *National Post*, where I worked at the time, about greenhouse gas emitted by the maple syrup industry. Touché.

Consumers have no way of knowing the carbon foot-print of their syrup. In stores you often get a choice of regular or organic. The distinction has to do with how the syrup is produced: Organic syrup-makers have to leave a greater per-centage of other species of trees in the forest, for example, and certain soaps to clean equipment are off limits. But the desig-nation tells the consumer nothing about how the syrup is boiled. Electricity is an environmentally friendly energy source to boil sap into syrup; wood fire is another carbon-neutral boil-ing choice since, in a well-managed forest, the minute you remove a tree, another begins to grow to take its place. Plus, if you're making syrup you are surrounded by forest, an excellent source of firewood. As the forest grows around you, it sponges up more carbon from the atmosphere. Érable du Québec, the promotional website of Quebec's syrup producers, notes that Quebec's sugar bushes capture the equivalent of the carbon produced by 220,000 cars. The maple syrup sector has in recent years also developed systems to recycle the vast amount of plastic tubing used to extract the sap.

Maple syrup marketing portrays the product as a pure and wholesome alternative to processed and refined sugars. High-fructose corn syrup results from a chemical reaction; cane sugar has a huge carbon footprint, given that ships haul the raw sugar from the Caribbean or further to refineries abroad. Maple syrup packaging sells us an image of a horse-drawn sleigh in a bucolic forest where buckets hang from trees and steam curls from the roof of the sugar shack. The reality, as we have seen, is far different. Syrup-makers, as they seek to mechanize and maximize production and profits, have work to do to ensure that they protect the health of the sugar bush for future generations and that they are part of the solution to climate change—and not part of the problem.

DOES THE FUTURE
TASTE AS SWEET?

Maple syrup producers' thirst for sap and their dedication to increases in production and efficiency through technology are natural impulses in our capitalist culture: This drive to expand extends through every industry, from automobiles to fashion. But I wondered whether something has been lost in the maple syrup industry over the years. What made me think of it was a remark from a nephew. I had brought my family a few bottles of maple syrup at Easter time, freshly produced in our tiny sugar shack in Madoc, Ontario. My nephew tasted my syrup. "I bought some syrup the other day from Temple's," he said, naming a sizable maple syrup producer in his area, Lanark County. "Yours tastes better."

It was a nice thing to say. Even so, I am not a skilled maple syrup producer. I suspect that he tasted not what I did to make my syrup but rather what I didn't do.

Temple's has around 5,000 spiles in sugar maple trees. Like most bigger producers, Temple's uses tubes in trees and vacuum technology to suck the sap out. Once the sap reaches the sugar shack, Temple's uses a reverse osmosis machine to extract much of the water. They then boil the sap concentrate to make maple syrup. I suspect that all of these steps take something away from the flavour of the maple syrup.

When you let sap drip into a bucket, and boil said sap over a wood fire for a long time, several producers say, more of the flavour from the maple tree stays in the maple syrup. The smoke also imparts a flavour. Perhaps, as with barbecue, different species of firewood change the flavour profile of the syrup as well, though I don't know anyone who has tested this theory.

The flavour that the production process imparts to maple syrup has troubled connoisseurs for a while. Already in 1896, Rowland E. Robinson, a Vermont writer and painter known for precise descriptions of the natural world and of the New England he loved, lamented the disappearance of the "old-time, dark-colored syrup." Robinson described subtle notes of smoke, the aroma of the woods, leaves, and a hint of bark imparted in the good old-fashioned maple syrup of his youth: a "wild, woodsy flavor" that Robinson said technological improvements had since removed from the syrup's taste profile. He compared this to how progress had stripped the twang out of the New England dialect. This homogenization displeased him: "One likes to know a Yankee by the flavor of his speech, and maple sugar by its taste."

One thing must be said about maple syrup in Canada: it is pure. In the United States more than a century ago packagers began to blend maple syrup with much cheaper cane syrup and other sweeteners, a practice that continues south of the border but that is against the law in Canada.

The enactment of laws to guarantee the purity of maple syrup dates to the early 20th century. As many Canadians moved to cities to work in the factories, they no longer made their own syrup and instead had to buy it at the grocery store. As the average person's distance from the farm grew, they became less able to distinguish between pure maple syrup and blends containing undisclosed quantities of cheaper cane sugar.

At a 1916 meeting of maple syrup makers, Gustave Boyer, member of Parliament for Vaudreuil and president of the agricultural association, spoke at length about adulteration. Boyer described the long journey, from his election to Parliament in Ottawa in 1906 to when Parliament passed An Act to Amend the Adulteration Act in 1916. The act reads, in part: "No person shall manufacture for sale, keep for sale, offer or expose for sale, or sell, any article of food resembling or being an imitation of maple sugar or maple syrup or which is composed partly of maple sugar or maple syrup, and which is not pure maple sugar or pure maple syrup."

At the same meeting, John H. Grimm, the maker of the famed Grimm evaporators, praised the Inland Revenue Department in Ottawa for punishing grocers under the amended Adulteration Act: "Since these grocerymen have been brought before the Courts of Justice there has been an increased demand coming from all parts of Canada for pure maple syrup and pure maple sugar," Grimm said. Syrup-makers were realizing their sweetener could not compete with much cheaper cane sugar as a commodity and had to succeed as a luxury good. In the meantime, in the United States blends of cane sugar and maple syrup took over much of the space on grocery shelves, a factor in the decline of syrup-making in the United States.

Regardless of the technology it uses, Temple's maple syrup is 100 percent pure and made only from sap extracted from trees in the Temple's sugar bush. In Quebec, while we know the maple syrup is pure, there is a lot of blending of syrup going on, another concern for some purists.

Most Quebec syrup goes in barrels to buyers or is stored in the warehouses owned by the Producteurs et productrices acéricoles du Québec (PPAQ), where it gets blended with other maple syrup. The end consumer will never know what forest or which producer the syrup comes from. This trend toward bigger, industrial syrup-makers has been happening for a while. Maple syrup, once a spring side hustle for farmers before they could get their crops in the ground, is big business. Today, Quebec counts fewer total syrup producers, but many of the ones still in action make syrup as a full-time occupation. And the province is ambitious: The PPAQ aims to triple syrup production by 2080.

The trend toward bigger producers extends elsewhere: For example, Black Bird Management Ltd., owned by Astina Forest AG of Feusisberg, Switzerland, has in the past few years put 250,000 taps in a forest near Sault Ste. Marie, Ontario, making it one of the world's biggest syrup-makers. Crown Maple of upstate New York, the sugar bush owned by private equity investor Robb Turner, expects to have 200,000 spiles in maple trees in New York and Vermont by the end of 2026.

Perhaps this is the way of all things. People at one time baked their own bread, knit their socks, grew their food; now we have bakeries and knitting mills and industrial farms. But is there something special about maple syrup, our national

"Because flavor is subjective using current assessment techniques, yet color can be objective and is more easily distinguished with light transmittance meters, all the grading systems have focused on the color of the syrup."

MICHAEL FARRELL,
The Sugarmaker's Companion, 2013

sweetener, the elixir of our Dominion, that holds it to a higher standard—that is to say, the vaunted purity and unique-on-earth flavour that comes from toil in the glory and mystery of our deep, dark, pristine forest? Trying to find the answer to this question has taken me on quite a jaunt through Central Canada: Does industrialization of every aspect of the syrup industry threaten the very thing we cherish: that caramelly, slightly smoky, mysterious, zesty sweet taste that reminds us of youth, wilderness and home?

A POSSIBLE CULPRIT, if we agree that maple syrup does not taste as good as it used to, are the rules that reward the palest syrup with the highest price. In a windowless room in a former furniture factory in Laurierville, I meet several women wearing white lab coats working out of Quebec's Global Strategic Maple Syrup Reserve. Lined up on tables in front of them are samples of maple syrup in small clear plastic cups, next to laptops and Melba toast. These women are the maple syrup tasters.

"We are like wine tasters," explains Vicky Vézina. "We smell it, we taste it." The tasters can detect different faults in the syrup, such as syrup made from sap that is too acidic or the flavour of defoamer (the product that syrup producers use to prevent the syrup from boiling over during evaporation) or a chemical flavour. Some syrup tastes fermented. Other undesirable flavours include manure, metallic, musty, mouldy, paint, plastic, ropy, sour, or soap. For each barrel of syrup, the tasters check the Brix (an indicator of sugar content), the light penetration and the taste. Each person tastes 140 barrels before lunch, and the same number again in the afternoon.

"I taste a bit of syrup," Vézina says. "If it's no good, I rinse my mouth and eat a bit of Melba toast and bring my taste buds back to neutral."

Syrup in Quebec leaves the sugar shack two main ways: (1) producers are permitted to sell their wares directly to consumers, which accounts for about 15 percent of syrup; and (2) producers package the syrup in 205-litre steel barrels, some of which goes directly to bottling plants and the rest to the strategic reserve. Here, workers taste and then re-boil the syrup to pasteurize it, and store it in other barrels. They classify the syrup at the warehouse by grade and year of production but not by region or producer.

Vézina is an employee of the Centre ACER, a non-profit maple syrup research group that employs eighty people across Quebec. Of those, fifteen are the taste testers of the inspection division, who work from March to September. Sometimes they work at the syrup warehouse in Laurierville, but often they are on the road. Despite the scale of the PPAQ's three maple syrup warehouses, most syrup never enters these warehouses at all, especially in the years when a warmer climate results in more moderate sap production. The Province of Quebec counts fifty-six authorized buyers of bulk maple syrup. Producers send most barrels of maple syrup straight to these bottling companies. The tasters then visit each buyer. They travel as a team: one inspector and two or three auxiliaries. "We class it before it is transformed," explains Micheline Faucher, a supervisor in the ACER inspection division. Every bottle of maple syrup over 1 gallon made in Quebec must first be classed by the Centre ACER.

Maple syrup makers fear the tasters because, says Faucher, "Payment is a function of classification." She adds, "It's a big responsibility. When we train a new taster, we accompany them for the first year. The hardest is to taste, to learn the characteristics of the syrup." But despite this emphasis on taste, the main way the system classes syrup is, in fact, in terms of light penetration.

Syrup comes in four classes: golden, which transmits 75 percent of light; amber, which transmits 50 to 75 percent of light; dark, which transmits 25 to 50 percent of light; and very dark, transmitting less than 25 percent light. The lighter the syrup, the bigger the rewards: In 2024, producers received $3.40 per pound for golden syrup, with the price dropping for darker grades. Flavour defects, when the tasters detect them, also affect the price paid for a barrel of maple syrup.

Many people buy syrup in small cans from farmstands that speckle the roadsides. Quebec rules allow this roadside sale and also allow producers to supply cans of syrup directly to their local grocery store. But in Quebec, even the artisanal production of syrup faces scrutiny.

"We send our people out to buy syrup from the side of the road or the grocery stores," says Faucher. "We buy 300 or 400 cans and bottles and taste it. And if it's not good, we report it." What happens next? The PPAQ told me that "ACER does an annual benchmarking through its inspection division, at the request of the PPAQ, in Quebec. If a problem is observed, it is analyzed and sent to the competent authority to be taken care of. For example, labelling issues go the Ministry of Agriculture, Fishery and Food of Quebec."

Sometimes producers disagree with the grade that the tasters give their syrup. In 2022, for example, the tasters classed almost 400,000 barrels of maple syrup. Of those, producers appealed the ruling on 2,000 barrels. The appeals process involves a blind taste test by three tasters. About 30 percent of the appeals came down in favour of the producers. Faucher understands why some producers get upset with the class given to a barrel of maple syrup, each of which is worth about $2,000.

"These guys have hundreds of millions of dollars invested," Faucher says. "I met two big employers who brought in their syrup. Some guys haven't slept much since Christmas. They are stressed out. I met a guy who had his holding tanks full of sap and was missing a piece for his evaporator. He had all this sap that he had to boil, and he didn't know what to do."

These farmers, up to their eyeballs in bank payments, are pushed in one inexorable direction: toward syrup that is as clear as possible. But is this the right way to do things? Some argue that as the industrial machinery of Big Maple floods the market, it risks turning maple syrup into a commodity, like corn or wheat, as opposed to a delicacy, like wine. You can end up losing the subtleties of maple syrup. On a visit to the Netherlands I sampled the pure maple syrup, labelled "Product of Canada," that friends had purchased in a Dutch grocery store. There was some maple flavour, but the rich, smooth, caramel taste that I associate with good maple syrup was absent.

Harsh criticism of the maple syrup rules comes from the historic heart of Quebec's maple syrup industry: the Citadelle Maple Syrup Producers' Co-operative, which celebrates its 100th anniversary in 2025. The co-operative, Cyrille Vaillancourt's beloved baby, had a pivotal role in the creation of Quebec's maple syrup bonanza. Citadelle created standards for pure, quality maple syrup, developed methods to preserve syrup, and built a market for Quebec maple products around the world. During my pilgrimage to the heartland of the syrup sector I stopped at Citadelle's head office in Plessisville, its front door flanked by sugar maple trees. At the entrance I found a plaque that designated the building a place of historical significance, which reads in part: "With the tradition of sugaring off in the spring, maple syrup symbolizes the end of winter and is associated with Canada's national identity and way of life at home and abroad."

If maple syrup has a spiritual home, Citadelle is it: The life-size marble statue of Our Lady of the Maples—the Notre-Dame-des-Érables—stands a mute vigil here on the second floor next to the boardroom. I spoke to Sébastien Roy, who took over in 2023 as general manager of Citadelle. Roy, trained as an accountant, oversees 275 people at two Quebec maple syrup bottling plants, plus a plant in New Brunswick. The co-op exports worldwide about nine of every ten bottles of syrup it fills.

But all is not well at Citadelle. Roy unleashed a blistering critique of the PPAQ, which as the 21st century dawned took over much of the relationship with syrup farmers that previously had been in the hands of Citadelle. Roy said that under the PPAQ, maple syrup quality has declined. "We're one hundred years old," said Roy. "For the first eighty years, things went well. For the past twenty years, *ça va mal*—things are going poorly."

Roy blames PPAQ's structure, where a third party (ACER) determines the syrup quality that dictates the price paid to syrup farmers, a price set through negotiation between PPAQ and syrup bottlers. This has stripped Citadelle, Roy said, of direct influence on its syrup supply.

"We lost our direct connection to the producers," Roy said. "Before, we looked a producer in the eye. Now in the syrup business it's all about volume. The reason we created the co-operative in 1925 was to develop methods to ensure good syrup quality. Now, we are going back to where we were in 1920. The Federation got too big. Citadelle would have preferred to not have a single-buyer mechanism. We no longer pay dividends to our members."

Roy also blasted the PPAQ rule that requires Citadelle to immediately open each barrel it receives for ACER to inspect. The syrup starts to spoil, and Citadelle loses a lot of it, he said. "It's like if you went to Loblaw's and they required you to open all the cans of tomatoes before you left the store. It's a pain in the ass."

Roy, himself a third-generation syrup producer in Quebec's Gaspé region, said that in producers' quest to increase syrup production, they threaten the health of the sugar bush. "There are more and more producers who don't respect the forest," he said. "A tree that's less than 12 or 16 inches [30 or 40 centimetres] diameter, I don't touch. But a lot of producers now are tapping trees much smaller than that."

The maple sap that drips into buckets or flows through tubing during syrup season is a clear liquid that contains about 2 percent sugar. When the buds start to open on the maple trees the sap becomes milky. Syrup-makers know not to boil this milky sap. But Roy tells me that these days, in their thirst for greater syrup volume, many syrup-makers don't know when to stop. Under the rules, syrup-makers get $3.40 per pound for the highest-quality syrup and $1.90 per pound for the poorest. "Twenty to twenty-five percent of the syrup made in Quebec now has flavour defects," he said. "The buyers buy the good syrup and the bad syrup, and they mix them together. All the bad-tasting syrup gets sold in Europe."

Charts on the PPAQ website indicate that in 2019, 16.5 percent of maple syrup made in Quebec had "flavour defects." In 2022, the most recent year reported, flavour defects affected 8.8 percent of maple syrup.

Roy ended his remarks to me with on a bitter note: "If Cyrille saw what was happening today he would not be happy. In the past ten years what's happened is really not good. This is serious stuff I am talking about."

Both the PPAQ and the Maple Industry Council, which bottles most of the syrup sold in bulk in Quebec, sent me extensive written replies to Roy's remarks. Louis Turenne, president of the Maple Industry Council—of which Citadelle is a member—is also general manager at The Maple Treat, a Montreal division of Vancouver-based Rogers Sugar and the world's largest maple syrup bottler. Turenne wrote that the fifty syrup bottlers in his council "have adopted rigorous quality management practices to guarantee excellent products that meet the requirements of different markets. Consumer preferences in terms of the taste and colour of maple syrup vary from country to country and our industries must be responsive in order to offer products that meet expectations." Turenne added that the most recent maple syrup grading report, for the 2024 season, found that 7 percent of syrups graded were "flawed in terms of flavour," adding, "however, there are markets for this type of product, which is used as an ingredient in processed food, such as marinades."

The PPAQ, in a letter to me signed by president Luc Goulet, said maple syrup has had massive global success in the past two decades thanks to the producers' work to stabilize the price of syrup through the creation of a sales agency, a strategic syrup reserve, syrup production quotas and research on syrup health benefits. Thanks to the PPAQ, maple syrup, which was exported to forty countries twenty years ago, now goes to sixty countries, and sales have more than doubled, wrote Goulet, who makes syrup with his wife at his farm south of Quebec City. He added that syrup producers are the best guardians of the health of their sugar bushes, and noted that in partnership with the PPAQ a minimum diameter of 23 centimetres, or 9 inches, is now prescribed to tap a maple tree on public land; he did not mention that the PPAQ opposed this rule and compromised only when the government allowed producers to grandfather their spiles in smaller maple trees on existing leases. Goulet said the syrup sector is growing and changing; the syrup made fifty years ago is not the same as syrup made today due to continuous improvement in production practices. He acknowledged that opening barrels to taste the syrup can depreciate the product and mentioned that, to solve the problem, the syrup sector is testing a "sampling stopper" as well as sampling at the sugar shack. "The PPAQ is proud of the progress it has made, and a serious evaluation of the sector shows important improvements in the production of Quebec syrup," he added. "The results of the last twenty years show a sector that works in concert for the number-one product of the Québécois."

A GOOD PLACE for a discussion of how syrup production techniques affect flavour is Kinnear's Mills in Quebec, the home of Édith Bonneau and Stéphane Guay. The couple met in 1990 while they studied biology at the Université Laval in Quebec City. "We were les petits amoureux de la biologie [the little biology sweethearts] because we got married during our undergrad," Bonneau told me. The pair initially found work in the livestock sector, bringing in technology from Germany to organically turn pig manure into compost, for example.

More recently, the couple has focused on maple syrup. Initially they built a sugar shack on the Île d'Orléans, an island in the St. Lawrence River that had been home to the first Bonneau family to sail from France in 1610. In 2023, their son decided to settle in the Beauce region. Bonneau and Guay followed him to the area and bought a sugar bush. "I cried a little and then we moved here," Bonneau said, sitting with Guay in their light-filled kitchen outside Kinnear's Mills, a sparsely populated, heavily forested valley in Quebec's Beauce syrup heartland. Attached to their airy, contemporary home, with its cathedral ceilings and plate glass windows looking out at the forest, is their sugar shack. From here the pair of tousle-haired, bespectacled researchers run their syrup consulting business, called Érable et Chalumeaux. "It's much quieter here because on the island there is a lot of bustle. We have lots of trees to do our projects," Bonneau said. The couple are now developing the sugar bush and filling their sugar shack with new equipment, including a wood-fired evaporator. Their plan is to produce organic, carbon-neutral maple syrup.

Guay and Bonneau, whose work these days gets funding from Les Équipments Lapierre, a major Quebec manufacturer of syrup equipment, have spent a long time studying syrup to try to understand what impacts its flavour. Many ask why syrup producers have not developed a terroir system, a classification by region, as exists in wine. The challenge is that (as in wine) the provenance of the sap (or grape) is only part of the story; syrup (or wine) gets much of its flavour from the way it is boiled (or fermented).

Guay and Bonneau devised an experiment to understand what effect the region of provenance might have on the flavour of maple syrup. "I realized that if we want to study terroir, we have to start with sap and concentrate it in exactly the same way, at the same place," Guay said. The pair took sap from four regions: Mirabel, the Beauce, Île d'Orléans, and Portneuf. They boiled the sap from each region the same way in their evaporator. Now the couple had four batches of maple syrup from four distinct forest regions, all boiled into syrup using identical methods.

The couple invited eighty people to come and taste the syrup. On each of four tables was a syrup that came from one of the four regions. The visitors got this challenge: Taste the syrups and class them correctly. Next to no one was able to put any syrup on the correct table. Based on this experiment, the biologists posit that the flavour of syrup comes not from the region where the sap originates but rather the method of boiling.

"We favour a long period of simmering because we find that it brings out the good taste of maple," said Bonneau. "But others like to make syrup quickly. They don't have time."

Bonneau and Guay have studied what's known as Maillard's reaction, identified in 1912 by the French chemist Louis Camille Maillard. Maillard's reaction is a series of chemical responses that transforms sugars and proteins in food, affecting flavour, colour and aroma. This reaction is lacking, their research shows, in the syrup that comes from newer evaporators, such as the EcoVAP used at the 5 Zef in Portneuf, which emphasize speed and efficiency.

"From an electric evaporator we took syrup that tasted almost of nothing, and we recooked it," Guay said. "We added maple sap, and we cooked it for longer. And we let several people taste it, and the woman who had made pale syrup using the electric evaporator tasted the syrup, which was her own syrup that we had recooked by adding maple sap, and she said that this was truly delicious."

Guay worries that consumers may waver in their fealty to authentic maple syrup, given changes in its flavour profile. "We have to remember what the syrup of our childhood tasted like," he said. "The product is hard to sell, but if it was always tasty, it would sell."

In his book *Histoire Acéricole*, Maxime Caouette is less critical of the high technology favoured by Big Maple, noting simply that contemporary syrup-making machinery "creates syrup with a more delicate flavour and a more pale colour." Others insist that innovations in equipment have led to better syrup. Robb Turner, the US private equity investor and sugarer, asserts in the *Crown Maple Guide to Maple Syrup* that his technology, such as vacuum suction of sap from trees, dissolved air flotation filtering, reverse osmosis and a fuel-oil-powered evaporator "has vastly improved the *quality* [his italics] of the maple syrup—a twenty-first-century route to a timeless food resource."

Quality and flavour are perhaps two different things. Guay and Bonneau are perplexed by Quebec's classification system for syrup, under which producers get the highest price for the palest syrup. The couple argues that, a century ago, governments set up these categories to encourage producers to clean their equipment and produce clearer syrup. But the pricing structure now has spurred equipment innovation that produces lighter and lighter syrup, they said. They worry that syrup producers will make something so clear it is flavourless and indistinguishable from refined white sugar.

"They give you less if your syrup is dark and very flavourful, and they pay you more if your syrup is pale and it tastes like nothing," Bonneau said. "Crazy, isn't it?"

Vaudeville of the PPAQ thinks the existing system works just fine. "We reward scarcity," he said. "It's harder to make golden syrup than amber. And the darker syrup is less desired. That's the syrup from the end of the season. We have to follow what the consumer wants."

ONE EVENING a few years ago, syrup-makers gathered in the Quebec town of Mirabel for tastings and discussions of flavour. Nathalie Desrochers, a specialist in maple syrup flavour, said that while the early electric evaporators created less flavourful syrup, the equipment is improving. But she made a plea for more care and education of consumers to promote flavour in maple syrup. Desrochers suggests two maple syrup markets: one for blended maple syrup—that is, more affordable syrup; the other for specialty syrup. She suggested a system of cuvées, as exists in wine, to make syrup more valuable.

Turner, who owns Crown Maple, had a similar thought in his *Guide to Maple Syrup*, suggesting that "just as there can be high-quality chocolate, honey or olive oil," producers could develop and market a range of quality levels in maple syrup.

Guay has a simple rule of thumb: "The buyers want it to taste like maple syrup," he said. When I visited, he and Bonneau were busy at their sugar shack in Kinnear's Mills installing a new wood-fired evaporator to prepare for spring. Though they have experimented with syrup for years, the upcoming season would be the first spring that Bonneau and Guay have quota to sell syrup in barrels through the PPAQ. They knew that if they made a clearer syrup, they would get more money, but the syrup would have less flavour.

"I think what is going to be hard for us is the day that we have to make a decision," Bonneau said. "Do we want our barrel to get a good price or do we want the barrel to taste good?"

The big question in all of this is whether a materially significant sector of the population will pay a premium for syrup made in a more labour-intensive way, one that might possibly taste more flavourful. Most grocery stores just have one or two choices of maple syrup. The selection at an independent grocery store where we shop in Toronto, Fiesta Farms, suggests that some consumers do want more maple syrup choice. Fiesta offers pure maple syrup from nine companies, five from Ontario and four from Quebec. Ontario single-source syrup costs more than Quebec blended syrup. The store stocks several grades of syrup from some of its suppliers. Canadian Heritage Organic of Béland, Quebec, offers amber, dark or very dark; each 500-millilitre, or 16-ounce, bottle is $16.99. Only one company, Carrick Bros. of Madawaska, a few hours drive northeast of Toronto, advertises that its syrup is "wood-fired," for which it charges a premium of several dollars more.

Some Canadians prefer syrup made using traditional methods. Heavily forested St. Joseph Island in Lake Huron, Ontario, has a number of maple syrup producers, including Indigenous producers.

Paul Cooper grew up on the island; he became a professor of wood science at the University of Toronto. When Cooper retired, he moved back to the island. There each spring Paul makes maple syrup with his brother Harold. Even as Big Maple expands across eastern Canada and the US northeast, smaller players like the Coopers fill a niche for those who prefer syrup made old-school.

In the same sugar bush tapped by their father and grandfather, the Coopers put in 500 to 600 spiles, connected to tubes that flow by gravity down the slope in their forest and into a reservoir. The Coopers boil their sap over a wood-fired evaporator. This system has one objective, Paul told me: more flavourful syrup.

"We make a few hundred litres," said Paul, "for ourselves and a few people who like the darker, heavier, thicker syrup that we make compared to the more commercial production. We don't use vacuum. We can only do it on the part of the slope that has gravity. It's not very productive, but we hope we aren't hurting the tree too much."

The brothers also shun reverse osmosis, the use of membranes that extract water and concentrate the sap before boiling. Paul Cooper conceded that reverse osmosis shortens the boiling time, and is thus friendlier to the environment, putting less carbon into the atmosphere. However, Cooper prefers the taste of syrup that spent longer over a flame. "The maple syrup producers association is educating people toward the lighter syrup," he said, which he dislikes. His neighbours, the Gilbertson family, producers on St. Joseph Island since 1936 and one of Ontario's largest syrup-makers, make this lighter syrup; they also own a pancake house.

"We joke that at Gilbertson's you pour syrup and it runs off your pancakes," Cooper said. "The other joke is, mix up white sugar with water, stir it with a maple branch, and call it maple syrup. Here people are brought up on the stuff that is boiled and boiled and boiled over a wood fire and develops more of the chemicals that provide the flavour. When you use reverse osmosis, the actual exposure to boiling temperature is a matter of hours, whereas in our case it's probably days that we're boiling it. It's almost a burnt taste to it. We produce for a group of people who don't like the lighter stuff. It's kind of like a coffee pot that has been on the heat for a while. It develops more flavour. The viscosity is higher. It's thicker."

"We don't do it for the money," Cooper added. "We do it for the fellowship. My brother, brother-in-law, assorted friends and relatives will show up and sit around and throw wood in the fire. It's just something we have always done and want to do. It gets in our blood. It's kind of like fishing. It doesn't pay, it's just something that people like to do."

SLEIGH RIDES AND STICKY HAIR IN THE LOVE SHACK

I n Canada, the hardest days of winter coincide with Lent, a period of penitence and fasting in a landscape where nights are long, dark, and cold. Everyone stays shivering at home for months on end, and no one goes out unless they must because the roads are too icy, the night is too cold, and you have to just keep loading wood into the stove to keep warm.

Then comes spring. The days lengthen. The snow starts to melt. The sap rises. Time to go out and tap the sugar maples. Time to see other people. Time to party.

Parties for sugaring-off season gained popularity at a time when winters were much fiercer than they are of late; this was long before shopping malls, movie theatres or television.

At Easter in Quebec a song accompanies the tolls of church bells:

Hallelujah, Lent is over.
We will eat no more
Pea soup.
We will eat nice
Fat lard.
Hallelujah.

A sugaring-off celebration I attended as a child launched my love affair with maple syrup. The party served as a crash course in the tight connection many feel between the rebirth of nature and the urge to shake one's tail feathers, with maple syrup serving as the lubricant to turn voices to song. The passion of this party's participants was more palpable because of the drab surroundings in which it took place: an industrial suburb halfway between the country and the city. You can take the people out of the bush, but you can't take the bush out of the people.

In the fall of 1969, my itinerant family—my mother, my stepfather, my two elder sisters and I—moved into a rented house on the main drag in Delson, a village on the south shore of the St. Lawrence River across from Montreal. We were poor; we had no furniture. The name Delson is a mashup derived from the Delaware and Hudson Railways, which ran through the village. It was a gritty, industrial place, a bit down on its luck. The local brick factory closed the year we arrived. In the spring of 1970, at around lunchtime one day, we went to the neighbouring village of Saint-Constant to attend a party. That day I made my first conscious connection between Quebec's sacred elixir, maple syrup, and the eminence in Quebec culture of the spring ritual of sugaring off, known in French as *le temps des sucres*. I got thrown, quite unprepared, into the centre of a collective joie-de-vivre experience that linked young and old in a bacchanalian celebration of spring, a *Big Fat Greek Wedding* type of gathering that is perhaps more common in Latin cultures. And what a party it was.

I don't remember many details—I was seven years old. What linger are more impressions than facts. My sister remembers that my mom's mother, my Oma, was on a visit from the Netherlands and joined us at the event.

Sugaring-off parties are a legendary Canadian rite. The Department of Agriculture writes in the 1913 book *The Maple Sugar Industry in Canada*: "With all the advances that have taken place in manipulation, sugar-making has not lost its romantic side. 'Sugaring Off' at the sugar camps in the woods is still looked forward to by young and old who regard the event as a social feature affording rare enjoyment. The tramp to the woods on a spring day, the aroma of the escaping steam, the partaking from a wooden paddle by means of a chip-like scoop the hot syrup just on the verge of solidifying into sugar or the tasting of the 'wax' that has been allowed to harden on the clean snow all serve to inspire the reminiscent story teller and to awaken the amorous instincts of the budding youths."

The tradition of parties when the maple sap runs long predates the arrival of settlers to the New World. In the Indigenous calendar, the Sugar Moon, the first full moon of March, marks the start of syrup season. Indigenous Peoples across the range of the sugar maple tree hold celebrations to welcome the spring and the bonanza that flows from the maple. With the Maple Dance, the First Peoples thank the Creator for nature's gift. The Haudenosaunee perform a sacred dance with words, not chants, that they keep for the longhouse, a traditional dwelling. Wasauksing's Sweet Water Ceremony, also known as Maple Fest, has over the years featured contests for who has the cutest baby, who can more quickly saw a log and who can eat the most pancakes.

Settler sugaring-off parties grew in the 19th century, when maple syrup makers began to build sugar shacks as somewhere to put evaporators and boil sap into syrup. These shacks became the sites for celebrations, offering a place for family and friends to gather after the isolation of winter.

By tradition, such parties were messy events, as Quebec ethnologist Jean-Claude Dupont portrays them in his book *Le temps des sucres*. Participants had to dress warmly in old clothes since the snow was still melting and the party always ended with people smearing one another in soot and taffy. Games of hide-and-seek in the forest and snowball fights were common. During sleigh rides someone would get pushed off the sled and those still on board would call the horse to trot ahead. Whoever had fallen into the snow had to chase the sleigh to get back on. By this point the weather had warmed to near or above freezing. The snow was soft and wet, and nobody got hurt.

Affection could bloom in syrup season, too. Many old maple sugar moulds, carved of wood, took the form of hearts. In old Quebec tradition, to woo his sweetie a young man would give her a heart-shaped maple sugar candy; her first bite served as a promise, usually to get married.

Benign enough, you say. Yet in the opinion of some, the Québécois youth of two centuries ago found a way to have perhaps too much fun in the sugar bush, and the sugar shacks ran the risk of turning into dens of licentiousness.

"It's the dance of the ducks, who, in rising from the marsh, shake their tail feathers and call 'quack, quack.'"

WERNER THOMAS
"La Danse des Canards," 1957

The vicar-general of the diocese of Quebec City, the Abby Alexis Mailloux, in his 1851 Manual for Christian Parents or Duties of Fathers and Mothers in the Religious Education of Their Children, had stern words about hanky-panky in the sugar shack:

> In the rural parishes where people make sugar, risks arise when parents let their young boys and young girls go to the sugar bush without going themselves. The greatest danger is to let girls or even women spend the night. To avoid all the problems of these gatherings in the sugar shacks, parents who want to offer their children the chance to eat fresh maple sugar, would be better off to buy it themselves, and have a little party at home.

This was hardly the first report of fooling around in the sugar shack; in one court case in Trois-Rivières in 1707, a woman sought a judge's ruling against her husband for having taken his lover to the sugar shack, where, the spurned spouse alleged, he "gave her many caresses and kissed her more than once."

These days the typical sugaring-off celebration is a G-rated affair held in a hall attached to a sugar shack. When my kids were teens, we took them to a sugar shack near Quebec City, the Érablière le Chemin du Roy. First we toured the snowy sugar bush on a wagon pulled by two horses. We peeked into the room where staff boiled the sap in the evaporator to make syrup. We then sat down for a feast, where a musician sang Quebec folk songs and a high-school group sang along. Afterward everyone trooped outside to eat maple taffy: The sugarer fills a trough with clean snow. The taffy, which is syrup that has been boiled a bit further, crystallizes when it is poured over the snow. You are to pick up your popsicle stick "like a soldier with his bayonet," as one sugaring song suggests, plunge the stick into a drizzle of syrup, and then roll the candy up into a ball and put it in your mouth. On our way out we stopped at the gift shop to buy maple syrup, maple sugar, maple candy, stuffed moose dolls and assorted trinkets and knickknacks.

As the maple syrup sector has industrialized, many syrupmakers have turned their backs on visitors who, for so many generations, have sought a spring outing to the sugar bush. One report said the number of sugar shacks in Quebec that welcome guests had slid from about 425 in 2010 to just 140 in 2022. Among the challenges, the COVID-19 pandemic forced *cabanes* to close to the public for the 2020 and 2021 seasons, leading to panicked calls from people who thought that, if the sugar shack was shut, there would be no maple syrup to buy. Since reopening, these surviving sugar shacks have faced other problems, including labour shortages and a tiny window of time to make money, just six to eight weeks. Most surviving shacks rely heavily on bus tours of seniors, tourists, and school kids to keep them in the black.

Even so, a visit to a *cabane* remains a spring ritual for many in eastern Canada. A story in *Le Journal de Montréal* a couple of years ago decried the rising prices of a sugar shack experience but noted nonetheless in its headline that "People Will Pay Anything to Get Their Sugar Rush," adding as a subhead: "Because of inflation, a family of four can pay $200 at a sugar shack." The story said that the price of a meal had jumped by about $10. On the plus side, many Quebec sugar shacks are all-you-can-eat.

In the eastern part of Quebec lots of people who live in towns have family and friends in the country who live on farms and make maple syrup. This is a less formal tradition: descending on relatives to "help out" with syrup season and get your sugar fix. "Quebec City just evacuates," says David Hall, the Cowansville farmer. "All these retired police officers and retired Hydro Québec workers go out and have a party for a month."

Ontarians also head out of town to celebrate maple syrup season. Families across the province take their children to the sugar bush for March Break to see how syrup is made and eat pancakes. A full-page ad in *The Globe and Mail* promises "Five Unique Maple Syrup Experiences Just Outside the Greater Toronto Area." One spa promises: "A maple body scrub treatment is the star of the show, which will leave you feeling relaxed and your skin revived." Hart House, a student centre at the University of Toronto, offers a March "Sugaring Off!" party at the Hart House Farm in Caledon north of the city. The students may need a lesson in the finer points of maple syrup season; they promoted the event with a photograph of oak leaves taken in fall.

For more than a century, come spring Montrealers have headed to the Meunier Sugar Bush in Richelieu. Philippe Meunier, with his wife Valérie Lajoie, is the third generation to run the sugar shack. The COVID-19 pandemic crippled a lot of sugar shacks that had bank payments, Philippe said; his family survived the pandemic through lots of work, patience, and creativity. The team puts about 4,000 spiles in trees and boils the sap with a wood fire. "We wanted to keep the traditional methods," Philippe told me. "We have tourists. They want to see how it's done." Over the years the Meuniers have added activities to make it a full-day trip for families. Along with food they also offer face-painting, bouncy castles, a petting zoo, tractor rides, Fat Bike rides, and a DJ dance party. In 2024, the sugar shack was open from the end of February to the third week in April. At the height of the season they employ about one hundred people, Philippe said.

The party we attended when I was little, in 1970, was different. Yes, maple syrup flowed. But the party was about a lot more than that. There was no sugar shack or sugar bush. The party began around noon, in a big drafty one-storey hall, like a community centre common room. Many people showed up. The enthusiasm of the participants was more noticeable given the drab nature of the setting. We entered a room with linoleum floors and fluorescent track lighting, furnished with long folding tables covered in plastic tablecloths.

Ontarians usually refer to the restaurant next to their sugar shack as a pancake house; that was roughly what I had been expecting. But when we went to the front, servers with big spoons loaded our plates with baked beans, ham, scrambled eggs, sausage, bacon, white bread and butter, and *oreilles de crisse*. Translated as "ears of Christ," this treat is deep-fried salted lard, or fatback. At the last station, a woman shocked us by drenching everything on our plates in maple syrup: the eggs, the beans and the meat.

Syrup on savoury stuff like eggs and beans tasted weird; I have gotten used to it over the years. The origins of this practice may come from the First Peoples; plenty of early accounts note that Indigenous Peoples and early settlers incorporated maple sap into just about every spring meal. The First Peoples used little salt in their cooking, instead seasoning their food with maple sugar. They used maple sap and syrup as cures for heart and stomach problems; in his 1724 book Father Joseph-François Lafitau, a Jesuit missionary in Quebec described a mixture of flour and maple sugar that Mohawk Nation members packed for provisions on trips. One Indigenous tradition, since copied by settlers, involves burying a pot of syrup-soaked beans in a fire pit to cook.

Quebecers adopted and over time modified the practice of cooking meat with maple syrup and sap. Back in the early days of the sugar shack, farmers in Quebec's Beauce region would cut thick slices of pork belly and throw them directly in the evaporator pan with the boiling sap, though others shunned the practice, saying it altered the flavour of the syrup. Other sugar-makers hung salt lard above the evaporator throughout sugaring-off season; the sugary steam that rose from the evaporator, mixed with the maple wood smoke from the fire, penetrated the meat and gave it a colour and flavour that regular smoking could not equal. It does sound rather good. There was another recipe, too: During a party at the sugar shack, after the guests had eaten maple taffy, the cook would crack two or three dozen eggs, beat them and cook them in taffy.

Drenching my eggs and meat in maple syrup is not a dining habit that I have ever copied at home, though we do use maple syrup for several dishes, such as in a marinade for salmon steaks, to sweeten salad dressing and as a topping for oatmeal.

In that St. Constant sugar shack in 1970, the crowd scarfed up syrup-soaked food—*oreilles de crisse* and pickled beets and onions compensated for the sweetness. After the main course finally came the pancakes, with more syrup. People sat packed together at long tables, all talking loudly and eating at the same time. I do not remember any alcohol.

Then everyone cleared the tables and moved the furniture to the sides of the room. A band took the stage and the dancing began. It was like a wedding. Everyone danced: young and old, women and men, and children, too. The room filled with twirling, swooping, spinning, laughing forms. Traditional Quebec instruments include the fiddle and the accordion, and knocking together two spoons for percussion. Probably those instruments were there, but this being 1970, the band actually played rock. Incongruously, I remember them belting out The Beatles' "Hey Jude." That was the only song we knew.

The other song I remember is "La Danse des Canards." (In English it's called "The Chicken Dance," typically played as an instrumental.) During the refrain, hold up your hands on both sides of your face and open and close your hands to imitate a duck quacking. Then tuck your hands under your arms and flap your bent arms like wings. Then bend your knees and shake your hind quarters like a duck shaking water off its back. Finally, clap your hands four times. Somehow, we all got swept up in this merriment. For another song we linked arms with strangers and twirled around the room. What has stayed with me from all this is a sense of cultural togetherness that I had never experienced before and that I came to value about Quebec in the years that followed.

In her teen years, my sister Noelle worked several seasons at the sugar shack of the Poulins, our farm neighbours in west Quebec. She refilled coffee cups and provided pitchers of syrup so people could dump even more on their food. She recalls a lot of daytime noise and merriment, and a huge cleanup at the end.

"My strongest memory is seeing an area cleared at some point on the dance floor, and an old man getting up and starting to jig," she recalls. "That means there must have been a fiddle player there. Jigging involves dancing on the spot, by one person in this case, while showing off their fancy footwork. The rest stand around watching, cheering and clapping in admiration. The dancer would be some older farmer, fifty or sixty years old, dressed in, at most, his best plaid shirt and clean jeans. Someone who wasn't necessarily rich, well-known or even popular. But this was his time to shine."

I asked Philippe Meunier of Meunier Sugar Bush about the future of the sugar shack as a place to celebrate. He thinks the tradition will endure, though the rich food does raise eyebrows.

"I compare it to apple-picking," he said. "These are like *incontournables* in Quebec: the sugar shack and the apple orchard. They are classics." (The word *incontournable* translates literally to "unavoidable"; he means more like a staple or essential or unmissable pilgrimage.) "It still works. You have to be passionate. We work evenings and weekends. A good team is the secret to my success. My wife works with me. Alone I could never survive."

ON THE ROAD TO
FIREFLY FARM

have lived in a lot of places over the years. In 1992, while living in New York City, I met the woman of my dreams, named Mimi. In 1994, Mimi and I moved to her hometown, Toronto. Even as we settled in the downtown of Canada's biggest city, Mimi understood even better than I did how important the countryside is to me. In 2010, after looking at a lot of places, we visited an eastern Ontario farm for which she had seen an ad, just north of a village named Madoc, in Hastings County halfway between Toronto and Ottawa.

The farm was perfect: 14 hectares, or 34 acres, with hay fields in the front, a barn to store our stuff, and mostly lots of forest, swamp and pine plantations in the back, including, the ad promised, "five acres [two hectares] of sugar bush." We bought it from the neighbours, who remained on their farm to the south—thankfully. They helped us in more ways than I can list.

As with all of Canada, Indigenous Peoples occupied this land before settlers came. The property sits in Treaty 57 territory, ostensibly covered by the Crawford's Purchase of 1783, a disputed claim that extends between the Ottawa River and the St. Lawrence River and that was one of the first treaties to be negotiated in Ontario. No paper documentation of this treaty exists. The Hastings and Prince Edward District School Board notes that its territory, which includes the land in Madoc, "is part of the traditional territories of the Haudenosaunee and Anishinaabe people." I am grateful for the opportunity to look after this land.

The first few years we camped during summer in a tent in the barnyard. At night fireflies sparkled in the hayfields and treated us to a light show, so Mimi named the place Firefly Farm. A few years later, in one of the hayfields, we built a cottage.

My personal adventure in the maple syrup business on our farm began slowly. One spring I tapped a few trees and hung buckets on the taps. I hauled the sap by toboggan to our fire pit, lit a wood fire, and poured the sap into a stainless-steel pan like the kind hotel breakfast buffets fill with scrambled eggs. I coaxed the sap to a boil. Our neighbour, Gunter Vierich, a retiree of German extraction, walked over for a chat.

"During the war we had no sugar in Germany," Gunter said. "We had beet juice, and we boiled it down over open fires. We had to stir for hours. We had to be very careful not to burn it!"

I assured him I would not burn it.

I burned it.

We boiled and boiled for days and eventually ended up with enough sap concentrate to fill one of Mimi's prized

Le Creuset cooking pots. We had a Coleman stove, left over from our first few years of camping in the barnyard. As evening fell, I put the stove on the front porch of the cottage, lit the flame and put the pot of concentrated sap on the stove. Then I went inside to join Mimi and the kids who sat curled up by a crackling fire watching *Ferris Bueller's Day Off.* A little while later I opened the front door. A pillar of black smoke rose from the pot. I had ruined the syrup. Several days' work went up in smoke; Mimi was livid about the Le Creuset. Bueller's day ended better than mine.

That summer I began to build a sugar shack. In my mind's eye I pictured the sugar shack of my childhood, a classic wooden structure with a peaked roof and a cupola. In the shack's centre stood a big, gleaming stainless-steel evaporator. Attached to the shack was a woodshed, into which my step-father corded dry stove wood.

Mimi found some plans online from Vermont for a sugar shack, which seemed legit. But I could not build it alone. Enter our son.

When our kids were small, we sent them to summer day camps: cheerleading camp, soccer camp, sewing camp, swim camp. We then devised a week when our son Frits would come with me out to our farm in Madoc; we called it Papa Camp. (Somehow our daughter Tallulah escaped Papa Camp.) This camp, in fact, morphed into sugar shack construction camp, an anodyne name to sanitize a sadistic endeavour.

The site we chose sits in the woods, next to the ruins of an old sugaring operation and a ten-minute walk from the house. We schlepped all tools and nearly all materials to the site in our arms or using a little wagon on the lawn tractor. In winter we hauled materials on a toboggan.

That first summer, my son and I tackled the labour-intensive excavation and cement work needed to install the four footings on which the shack would sit. Unfortunately, Papa Camp coincided with the worst time of year for mosquito infestation—a suitable time to stay *out* of the woods. We bought Frits a bug shirt. I also pitched a tent near the building site as our bug-free break spot. We forbade entry to Coco, our chocolate lab, so she would park herself at the screen door of the tent and peer through forlornly. Frits would pantomime "But I want to be tent doggie."

After pouring the footings, we framed the floor and laid the floor joists. There is no electricity at the site, so we had to saw all the lumber by hand. My wife stayed in Toronto and worked her ass off, showing no end of patience with all my quixotic drudgery.

I realize now that whoever drew the sugar shack designs I used intended the structure to be more visually pleasing than functional. The main flaw is the wood floor. A sugar shack floor must bear a lot of weight—that is, an evaporator filled with sap and stove wood. More critically, the fire one stokes to boil sap produces tremendous heat and flying sparks. Ergo, most sugar shacks have poured concrete floors to minimize the risk of fire. Typically, builders situate the shack at a spot with a hill behind, onto which one can drive a vehicle and also easily transfer sap, pulled by gravity, to a vessel in the shack. I neglected these details, too.

Once the floor was complete, I moved on to the walls. The project advanced slowly, but I was in no rush. A friend suggested a company down the highway who could build the roof trusses. I took the blueprints there and a young woman drew the trusses in AutoCAD, a useful piece of design software, in half an hour. The company delivered the trusses to our farm, and I loaded them into a wagon pulled by a tractor, which was driven by my generous neighbour Gunter, who was by then in his late eighties. A local carpenter raised the trusses on the frame.

The kindness of neighbours was central to this passion project. As winter loomed, I realized I had no hope of putting on a roof before the snow fell, so another neighbour, Kelly Cook, consented to help me stretch a tarp over the sugar shack frame. Dawn broke on the chosen November morning with an evil wind out of the west and torrential rain. Kelly rolled into the forest on his four-wheeler, dressed in camouflage rain gear, knee-high steel-toe rubber boots, gloves, and a smile that hid a grimace. Somehow, we climbed onto the roof frame. Like mariners on a galleon tossed in a foaming ocean tempest who clamber up the masts and cling to the rigging, we clutched the wildly flapping tarp and used rope to lash it to the trusses. A lifetime's supply of maple syrup may not compensate Kelly for his valour on that day.

The next summer my sister Lola came by with her cordless drill; she and another contractor and his son helped affix the tin roof. By this point the project had become a constant preoccupation for me. When I was back in Toronto walking the dog, I dreamed of my sugar shack. On a neighbour's lawn I came upon a house's worth of windows. I carried the windows home in several trips, strapped them to the car roof to bring to the farm, and then dragged them on a wagon to the building site. Canadians obsessively insulate structures to keep out cold and heat; a sugar shack should be the opposite of airtight, to let out steam. The more windows the merrier, especially since, with no electricity, I needed maximum natural light.

Then the COVID-19 pandemic hit. Frits could find no summer job, so I employed him again on the sugar shack project. With the frame of the shack now in place, we needed wood. Some of our forest is red pine trees that the previous owners, the Vieriches, planted in 1995 in rows. The pines, now the height of houses, needed thinning. But there was a problem we didn't foresee. In such a forest when you cut down a tree it catches its top in the branches of its neighbours and remains upright. When the first tree we cut got stuck, we walked sheepishly over to Gunter's for help. He tied a rope to the trunk and the other end to his tractor and pulled the tree down. We knew from his face he would not do that a second time. So, we innovated. First Frits climbed each tree and tied a rope halfway up. We tied the rope to the lawn tractor, positioning the tractor out of range of the falling tree. I cut the tree with the chainsaw, and Frits gunned the tractor and sometimes the tree fell. Some logs proved too heavy for the tiny machine to move. Then we would place a log crossways under the log, and roll one log over the other. We described our technique to Gunter. "You guys are going back to the Stone Age," he said. Laughter is a great balm in such travails.

We hired a guy with a portable sawmill to cut the pine into planks, which became the walls of the sugar shack.

The Home Hardware store in Madoc, come spring, displays an aisle of equipment for the backyard sugaring-off enthusiast: spiles, both plastic and metal; buckets and lids, also in one's choice of plastic or metal; filters for purifying the syrup; and glass bottles in several sizes, including bottles in the form of a maple leaf.

Such stores catering to the amateur syrup-boiler are common across eastern Canada. David Briggs of Briggs

"There are places in the maple forest that bring back memories, such as the place where the horse got stuck, the big rock under which a mother bear was hiding with her cubs, and the crows' corner."

JEAN-CLAUDE DUPONT,
Le temps des sucres, 2004

Maple in New Brunswick is the Moncton distributor for Lapierre, a Quebec syrup equipment maker. He sells everything from tubing for bigger producers to buckets and spiles for hobbyists. He warned of the addictive attraction of the sugar bush.

"It's the maple disease," David said. "There's no cure. I always tell people when they come in the door. They buy ten pails and I say, 'I warn ya. It's ten this year, and next year you'll be looking at your neighbour's trees.' A year later they come in again, laughing, and admit that I was right."

Dr. Tom Beckley, a sociologist in the Forestry faculty at the University of New Brunswick, is another maple syrup hobbyist. On their land in Keswick Ridge, he and his partner put in one hundred taps to collect sap for syrup. He has type 1 diabetes. "I wondered whether that would affect my enjoyment of making maple syrup," he said. It turns out, although he doesn't consume much syrup, he loves to make it. He has the maple fever. "We bought a portable sawmill and now we are going to build a sugar shack," he told me. He's teamed up with his neighbour to buy an evaporator. "We gift a lot of the syrup away," Beckley said. "We supply my partner Louise's family in Ottawa and my family in Maine. My neighbour is a trapper. We traded trapping services to get woodchucks and raccoons out from our garden in exchange for garlic and maple syrup. And he gave us some venison, too."

Maple syrup these days has a cachet that is attracting a new generation. Karen Ennis, who makes maple syrup at her farm in Lanark County, Ontario, mentioned her granddaughter Jessica's involvement in the family's maple syrup business. Jessica spent time in the sugar shack during the season, helping to fill containers with hot syrup.

"When she was in grades seven, eight and nine, her dad would take her to the local farmers' market and she would sell maple syrup," Karen says. "Totally proud. When I was growing up, I was a country bumpkin. Now people are proud to produce maple syrup."

As my sugar shack construction project crept along, I began to make maple syrup beside the new structure, on the ruins of the old sugaring-off operation. These ruins consist of a U-shape of crumbling concrete about waist height, with various discarded buckets and lengths of stovepipe, rusted beyond use and half-submerged in generations of dead leaves. I found iron bars among the detritus, laid them across the U and put a new sap pan, about the size of a writing desk, on top. Each spring I would excavate my boiling spot, digging a car-size heap of snow from the ruins. Then I'd lie in the snow and light a fire. My sister Sylvia and her husband Franc, who live down the road near Perth, would come over—cans of beer in hand—to help gather and boil sap. As we stood shivering in the inevitable snowfall, trying to get cozy in a snowbank while coaxing the sap to a boil, my sister would look over at the building project and ask, "Hey, Pete, are you ever going to finish the sugar shack?"

Sometimes when I am struggling to make maple syrup with my limited knowledge and primitive methods, I go to a neighbour for solace, inspiration, camaraderie and beer or whisky. Steve Needham is owner of O'Hara Sugar Maples, just east of our farm; his sugar shack sits in a clearing in the forest. One Saturday in early February I paid a visit. A beagle puppy greeted me with a happy bark. Although no smoke rose from any of the many chimneys jutting out of the jaunty red tin roofs, I guessed there was probably someone inside.

I walked past a vintage yellow Ski-Doo half-covered in snow to a door with snow shovels beside it that read "Kitchen." I knocked and a voice said, "Come in."

At the end of a long pine table sat a big man, writing something on a piece of paper. His left hand held a lit cigarillo. He wore a dark blue sweatshirt embroidered with "O'Hara Sugar Maples." A beckoning warmth came from the woodstove.

"Hello," said Steve, whose friends call him Bubba. "Would you like a beer?" He motioned behind his back. "Grab one out of the door of the fridge."

I opened a beer, tossed my coat on a couch and sat down on a long bench that flanked the table. Daisy, the puppy, stood with her paws on the bench looking for more rubs. On a wall a TV played a news channel. Bottles of maple syrup lined the shelves beside the TV. Strewn on the table were bottles of ketchup and relish, water bottles, several TV remotes, a can of Deep Creep lubricant, rolls of labels for O'Hara Sugar Maple, a jar filled with Sharpies, gloves, a tin cash box and a box containing 1,000 plastic spiles mailed from the manufacturer, Ératube of Saint-Hyacinthe, Quebec.

A mural on the wall depicted a sugar bush in early spring, with wooden buckets hanging from the trees, snow melting on the ground, a barrel and steam rising from the cupola of a sugar shack—a stark contrast to maple syrup season in this forest today. On my way in I'd passed groves of sugar maples linked by a webwork of blue plastic tubing. A man in a high-visibility vest used a mallet to tap a spile into a hole in a maple tree. The tubes stay up all year; each spring, Needham's crew drills a hole in each sugar maple tree to insert a new plastic spile.

"I have six guys out there tapping the south side right now," Needham told me. "This is the earliest I've ever tapped."

The evaporator stood cold and dark in the big boiling room next door. Needham said he expected to light his evaporator later in the week.

Needham first made maple syrup at age fourteen, in the maple forest of the farm next door to his home. It was a dairy farm, and Needham worked there part-time; he helped to milk forty-five cows morning and night. One spring Needham asked the farmer for permission to dig some sap buckets out of his barn and tap some trees.

"I had a '68 Ski-Doo, which is the year I was born. It's parked outside. And a sleigh. I filled 5-gallon pails with sap. I stacked some concrete blocks in the driveway of my house and set a potash kettle [a big black iron kettle] on them. I sat out on the driveway, boiled sap, and did my homework and listened to the hockey game on the radio."

The scene sounds idyllic; the result proved less so. "I made the most horrible-tasting shit," said Needham. Unbowed, Needham became a subcontractor. A farmer nearby bought maple sap. Needham borrowed his tractor. He converted a manure spreader into a trailer, which held ten drums of sap. Needham tapped his trees, collected the sap and hauled it to the farmer, who tested the sap and paid Needham based on its sugar content. Needham could make $300 for a season with this toil—okay money in the 1980s, he noted. But he realized that the farmer was making a lot more for the syrup.

In his early twenties Needham built his first sugar shack. The facility in which he now works is his third. Needham today is one of the bigger maple syrup producers in this part of Ontario. Needham sits on the board of the Ontario Maple Syrup Producers' Association, which represents 600 maple syrup producers in the province.

Dwarfed by the scale of Quebec's syrup industry, Ontario makes just 3 percent of Canada's maple syrup. Even so, this syrup supplies some of the province's demand. Needham is trained as a plumber, which, when you think of all the pipes, hoses, tanks, pumps, valves and assorted tubing required to make maple syrup at any scale, is a useful skill set. He has been so successful that several years ago he quit plumbing to focus on syrup. O'Hara Sugar Maples syrup fills the shelves of grocery stores throughout the region; once a week Needham drives to deliver to Metro supermarkets in Toronto.

Needham looked down at his smartphone. "I may have to go pick up the boys," he said. He dialled and spoke to his son, Jager, a plumbing apprentice at a college nearby.

"Do I need to come and get you?" Needham asked.

"No," came a voice. "We have the bike. I will walk."

A few minutes later, the kitchen door opened and a teen boy came in. He wore a black top hat with a wide brim, blue overalls, black vinyl chaps and what resembled a bright orange Mexican serape. I was taken aback: he looked dressed for Halloween.

Needham introduced me to the boy, explaining that he is Amish. Soon the kitchen filled with teen boys; two others wore similar top hats. The Amish wear straw hats much of the year; in the winter they protect the straw with a black hat-cover. The boys stacked yellow cordless electric drills in a box and threw their orange tapping vests on top of my coat on the couch. Each went to the fridge, took a beer and sat around the table.

The three Amish boys in hats were brothers; the other three, Madoc high-school students, wore baseball caps. The Amish boys lit cigars and sat sipping beer, puffing and grinning. Wood chips from the tree-drilling job clung to their sleeves.

I asked the first boy about his chaps. "They keep my pants dry," he said. His twin brother, across the table, said of his chaps, "Mine have holes in them from shoeing horses." Poking out from beneath them he wore insulated black rubber boots. This was the clothing I wish we'd had as kids in Quebec.

Needham ran over the agenda for the next few days: cleaning extractors, cleaning the concentrate tanks, and lots more tapping. The boys had already been tapping for several days.

The assembled discussed the day's work: They had begun at nine and finished at four. They agreed they had worked six hours. Needham also threw in hot dogs for lunch, beer and cigars, and transport in his truck.

"Six hours at $20 an hour, $120," Needham said. He opened the cash box and pulled out three $100 bills and three $20s, and handed them to the boy with the horseshoe-nail holes in his chaps.

That quintessentially Canadian spring activity, tapping maple trees and collecting sap to boil into syrup, relies today, even as it did when Needham was a boy, on the labour of teenagers.

"I always liked having money in my pocket," Needham says, to explain what lured him into making maple syrup before Ontario allowed him to have a driver's licence. The boys around the table here appeared to feel the same way. They were all smiles as they filed out of the sugar shack. The sun had turned orange in the west and long shadows of the bare sugar maple trees spread across the snowy lot as the boys piled into Steve and Jager's pickup trucks for the drive to their homes.

This is Needham's favourite time of year. He is filled with excitement about what the season will bring. "I just took a notion to it," he says, of sugaring off. "It's a disease. I just like the flavour of maple syrup. And there is something about the sun in the spring. It's beautiful being in the bush."

In 2023, my sugar shack was finally ready for inauguration. Then I caught COVID. I went to Madoc to recuperate with the dogs. The frigid air, snow and sunshine revived me. I charged my cordless drill, put it in a backpack, put on my cross-country skis and took the dogs with me to the sugar shack. Over a few days I hung forty buckets on maple trees. Some of this work took place in a blizzard.

After ten days of night sweats, soup, Kleenex and Somerset Maugham's *Collected Short Stories: Volume Two*, I tested negative. Back in Toronto I watched the weather report for Madoc. The temperature rose above freezing for a few days. It was not weather for much sap to run. So, at the beginning of March when Mimi and I drove out to Madoc, my expectations were low. To my surprise, in the woods we found many buckets overflowing with sap, frozen solid. This foreshadowed a classic high-octane drama of maple syrup season, with more variables than my little brain could handle. Such is syrup season: the collision of many forces, some of which one cannot control: weather, visitors, dogs, snow, ice, fire, family, alcohol.

Frits, our son, planned to come for the weekend from Kingston, where he studied at Queen's University. He drove up with his roommate in her low-slung Honda Civic with tinted windows, big speakers and BC plates. Another of Frits's roommates announced he would ride his bicycle from Kingston through the snow, about 120 kilometres, or 74 miles—a bad idea. But who can talk sense to kids?

Bless Mimi, who had come for the weekend laden with food. Next variable: In the sugar shack was a brand-new evaporator, a gift from Mimi for my sixtieth birthday, made by a blacksmith in French-speaking eastern Ontario. It's good for up to one hundred spiles, I think. The thing sat in pieces in my sugar shack for months because, having built a sugar shack, I never considered the job of punching a hole in the roof to install an evaporator chimney to exhaust smoke from the fire.

Again I leaned on a neighbour. Kelly and Shirleanne Cook have a son named Kyle who is a millwright. Kelly said Kyle could come over with his electric saw and cut a hole in the roof. But when the day arrived, I learned that Kyle had been out late with friends and was taking it easy that morning. At some point he roused himself to come over on his four-wheeler. On arrival, Kyle climbed a ladder without much comment and cut a hole in the sugar shack roof.

Outside the sugar shack I had built a platform. A flight of wooden stairs go up to the platform where a barrel sits. From the barrel a pipe runs through a hole in the wall into the evaporator. In theory, pour the sap in the barrel and it flows to the spot where you boil it. But the sap was frozen solid in the buckets; ice chunks will not flow into an evaporator. I also needed to line the firebox of the evaporator with fire bricks, which I didn't have yet. My to-do list for getting the sugar shack finished was growing.

Throughout the process, our dogs provided humour and entertainment to lift our spirits. They love to stick their schnozzes in the collection pails and drink the maple sap. Sometimes I would ski over to the neighbours with our puppy Rook in tow to pick up their two-year-old yellow lab, Norman. Norman and Rook are like brothers: they love to jump and push each other into a snowbank. Each lunge ends with one dog lying on his back in the snow. The other jumps on top and chews the face. This lasts a long time.

Frits and his friends gathered the buckets of frozen sap using toboggans and pails. It is a bit of a trick to collect frozen sap. Sometimes you have to bang on the aluminum bucket to dislodge the sap. We have done this over the years and our buckets are dented.

Now we had a lot of frozen sap. What to do? Light a fire in the evaporator and transfer the blocks of frozen sap into the pan. The chunks of sap will melt, and at some point you have an evaporator full of sap.

This was my technique for years. Then I read how Indigenous Peoples made maple sugar. Because water freezes before sugar does, they often would let the sap freeze and toss out the ice, leaving a small amount of sap concentrate. So I dumped each frozen sap block out of the bucket and then punctured each block with a blow from a hammer. There was indeed some sweet liquid inside, which I poured into the evaporator, discarding the ice. Not that this sped up the sap-boiling process much. Making syrup always takes longer at the start of the season. You start with sap that is 2 percent sugar; you need to get it to 66 percent sugar. After two days of hauling sap Frits and his friends had to return to school, but the syrup was not ready. We had to pay them off in last year's syrup.

Two weeks later our daughter Tallulah came from Montreal with her boyfriend José; three of her friends came from Toronto. Now we had lots of help. During their visit the sugar shack saw its inaugural rager, but I was too tired to attend. After supper, the five of them loaded a toboggan with lanterns and food and drink and games and a portable speaker. From the cottage Mimi and I watched the lantern lights bob across the dark field of snow and into the forest. The sugar shack filled with laughter, merriment, dancing and a drinking game of Jenga. They found some gin. They scooped hot sap concentrate from the evaporator and added gin. "It was delicious," said Tallulah. "Sugar shack elixir." I had asked them to please keep the fire roaring under the syrup pans. In the morning I found the fire stone-cold, and the concentration of sugar in the evaporator pan not much changed. It turns out in spite of many inebriated attempts to stoke the fire, it spluttered because the firewood I'd gathered was still a bit green and burned poorly. I still have much to learn about making maple syrup.

I found some dry wood, lit the fire and hunkered in for a day of boiling. Tallulah and her friends hauled sap to the sugar shack and washed empty bottles. Pizza was ordered. At dusk the syrup was ready: I opened the evaporator tap to pour out the molten prize. We filtered, and bottled, and videoed, and laughed and hauled sleighs of jars filled with hot syrup through the woods in the dark night back to the house. In my childhood, neighbouring farmers on our road gave us their empty rum and whisky bottles, which we would sterilize and fill with syrup. Old habits die hard. These days I reuse every jar, be it from chicken korma or Dijon mustard, for my syrup. My friends and neighbours know of this habit; it's not uncommon for me to find empty bottles in my mailbox from those who want a refill.

After a four-day visit by Tallulah and her posse, we wound up with a great deal of maple syrup. We proudly lined up dozens of bottles on the front porch.

A year later it was sugaring-off season again. But spring 2024 was like none I had ever seen—the snows of February and March never came. In February I stayed a few days at

Firefly Farm on the pretext that I would work full-time on my manuscript, by that point almost due. Of course I had to slip out and tap some maple trees. After I returned to the city, the neighbours gathered my sap and filled the evaporator. (Thanks, neighbours.) In March I visited again. I lit a fire in the evaporator and boiled the sap, but not to the point of syrup. That week, the temperature stayed above zero every night. What snow there had been melted. The sap ran hardly at all.

My sister Sylvia drove over with a friend. We lit the fire in the sugar shack, mostly because it was cozy. Sap was scarce. We picked up a few thimbles full and then went back to the cottage for lunch, leaving what sap there was boiling in the evaporator. After lunch Sylvia asked, "Should we walk back out to the sugar shack?" I demurred. I thought the fire would go out and the sap would cool without becoming syrup.

I returned to the shack the next morning. I had burned the syrup once again. I realized that with my book deadline looming I was trying to accomplish too much. Black hunks of carbonized sugar coated the bottom and sides of the pan. By some miracle, there was some syrup in the pan, too. I managed to fill several jars with the sweet stuff. Then I filled the pan with water and left it to soak overnight. The next day I scraped the pan with a nail bar. A neighbour came out and helped me pour the burned gunk onto the forest floor. After another good wash, the pan was as good as new.

I was undeterred. I would try again. I know I will never excel as a syrup producer. That is not my goal. I have fun, friends and family gather, some syrup results. This is everything that I want.

WHAT IT BOILS DOWN TO

In 1913, Frances Densmore, an American ethnographer working for the US Smithsonian Institution, published a 314-page book, *Chippewa Music—II*, in which she catalogued 180 songs of the Chippewa Nations of Wisconsin and Minnesota. (Chippewa is a US.spelling; Canada uses the term Ojibwe. The Chippewa and Ojibwe are one First Nation.) Densmore used a phonograph to record, and then transcribe, all manner of song, from dream songs to war songs to love songs to moccasin games songs and songs connected with the gift of a pony, among others. On page 231, one can find the "Maple Sugar Song," in which Mec'kawiga'bau, a Chippewa performer whose name translates to "stands firmly," sang *Sin-ze-ba-kwat e – ta me-no-ka-go-yan*. Translation: "Maple sugar is the only thing that satisfies me."

When I was a child, growing up in a sugar bush in Quebec, I developed my own reverence for maple syrup, but it was only in researching this book that I came to truly appreciate the debt that Canada owes to the First Peoples—school had never taught me the Indigenous origins of our emblematic condiment.

The importance of maple sugar to the Indigenous Peoples cannot be overstated. Each spring for thousands of years, the First Peoples moved their camps into the maple forests. They would tap the trees to reap the sap or sweet water, used as a medicine, and boil this sap to make maple sugar, a prized sweetener. On a page adjoining the words and music in Densmore's book, black-and-white photos depict *ma'kuks*, conical containers made from birch bark and sewn with spruce roots—the containers that the Chippewa/Ojibwe on both sides of the Great Lakes used to store and trade maple sugar, which the First Peoples called *nasa'igun*.

Like the "Maple Sugar Song," other song titles in the book, such as "Two Foxes Face Each Other," "The Thunderbirds" and "Song of the Deer Dancing," remind us of the intimate relationship the First Nations share with the natural world.

Brenda Murphy, a professor of society, culture and environment at Wilfred Laurier University, tells us that the First Peoples view maple trees as active agents who unselfishly share their sap with us each spring. "In return," she notes from Indigenous teaching, "the sugarbush needs to be treated with respect and honoured through ceremony and good stewardship practices."

The First Peoples taught European settlers how to process maple sap into sweetener, but sadly we did not honour the natural world in the same ways. Instead we silenced Indigenous song, forced Indigenous children into schools that stripped them of their culture, pushed Indigenous communities onto reservations and cut down many of the forests in which they thrived.

Each day all around us we see signs, in the form of floods, droughts and wildfires, that our exploitive economy, which views the natural world as an inexhaustible resource we may plunder for our own comfort, has wreaked havoc on our environment and left the planet in a precarious state, threatening our survival. At the University of Toronto, where I teach forestry, we strive to integrate the First Peoples' Traditional Ecological Knowledge into the curriculum, which is a component of our efforts, in the Masters of Forest Conservation, to train the next generation of foresters who will nurture the natural environment into the future.

Transforming our approach to one that respects our ecosystems is a challenge that extends well beyond the sugar bush, and yet the lens of sugaring is as good as any to remind us that it is only through the tender, loving care of our forests and their inhabitants that we can thrive.

Indigenous Peoples and settlers have made and enjoyed maple syrup for a long time. We will keep making maple syrup for a long time to come. The maple syrup made across Canada today is pure and delicious.

Yes, we can have adult conversations about flavour and tend the sugar bushes with care. Most of all, however, we need to transition to a low-carbon economy and lead the world out of a dependence on fossil fuels to reverse climate change and save maple syrup season.

The First Peoples use song, dance and celebration to venerate the sugar bush. Quebec maple syrup producers in the 1950s embraced Our Lady of the Maples, a Madonna who has brought them much good fortune. In my sugar shack I keep a white plaster bust of Winston Churchill, given to me by a friend. The former prime minister sits on a windowsill and glowers at my evaporator.

Churchill famously pledged to never surrender. I agree. I suggest we channel the Churchillian stiff upper lip and get to work preserving and restoring our nation's natural splendour: our majestic forests. Canada is a nation of unmatched beauty. To paraphrase Churchill: We must not flag or fail. We must go on to the end. We must defend our maple trees, whatever the cost may be.

GLOSSARY OF MAPLE SUGARING TERMS

Acériculture This Quebec-born word fuses *agriculture* and *acer*, the Latin word for "maple." *Acériculture* translates to "sugaring." An *acériculteur* is a man who makes syrup; an *acéricultrice* is a woman syrup maker.

Evaporator A stove used to boil maple sap into syrup. Traditionally one lights a fire of stovewood in the evaporator to boil the sap that sits over the fire in pans. Excess water rises as steam into the air. Forty litres of sap yields one litre of syrup. Newer evaporators use natural gas, propane, fuel oil or electricity to boil the sap; the most advanced evaporators recycle the steam to further heat the sap.

Maple syrup barrel Most producers ship the bulk of their maple syrup in barrels that hold 205 litres, or 53 gallons. Counting quantities of syrup can get tricky. Quebec producers measure syrup in pounds. A barrel contains 330 pounds of syrup. Ontario uses litres.

Maple taffy A candy made from thickened maple syrup. Also called *sugar-on-snow*; in French, *la tire*. To make maple taffy: fill a large container with snow and compact the snow. Boil maple syrup in a pan until a drop of syrup in a glass of cold water forms a ball. Pour the hot syrup in strips on the snow. Guests each poke a popsicle stick into a strip of cooling syrup and wind into a lollypop of warm sticky candy.

Mockuks or *makaks* The Anishnaabe word for containers made from birch bark, sewn with spruce roots and sealed with pine resin, made by Indigenous Peoples to collect and transport sap as well as to store and ship maple sugar. Used up to the early 20th century.

PPAQ Acronym for Producteurs et productrice acéricoles du Québec, or Quebec Maple Syrup Producers. This legal cartel of maple syrup farmers in Quebec controls three quarters of the world's maple syrup, sets production quotas and fixes the price of maple syrup, in negotiation with syrup bottling companies, based on its grade.

Reverse osmosis A mechanical process by which pumps send maple sap through a semi-permeable membrane that retains the sugar molecules and expels a demineralized water. This process removes most water from the sap, reducing the amount of time needed to boil the liquid into maple syrup.

Spile A spout, or tap, inserted into a hole drilled in a maple tree to extract the sap. The word *spile* possibly comes from the Dutch word *spijl*, for peg.

Sugaring off The six-week period, sometime between early February and the end of April (depending on latitude), during which one can tap sugar maple trees, thanks to freeze–thaw cycles, to obtain their sap. The Anishnaabe say *iskigamizige* or "sugaring off" takes place during the "sugar moon." Before canning technology, Indigenous Peoples and colonists mostly made maple sugar—by boiling maple syrup until it crystallized. Maple sugar was easier to preserve and to trade. This begat other terms such as "sugar bush," "sugar shack," "sugar maple" and "sugaring." In French, sugaring-off season is *le temps des sucres*.

Tapping The process of drilling holes in maple trees in order to insert spiles to extract sap. Tapping takes place before the start of syrup season, sometime in January through March. Metal spiles require a 7/16-inch hole; plastic spiles used for vacuum tubing sap extraction systems are typically 5/16 inch. A large maple can support two or even three spiles. The industry in both the US and Canada uses Imperial measurements for spile and tubing diameters.

ACKNOWLEDGEMENTS

This book owes a great debt to syrup producers who took their time with me, including Chris Chomyshyn and his team at Wasauksing Maple Products, Angèle and Nelson Grenier (for interviews and meals), Alain Gauthier and everyone at Les 5 Zef, Édith Bonneau and Stéphane Guay, Randall Goodfellow, David "Fish" Hall, Philippe Meunier and Valérie Lajoie, Steve Needham (for his thoughts, rye whisky and books), Brian Bainborough and Tom Shaw, Karen Ennis, David and Sherry Briggs, Jean-Francois Laplante, Éric Caron and Philippe Meunier, plus, at Érablière Sigewigus, Sébastien Roy, Jonathan Desjarlais and Frédéric Basque, among others.

Thank you to Terry Shaw of the Nation Micmac de Gespeg, Dominic Beaudry of Wiikwemkoong Unceded Territory and Dave Rice of Wasauksing First Nation, for wisdom.

The Toronto Public Library weathered a denial of service attack while I was writing this book. This attack crippled the library and drove home how much I rely on one of the world's most extensive public libraries, with its millions of books stored at one hundred branches. The library also brought me books from as far away as the Library of the University of Regina through the free inter-library loan system.

Thank you to Geneviève Martineau at the Producteurs et productrices acéricoles du Québec and Lynne Faubert, a writer in Montreal.

Thank you to Narissa Somji and Toby Sanger, who put me up in Ottawa during my research at the glorious Library and Archives Canada, where I got help from Indigenous archivist Mélanie Benard, and archivists Patricia Bergeron and Gaya Déry. In Montreal librarians at the inviting Bibliothèque et Archives nationales du Québec helped a great deal. In Saint-Romuald, Quebec, thank you to the Gar family for shelter and sustenance. Thank you, Dave Pott, woodworker in Trois-Rivières, for support.

Thank you to Julien Beauchamp-Laliberté, Crown prosecutor in Trois-Rivières, retired Sûreté du Québec detective Luc Briand and Yves Charlebois, mayor of Saint-Ferdinand, Quebec. At the Institute of Forestry & Conservation, University of Toronto, thank you to Dr. Sandy Smith, Dr. Sean Thomas and Eric Davies. Thanks to Kim Allen at Forest NB and Louise Poitras at the New Brunswick Maple Syrup Association.

Luc Dupont mailed me out-of-print books from his father, the remarkable ethnologist Jean-Claude Dupont from Laval University, whose book *Le temps des sucres* is an inspiration for this one.

Thanks a lot to my sister Noelle MacFarlane, who read an early draft of the book. Thank you to Jay Sheeks, who taught me to make and to respect maple syrup. Thank you to my mom, Marianne Dekking. At her insistence I attended École Sainte-Jeanne-d'Arc in Papineauville, Quebec, where I learned French. French was vital for this project. I interviewed many French-speakers in Quebec and New Brunswick, and many of the scholarly works, books, magazines, newspapers and websites I consulted in my research are in French. *Merci, Madame Séguin et Madame Bissonnette!*

Thank you, Mimi Maxwell, my wife, best friend and most loyal supporter, whose professional success has floated us through my quixotic periods, and who found our farm and bought me an evaporator.

Thank you to our children, Tallulah and Frits Kuitenbrouwer, for unwavering love and for bringing friends to help gather sap and make syrup.

This book started with an email from Anna MacDiarmid, publishing manager at Doubleday Canada, whose writing skills were clear from her first note, which began, "Please allow me to introduce myself." Anna's vision made *Maple Syrup* possible. Thank you, Anna.

Thank you to Michael Mouland, my agent whom I pay in maple syrup. Thank you to author John Zada, who helped with my proposal and with counsel throughout. Thank you to Matthew Thomas, PhD, whose maple research is impeccable. Thanks also to Andrew Munger for support and to Lars Christiansen, who gave us so many buckets and spiles and lids. Thank you to our neighbours, the Cooks—Shirleanne, Kelly, Kyle and Taylor—for help with sugaring, and Gunter and Elsa Vierich, for support throughout.

BIBLIOGRAPHY

Austen, I. (2012, December 19) In $18 million theft, victim was a Canadian maple syrup cartel. *The New York Times.*

Baril, H. (2019, April 14). Dix ans pour rendre le sirop d'érable plus vert. *La Presse*, p. 4.

Beauchamp-Laliberté, J. (2022, March 31). L'argent, c'est le nerf de la guerre du crime organisé. (M. Dumont, Interviewer)

Beaudry, D. (2023, November 15). Associate Vice-President, Academic and Indigenous Programs, Laurentian University, Sudbury, Ontario. (P. Kuitenbrouwer, Interviewer)

Beckley, D. T. (2024, January 22). Professor of natural resource sociology, Department of Forestry and Environmental Management, University of New Brunswick. (P. Kuitenbrouwer, Interviewer)

Bigras-Dutrisac, H. (2022, February 28). Quebec's treasured sugar shacks face a sticky future. *CoStar News*. Retrieved from www.costar.com/article/1446286355/quebecs-treasured -sugar-shacks-face-a-sticky-future.

Bonneau, É., & Guay, S. (2023, October 25). *Érable &*
Chalumeaux. (P. Kuitenbrouwer, Interviewer)

Boswell, H. D. (1966). *Legends of Quebec: From the Land of the*
Golden Dog. Toronto, Ontario: McClelland & Stewart Ltd.

Bowley, P. (2015). Farm forestry in agricultural Southern
Ontario, ca. 1850–1940. *Scientia Canadensis, 38* (1), pp. 122–49.

Briggs, D. (2024, January 22). Co-owner, Briggs Maple,
Hillsborough, New Brunswick. (P. Kuitenbrouwer,
Interviewer)

Briggs, S. (2024, January 14). Co-owner, Briggs Maples.
(P. Kuitenbrouwer, Interviewer)

Bruchac, J., Bruchac, J., & Bruchac, J. (2024). *Gluskonba and*
the Maple Trees. Summertown, Tennessee: 7th Generation
Book Publishing Company.

Caouette, M. (2023). *Histoire acéricole: Anecdotes, procédés tech-*
niques, chalumeaux. St. Marcel: Édition La Plume d'Oie.

Caron, É. (2024, January 12). Co-owner, Sylvacer.
(P. Kuitenbrouwer, Interviewer)

Chapman, W. (1904). *Les aspirations: Poésies canadiennes.* Paris:
Librairies-imprimeries réunies.

Charlton, D. (2024, January 20). The sugar maple and social protest. *Tyler Arboretum.* Retrieved from https://tylerarboretum
.org/the-sugar-maple-and-social-protest/.

Chenevert, B. (2021). *Maple Sugaring Among the Abenaki and*
Wabanaki Peoples. Barton, Vermont: Nulhegan Abenaki
Historical and Cultural Preservation Dept.

Chouinard, J.-M. (2024, January 24). Secrétaire corporative
retraité, Citadelle, coopérative de producteurs de sirop
d'érable. (P. Kuitenbrouwer, Interviewer)

Citadelle Maple Syrup Producers' Cooperative: The beginnings
of the cooperative. (2023, November 2). Retrieved from
https://expositioncitadelle.wixsite.com/expositioncitadelle
/beginnings.

Cloutier, E. (1953). *Canadian Government Publications Consolidated Annual Catalogue 1953.* Ottawa, Ontario: The Queen's Printer: Office of the Supervisor of Government Publications.

Coons, C. (1992). *Sugar Bush Management for Maple Syrup Producers.* Toronto, Ontario: Ontario Ministry of Natural Resources.

Cooper, P. (2024, January 11). Professor emeritus of wood science, University of Toronto. (P. Kuitenbrouwer, Interviewer)

Coté, J., & Simard, F.-X. (1997). *Le livre du sirop d'érable.* Outremont, Québec: Les Editions Québecor.

Croteau, A. (1997). *L'érabliere et sa cabane: Le quatres saisons.* Saint-Laurent, Quebec: Éditions du trécarré.

Cummings, E.C. (1892). *The Mission of Father Rasles as Depicted by Himself—A Translation from "Lettres Édifiantes et Curieuses," J.G. Merigot le jeune, Paris, 1781,* p. 27.

Dekking, M. (2023, August 17). Longtime maple syrup maker. (P. Kuitenbrouwer, Interviewer)

Demande de faire enquête et d'émettre certaines ordonnances en vertu des articles 43, 163 et suivants de la Loi sur la mise en marché des produits agricoles. (2007, July 10). *Décisions de la régie des marches agricoles et alimentaires.* Montréal, Québec: Gouvernement du Québec.

Densmore, F. (1913). *Chippewa Music—II* (Bureau of American Ethnology Bulletin 53). Smithsonian Institution, Washington D.C.

Desjardins, P.-M. (2024, February 2). Professeur d'économie et directeur de l'École des hautes études publiques, Université de Moncton. (P. Kuitenbrouwer, Interviewer)

Desjardins, P.-M., & Leclerc, A. (2024). *Impact économique de l'industrie acéricole au Nouveau-Brunswick.* Grand Falls, New Brunswick: Association Acéricole du Nouveau-Brunswick.

Dillon, L. (2024, May 30). *Historical Demography of Canada, 1608–1921.* Retrieved from Open Text BC: https://opentextbc.ca/postconfederation2e/chapter/1-2-historical-demography-of-canada-1608-1921/.

Dunne, N. (2023, March 14). Billions have been made on Robinson Huron Treaty lands: First Nations could finally get a fair share. *The Narwhal.* Retrieved from https://thenarwhal.ca/robinson-huron-treaty-explainer/.

Dumont, J. (1993) *Caractéristiques chimiques et nutritives du sirop d'érable.* Saint-Hyacinthe, Québec: Centre ACER.

Dupont, J.-C. (1975). *Le sucre du pays.* Ottawa, Ontario: Les Éditions Leméac Inc.

Dupont, J.-C. (2004). *Le temps des sucres.* Sainte-Foy, Quebec: Les Editions GID.

Eagleson, J., & Hasner, R. (2006). *The Maple Syrup Book.* Richmond Hill, Ontario: Firefly Books Ltd.

Ennis, K. (2023, September 8). Owner, Ennis Maple Products, Lanark County, Ontario. (P. Kuitenbrouwer, Interviewer)

Farrar, J. L. (1995). *Trees in Canada.* Ottawa and Markham, Ontario: Natural Resources Canada, Canadian Forest Service, and Fitzhenry & Whiteside Ltd.

Faucher, M. (2023, March 16). Supervisor, ACER, Inspection Division. (P. Kuitenbrouwer, Interviewer)

Fédération des producteurs acéricoles du Québec c. Monsieur Richard Vallières, Les exportations R.J.S., Inc., 9246-2655 Québec Inc et Régie des marches agricoles et alimentaires du Québec, 200-05-018526-074 (Cour Supérieure August 23, 2007).

Fortin, J.-É. (1919, March). La bénédiction des érables. *Le Terroir*, pp. 25–33.

Friend, D. (2023, June 18). Canada, Ontario reach historic $10-billion proposed First Nations treaty settlement. *Canadian Press.* Retrieved from https://www.theglobeandmail.com

/canada/article-canada-ontario-reach-historic-10-billion
-proposed-first-nations-treaty/.

Godfrey, H.H. (1897) The land of the maple: patriotic song.
Mason and Risch Piano.

Goodfellow, R. (2023, October 2). President, Ontario Maple
Syrup Producers' Association. (P. Kuitenbrouwer, Interviewer)

Government of Canada. (1873–81). *Census of Canada—
Recensement du Canada 1870–71.* Ottawa, Ontario.

Government of Canada. (1881, July 14). *An Act to Amend "The
Indian Act, 1880."* Ottawa, Ontario: Queen's Printer.

Government of Canada. (1883). *Census of Canada 1880–81
Recensement du Canada Volume III.* Ottawa, Ontario.

Government of Canada. (1904). *Fourth Census of Canada 1901.
Volume II: Natural Products.* Ottawa, Ontario.

Grenier, A., & Grenier, N. (2023, October 25). Former maple
syrup producers, Sainte-Clotilde-de-Beauce, Quebec.
(P. Kuitenbrouwer, Interviewer)

Grenier, D. (2024, January 6). Maple syrup producer, Sainte-
Clotilde-de-Beauce, Quebec. (P. Kuitenbrouwer,
Interviewer)

Hall, D. (2023, March 17). Owner, Hallacres Farm, Cowansville,
Quebec. (P. Kuitenbrouwer, Interviewer)

Hamilton, G. (2017, January 13). Leader's guilty plea brings to
an end syrup heist case. *The Gazette*, p. NP3.

Henry, A. (1921). *Alexander Henry's Travels and Adventures in the
Years 1760–1776.* Chicago, Illinois: The Lakeside Press.

Her Majesty the Queen v. Richard Vallières, 2022 CSC 10
(Supreme Court of Canada March 31, 2022).

Herd, T. (2010) *Maple Sugar.* North Adams, MA: Storey
Publishing.

Huron, R. (2014). *Historical Roots of Canadian Aboriginal and
Non-Aboriginal Maple Practices.* Waterloo, Ontario: Wilfred
Laurier University.

Kiger, P. J. (2021, September 29). When Benedict Arnold tried to capture Quebec. *History*. Retrieved from www.history.com /news/benedict-arnold-canada-invasion-revolutionary-war.

Kuitenbrouwer, P. (2004). *Our Song: The Story of "O Canada," the Canadian National Anthem*. Montreal, Quebec: Lobster Press.

La Reine c. Avick Caron, 400-01-075233-148; 400-01-084989-177 (Cour du Québec, district de Trois-Rivières avril 21, 2017).

Lafrenière, M. (2016, October 21). Vol de sirop d'érable: "Il m'a refilé 1000 $ pour que je ferme ma gueule." *Le Nouvelliste*.

Lafrenière, M. (2017, June 16). La saga du vol de sirop d'érable est terminée. *Le Nouvelliste*.

Lagarde, N. (2023) *Réflexions sur le bord de la bouilleuse*. InfoSirop Magazine, été.

La langue française, s.v. "Revanche des berceaux," accessed July 20, 2023, www.lalanguefrancaise.com/dictionnaire/definition /revanche-des-berceaux.

Lamarche, J. (1979). *Cyrille Vaillancourt: Homme d'action, homme d'unité, co-opérateur émérite (1892-1969)*. Montreal: La Fédération de Québec des Caisses Populaires Desjardins; Distribution pour Les Éditions du Jour.

Lamond, R. (1821). *A Narrative of the Rise & Progress of Emigration, from the Counties of Lanark & Renfrew, to the New Settlements in Upper Canada, on Government Grant, comprising the proceedings for the Glasgow Committee for Directing the Affairs & Embarkation*. Glasgow, Scotland: Chalmers & Collins.

Lange, M. A. (2017). *Meaning of Maples*. Fayetteville: University of Arkansas Press.

Langlois, M. (2023, March 16). On veut se sucrer le bec à n'importe quel prix. *Le Journal de Montréal*, p. 2.

Lafitau, J. F. (1724): *Mœurs des sauvages amériquains*. Paris: Saugrains.

Lawrence, J., & Martin, R. (1993). *Sweet Maple: Life, Lore and Recipes from the Sugarbush*. Montpelier and Shelburne,

Ontario: Vermont Life Magazine and Chapters Publishing Ltd.

Leclerc, P.-A. (1991). *La belle histoire des sucres*. La Pocatière: Musée Francois-Pilote.

Létourneau, G., & Sames, J. (2013). Ash to cash: The untold story. *Histoire Québec, 18*(3).

Les expertises confirment l'incendie criminel: La cabane à sucre de Pierre Lemieux a bien été victime de vandales. (2000, March 31) *Le Nouvelliste*, p. 2.

Locklin, D. R. (2024, January 16). Associate professor, Department for the Study of Religion, University of Toronto. (P. Kuitenbrouwer, Interviewer)

MacDonald, J. (1953). *Maple Products: Investigation into an Alleged Combine in the Purchase of Maple Syrup and Maple Sugar in the Province of Quebec*. Ottawa, Ontario: Government of Canada, Department of Justice.

Manitoulin Island Agency—Correspondence Regarding Land Sales in Howland Township That Was Being Used as a Sugarbush by the Indians (1876–1924). Collection of Library and Archives Canada, Ottawa.

Massicotte, N. (2015, December 2). Vol de sirop d'érable: dix-huit mois avec sursis pour Steve Picard. *Le Nouvelliste*.

Massicotte, N. (November 13, 2015). Vol de sirop d'érable: Sébastien et Gaétan Jutras plaident coupable. *Le Nouvelliste*.

Ménard, M. (2023, July 7). Décroissance importante des ventes mondiales de sirop d'érable. *La Terre*. Retrieved from www.laterre.ca/productions/acericulture/decroissance -importante-des-ventes-mondiales-de-sirop-derable/.

Messier, C. (2021, December 12). Professeur, Département des sciences biologiques, Université du Québec à Montréal. (P. Kuitenbrouwer, Interviewer)

Meunier, P. (2024, February 12). Owner, Érablière Meunier. (P. Kuitenbrouwer, Interviewer)

Miller, H. (1980, April). Potash from wood ashes: Frontier technology in Canada and the United States. *Technology and Culture*, pp. 187–208.

Morgan, L. H. (1962). *League of the Iroquois*. Secaucus, New Jersey: Citadel Press, Inc.

Morin, G., Murphy, B., & Chrétien, A. (2014). *Maple Syrup Value Systems and Value Chains*. Brantford, Ontario: Wilfrid Laurier University.

Morin, J.-R. (2015). *Chalumeaux, brevets et objets acéricoles d'autrefois*. Éditions La Plume d'Oie.

Morrow, A., & York, G. (2023, May 13). The true cost of chocolate. *The Globe and Mail*, p. B4.

Murphy, B. (2014). *Maple Syrup Value Systems and Value Chains—Considering Aboriginal and Non-Aboriginal Perspectives*. Waterloo, Ontario: Wilfred Laurier University.

National Indigenous Diabetes Association. (2020). *Gifts from our Relations: Indigenous Original Foods Guide*. Indigenous Services Canada. Retrieved from https://nada.ca/wp-content/uploads/NIDA_TRADITIONAL_FOODS_GUIDE-2019-English.pdf.

Nearing, H., & Nearing, S. (1950). *The Maple Sugar Book*. White River Junction, Vermont: Chelsea Green Publishing Company.

New Brunswick, Legislative Assembly. (2022, November 2). *Journal of Debates (Hansard)*, Second Session, 60th legislature. Fredericton, New Brunswick.

Oneida Indian Nation (2025, February 1). Haudenosaunee dance. Retrieved from https://www.oneidaindiannation.com/haudenosaunee-dance/.

Ontario Provincial Government. (2023, September 26). Governments investing in Ontario's maple syrup sector [News release]. Retrieved from https://news.ontario.ca/en/release/1003551/governments-investing-in-ontarios-maple-syrup-sector.

Pelchat, M. (2000, March 30). La mafia du sirop frappe. *La Presse*, pp. 1–2.

Pendergast, J. F. (1982). The origins of maple sugar. *Syllogeus* (36). Ottawa: National Museums of Canada.

Perrault, F. (2023, Autumn). L'acériculture en forêt publique: Cruciale pour la croissance de l'industrie. *InfoSirop*, p. 22.

Pilon, J.-L. (1998). *Gather Around This Pot.* Canadian Museum of History. Retrieved from www.museedelaguerre.ca/cmc/exhibitions/archeo/ceramiq/cerart4e.html.

Producteurs et productrices acéricoles du Québec. (2020). *Si l'érable m'était conté, 1920–2020: Un siècle d'acériculture au Québec.* Longueuil, Quebec: PPAQ.

Quessy, G. (2023, October 5). Les différentes saveurs du sirop présentées à la Soirée de l'érable. *La Terre de Chez Nous.*

Ramsingh, B. (2018). *Liquid Gold: Tapping into the Power Dynamics of Maple Syrup Supply Chains.* Dublin Gastronomy Symposium: Food and Power. https://clok.uclan.ac.uk/23159/.

Report of the Proceedings of the Fourth Annual Meeting of the Pure Maple Sugar and Syrup Co-Operative Agricultural Association. (1916). Rigaud, Quebec.

Robinson, R. E. (1896, April). Old-time sugar-making. *The Atlantic Monthly*, pp. 466–71.

Roy, S. (2024, March 4). Directeur général, Citadelle, coopérative de producteurs de sirop d'érable. (P. Kuitenbrouwer, Interviewer)

Rush, B. (1791). *Third Volume of the Transactions of the American Philosophical Society.* Philadelphia, Pennsylvania: R. Aitken & Son.

Strickland, S. C. (1853 [reprinted 1970]). *Twenty-Seven Years in Canada West or The Experience of an Early Settler.* Edmonton, Alberta: M. G. Hurtig Ltd.

Sa majesté la Reine c. Étienne St-Pierre, 400-01-069892-123 (Cour supérieure, province de Québec, 28 avril, 2017).

Sa majesté la Reine c. Raymond Vallières, 400-01-070345-137 (Cour supérieure, province de Québec, district de Trois-Rivières 28 avril, 2017).

Sa majesté la Reine c. Richard Vallières, 400-01-069882-124 (Cour supérieure, province de Québec, district de Trois-Rivières, 28 avril, 2017).

Sa majesté la Reine c. Sylvain Bourassa, 400-01-079812-152 (Cour supérieure, 16 juin, 2017).

Shanahan, D. D. (2018, November 6). The accidental treaties. *Anishinabek News*. Retrieved from https://anishinabeknews. ca/2018/11/06/the-accidental-treaties/.

Shaw, T. (2024, January 8). Co-owner, Shaws Maple Syrup. (P. Kuitenbrouwer, Interviewer)

Silverman, A. (2022, February 7). Forest industry says expanded maple production could strain hardwood supply. *CBC News*. Retrieved from www.cbc.ca/news/canada /new-brunswick/new-brunswick-maple-syrup-forest -industry-1.6340336.

Simard, J., & Brault, F. (1989). *Les arts sacrés au Québec*. Boucherville, Quebec: Les Editions de Mortagne.

Smith, C. (1996). *When the Sugar Bird Sings: The History of Maple Syrup in Lanark County*. Burnstown, Ontario: General Store Publishing House.

Smith, W. L. (1923). *The Makers of Canada: The Pioneers of Old Ontario*. Toronto, Ontario: George N. Morang.

Soubeyrand, M., & Gennaretti, F. (2023, November 22). Au Québec, les feuillus pourraient se déplacer vers le nord. Voici les conséquences potentielles sur le paysage forestier boréal. *The Conversation*.

Suzor-Coté, M-A. (c. 1914). Bénédiction des érables (Blessing of the maples). Alan Klinkhoff Gallery. Accessed at https://www.klinkhoff.ca/viewing-room/57/works/artworks

-9937-marc-aurele-suzor-cote-benediction-des-erables
-blessing-of-the-maples-sketch-1914-circa/.

Theodat, F. G. (1865). *Le Grand Voyage du Pays des Hurons.* Paris: Librarie Tross.

Thomas, M. M. (2019, March 11). Evaporator company histories: Dominion & Grimm. *Maple Syrup History.* Retrieved from https://maplesyruphistory.com/2019/03/11/evaporator-company-histories-dominion-grimm/.

Thomas, M. M. (2001, January). The archeology of Great Lakes Native American maple sugar production in the reservation era. *The Wisconsin Archeologist,* pp. 139–66.

Thomas, M. M. (2018). *Maple King: The Making of a Maple Syrup Empire.* Bolton, Ontario: Matthew Thomas.

Timothy D. Perkins, R. B. (2022). *North American Maple Syrup Producers Manual, Third Edition.* Burlington, Vermont: University of Vermont.

Traill, C. (1855). *The Canadian Settler's Guide.* Toronto, Ontario: The Old Countryman Office.

Traill, C. P. (1832 [reprinted 1989]). *The Backwoods of Canada: Being Letters From the Wife of an Emigrant Officer, Illustrative of the Domestic Economy of British America.* Toronto, Ontario: McClelland & Stewart Ltd.

Tremblay, J. J. (2023, June). 200,000 hectares pour l'acériculture. *InfoSirop,* p. 25.

Turner, R., & Carbone, J. (2016). *The Crown Maple Guide to Maple Syrup.* New York, New York: Abrams.

Vaillancourt, C. (1927). *Nos érablières: Pourquoi les conserver, comment les exploiter.* Québec, Ontario: Ministère de l'Agriculture.

Vaillancourt, C. (c. 1932). *The Maple: Pride of Quebec.* Lévis, Quebec: The Maple Syrup Producers of Quebec.

Vaillancourt, C. (1932, January 1). *L'Érable: Organe officiel de la société des producteurs de sucre d'érable.*

Vaillancourt, Cyrille (n.d.). *Répertoire du patrimoine culturel du Québec*. Retrieved August 4, 2023, from www.patrimoine -culturel.gouv.qc.ca/rpcq/detail.do?methode=consulter &id=26483&type=pge.

Valeriote, E. (2023, December 13). For US maple syrup producers, climate change and competition threaten a way of life. *Modern Farmer*. Retrieved from https://modernfarmer.com /2023/04/for-us-maple-syrup-producers-climate-change -and-competition-threaten-a-way-of-life/.

Wade, S. D. (2021, August). Ojibwe women and maple sugar production in Anishinaabewakiing and the Red River Region, 1670–1873. *Minds@UW*, University of Wisconsin, Milwaukee. Retrieved from https://dc.uwm.edu/etd/2744/.

Why maples matter! (n.d.). *Maple Leaves Forever*. Retrieved December 12, 2023, from https://mapleleavesforever.ca /why-maples-matter/.

INDEX

curl $\qquad$ $\mathbf{curl\ A} = \begin{vmatrix} \mathbf{e}_r/r^2\sin\theta & \mathbf{e}_\theta/r\sin\theta & \mathbf{e}_\varphi/r \\ \partial/\partial r & \partial/\partial\theta & \partial/\partial\varphi \\ A_r & r\,A_\theta & r\sin\theta\,A_\varphi \end{vmatrix}$

Laplacian $\quad \nabla^2\psi = \dfrac{1}{r^2}\dfrac{\partial}{\partial r}\left(r^2\dfrac{\partial\psi}{\partial r}\right) + \dfrac{1}{r^2\sin\theta}\dfrac{\partial}{\partial\theta}\left(\sin\theta\dfrac{\partial\psi}{\partial\theta}\right) + \dfrac{1}{r^2\sin^2\theta}\dfrac{\partial^2\psi}{\partial\varphi^2}$

Triple Products

$\mathbf{A}\cdot(\mathbf{B}\times\mathbf{C}) = \mathbf{B}\cdot(\mathbf{C}\times\mathbf{A}) = \cdots = (\mathbf{A}\times\mathbf{B})\cdot\mathbf{C} = \cdots$

$\mathbf{A}\times(\mathbf{B}\times\mathbf{C}) = \mathbf{B}\,(\mathbf{A}\cdot\mathbf{C}) - \mathbf{C}\,(\mathbf{A}\cdot\mathbf{B})$

Derivatives of Products

$\mathbf{grad}\,(\psi\varphi) = \psi\,\mathbf{grad}\,\varphi + \varphi\,\mathbf{grad}\,\psi$

$\mathbf{grad}\,(\mathbf{A}\cdot\mathbf{B}) = \mathbf{A}\times\mathbf{curl\ B} + \mathbf{B}\times\mathbf{curl\ A} + (\mathbf{A}\cdot\nabla)\mathbf{B} + (\mathbf{B}\cdot\nabla)\mathbf{A}$

$\mathrm{div}(\psi\mathbf{A}) = \psi\,\mathrm{div}\,\mathbf{A} + \mathbf{A}\cdot\mathbf{grad}\,\psi$

$\mathrm{div}(\mathbf{A}\times\mathbf{B}) = \mathbf{B}\cdot\mathbf{curl\ A} - \mathbf{A}\cdot\mathbf{curl\ B}$

$\mathbf{curl}\,(\psi\mathbf{A}) = \psi\,\mathbf{curl\ A} - \mathbf{A}\times\mathbf{grad}\,\psi$

$\mathbf{curl}\,(\mathbf{A}\times\mathbf{B}) = \mathbf{A}\,\mathrm{div}\,\mathbf{B} - \mathbf{B}\,\mathrm{div}\,\mathbf{A} + (\mathbf{B}\cdot\nabla)\mathbf{A} - (\mathbf{A}\cdot\nabla)\mathbf{B}$

Second Derivatives

$\mathrm{div}\,\mathbf{curl\ A} = 0$

$\mathbf{curl\ grad}\,\psi = 0$

$\mathbf{curl\ curl\ A} = \mathbf{grad}\,\mathrm{div}\,\mathbf{A} - \nabla^2\mathbf{A}$

Integral Theorems

Gauss' (divergence) theorem $\qquad \displaystyle\int_V \mathrm{div}\,\mathbf{A}\ dv = \oint_S \mathbf{A}\cdot\mathbf{n}\ dS$

Stokes' (curl) theorem $\qquad \displaystyle\int_S \mathbf{curl\ A}\cdot\mathbf{n}\ dS = \oint_\Gamma \mathbf{A}\cdot d\mathbf{l}$